Tony Gates was born in England and now lives in South Australia. His working life has included merchant seaman and army service, personnel and training, tour leading and extensive personal travel.

His interests include fly-fishing, classical music, railways, writing, language, travel, history, theology and art.

He has long been in love with Italy and does not know how many times he has visited the Italian Peninsula.

Father of two adult sons and an adult daughter, he is married to his beloved Ruth.

To my precious wife, Ruth, whose comments and careful reading of the manuscript led to this being a better book than it would otherwise have been.

Tony Gates

UNPACKING ITALY

Passions of a Traveller

AUSTIN MACAULEY PUBLISHERS™

LONDON ∗ CAMBRIDGE ∗ NEW YORK ∗ SHARJAH

A CIP catalogue record for this title is available from the British Library.

ISBN 9781528995245 (Paperback)
ISBN 9781528995252 (Hardback)
ISBN 9781528995269 (ePub e-book)

www.austinmacauley.com

First Published 2022
Austin Macauley Publishers Ltd®
1 Canada Square
Canary Wharf
London
E14 5AA

I express my sincere gratitude for the fellowship and critical comments of fellow members of the Sand Writers group in South Australia, to BH who read my early reflection on the Villa San Michele while he was there at Anacapri, and whose response encouraged me more than he can know to continue writing, and to Austin Macauley Publishers who decided the book was worth launching into the market.

Table of Contents

Introduction

I have the Italian disease. I'm not sure that it is fatal, but it is certainly incurable. If you want to avoid contracting it, my advice is to give a wide berth to anything like an interest in this Mediterranean peninsula until you are comfortably into middle age. By then, you should be well set in your ways, which is the best of all immunities to the Italian virus.

My downfall was the early age at which I succumbed. I was ten. It started with a love of bluebell woods. At that tender age, I discovered an enchanting one on the northern edge of London and found within it an old, black, single-decker bus which had been converted into a home. Harold, the elderly man who lived there, became my firm friend until his death. It was Harold who introduced me to 'The Story of San Michele', the Swedish doctor Axel Münthe's literary *tour de force* in the English language. How could I possibly have found that book interesting at the age of ten?

How I even finished it I cannot understand now, but the fact is I couldn't put it down.

Münthe's dream, centred on the isle of Capri, captivated me.

The result was that the ten-year-old boy developed a burning desire to go to Capri. I wanted to walk the byways of Anacapri where old illiterate *Maria Porta Lettere*, unable to read the envelopes, used to deliver the post to *Capolimone, Zopparella, Rosinella Pane Asciutto* and other colourfully nicknamed inhabitants of the high village, each one a part of Münthe's world. I needed, as much as I needed air, to visit San Michele, the villa built on the site of one of Tiberius' residences, the fulfilment of Münthe's dream. I yearned to sit in the sun where *La Bella Margherita* had served macaroni and red wine, though red wine meant nothing to me then, but what romantic notions, even for a ten-year-old, clung to the words—*La Bella Margherita*!

Since then it has been my joy to visit Italy many times and to make a number of visits to Capri, an island I seem to love more each time I set foot on it. I first saw it as a seaman at the age of seventeen, though from a distance. I stepped ashore from a cargo ship in Naples and walked as far as I could along the northern arc of the bay. Then I turned and looked back. Immediately I knew I had never seen anything as beautiful anywhere. I have seen nothing lovelier since.

The city seemed to have its feet in the water, forming a curve of an extraordinary collection of buildings lining the deep blue of the bay. Ferries were coming and going from Mergellina and Beverello. The Angevin and Aragonese fortress of Castel Nuovo stood menacingly over the waterfront, dominating Stazione Marittima. Vessels were everywhere on the water. As my eye followed the line of the bay, there in the distance twin-cratered Vesuvius, with just a trace of barely visible smoke idly curling into an azure sky, stood as a reminder to Neapolitans that beauty is not always without its darker side. From Vesuvius, the Sorrento peninsula stretched westwards, pointing invitingly to Capri, with its two distinct massifs joined by a gently sloping saddle. So near and yet so far! Soon it was back to the ship, but I had experienced some hours of excited imagination. My determination to set foot upon the island was firmed.

Some day, some day!

Too soon, the hour came for casting off and it was back to work for that seventeen-year-old seaman.

The Bay of Naples receded into the distance and something of Tony Gates was left behind.

I keep returning to Italy. Sometimes I ask myself why. Answers do not come easily. It is, I think, because Italy refuses to be neatly classified. Whenever I think I am getting close to understanding the kind of place it is, I find that it becomes elusive all over again. Is it the beauty of the language? The chaos of the political system? The bustle and noise of Rome? The ancient roots of the land? The country-wide art gallery seen in the churches, the museums, the architecture, the public sculptures? The beauty of the Tuscan hills, rolling, green and inviting? The extraordinary mix of cultures born of Etruscans, Greeks, Romans, Lombards, Spaniards, Frenchmen and a host of others?

Or is it perhaps because every time I go to Italy, I discover something more about myself, my roots as a European?

It just may be that I have never grown up and can't resist travelling on Italian trains. I still get a thrill from wandering the stations of the great cities, reading the destinations of the trains and travelling on such romantically named services as the Napoli Express or the Cisalpine Express, a title which always brings to mind Cisalpine Gaul and Julius Caesar's fateful crossing of the Rubicon, that tiny stream which runs into the Adriatic and has the nerve to call itself a river.

Having said that, I find that another magnetic field of Italy draws me in—so many world-shaping events have taken place there. Get off almost any train at almost any station and you are not far from the making of history.

In the end, I have to admit that I don't know why the country lures me back again and again. Its call is as irresistible as that of the sirens to Ulysses—but I have no intention of being tied to the mast. I am very happy to be among the seduced.

This perspective of Italy is through the eyes of an incurable romantic. I make no apology for that. In this world where value is too often measured in compound interest and technological development, the need for romantics is critical. My own romanticism might best be explained by another cameo from boyhood. School was not a source of pleasure to me, and in order to relieve the tedium of sitting in a classroom during the precious hours of the day when better things could be done, I made good use of my bike. Leaving home at the correct time for a boy going off to school and arriving home at just the expected hour, from time to time I pointed the handlebars southwards towards central London.

There a day of sheer delight awaited me as I spent happy moments on London Bridge gazing at the Pool of London, or sometimes heading for the Isle of Dogs and the non-tidal docks. In both places, I would study intently the ships in port, their names, their flags, and wonder where they had been and where they might be going when at last they set their heads downriver towards the Thames estuary and North Foreland. On those days away from school the firm plan to go to sea took shape. There was a world that was bigger than the London I loved and still love, and those vessels were my indications of it. I would see that world and fill my life with experiences Marco Polo never dreamed of!

Most people leave their boyhood or girlhood dreams behind them. I have been fortunate in having mine remain with me. In the ways that really matter, I am still the boy sitting on London Bridge looking at an ocean-going ship, ready to sign on at a moment's notice to see where it will take me. I make this point because sometimes I feel sorry for those whose romanticism has become lost in the sophistication and cynicism of maturity. Shirley Valentine expressed it well in the film surely designed for all romantics when she asked, "What happened to Shirley Valentine in all this living?"

T.S. Elliot put it perhaps more elegantly, "Where is the life we have lost in living?" If you've lost the zest for life and the need to know what lies over the hill, you may never set foot in Italy. You may never do anything which diverts you from the road well-travelled.

Having made that point, I need to state that I am a man who appreciates not only the romantic but also the harder facts of history. The vision of Italy in this book therefore is inclusive of both. Yet I hope you will find that it increases the ease and pleasure of reading and travelling in that finest of vessels, your armchair. I have certainly had enormous pleasure in writing it. My passion is on the paper. I hope my pleasure in wandering from the tried and tested roads is also here.

I was talking recently with a travelling man. He and his wife join many tours and have travelled to a good many countries of Europe and elsewhere, but never to Italy. 'We've heard bad stories about Italy,' he told me, 'and we've been put off because we like to travel with as little risk as possible, and we like things to run like clockwork.' He didn't specify what the perceived risks in Italy were, but he had said enough. He was surely right never to have been there. A man who likes things to run like clockwork is not a man for Italy. There, a more laid-back style is preferred. That is the genius of the country.

If you are prepared to take the risk of contracting the bug, then plan today to make a trip. In the meantime, join me in your armchair in looking through romantic eyes at my Italy.

Chapter 1

Through Simplon to Eden

There are many ways to enter Italy. Some fly directly into Fiumicino and attack Rome directly. Others enter by train from Provence. Some drive into the north via, say, the St Gotthard Pass and motor down into Lombardy. I've enjoyed them all, but the entrance I like the most is by train through the Simplon tunnel down into Domodossola and Stresa via the rugged mountains which divide Italy from Switzerland.

To gain the most from the journey you commence it at Gare de Lyon in Paris, taking the TGV (*Train à Grande Vitesse*—Very Fast Train) to Lausanne, up to 300 km per hour (186 mph) of comfortable travel. There you leave the TGV to take a rather more down-to-earth but no less interesting train, which will be heading for Milan. Before entering the Simplon tunnel, you enjoy a scenic journey around the northern and eastern shores of Lake Geneva, often glimmering with reflected sunlight like a giant mirror, and then follow the Rhone valley to Brig, a delightful interlude in Switzerland before getting down to the major business of Italy.

Of course, there's nothing marvellously scenic about the Simplon Tunnel. Just the reverse. After all, you are in darkness during the journey through the mountain. 'So,' you might ask, 'why are you excited about a train journey through a tunnel?'

My reply is that I find it so exciting that I have made the journey in both directions many times. It offers me, and I hope you, an opportunity to let imagination paint the pictures, because we are now, in the darkness, part of great things which took place in the Alps a century or so ago. We are boring our way through a remarkable piece of history. Given that its length in the southbound tunnel is twelve and a quarter miles, or approximately twenty kilometres, we have ten to fifteen minutes to think about the wonder of its cutting as we pass through. It runs from Brig to Iselle, so we enter it in Switzerland and leave it in Italy. It was opened in 1906 after seven years of construction and made possible a spectacular train route into a veritable Eden.

The Alps have always been a considerable barrier to railway travel. The steepest gradients are well beyond the capabilities of locomotives using steel wheels on steel rails. For any useful route to be found into northern Italy, tunnelling was inevitable. But no ordinary tunnelling was called for. The challenge of boring through solid rock towering thousands of feet above the tunnel was quite different from the task of piercing lower hills through which shafts could be put down, for facilitating tunnelling with men working outwards in both directions from those shaft bases. With the Simplon tunnel, separate crews worked from the Swiss and Italian ends, meeting in the middle, in what was, at its time of cutting, the most difficult engineering task the world had seen.

It was not the first tunnel to have been cut in the Alps. In 1871, after thirteen years of work, the Mont Cenis tunnel was opened to allow trains to run from Paris to Turin. The thirteen kilometres bore was completed by men, stripped to the waist, using only picks and shovels. A year after its opening, the St Gotthard tunnel, entirely within Switzerland, was commenced. On completion it was 14 kilometres long with double tracks. The engineer for the project, Favre, died inside the tunnel while working on the enterprise. Poor Louis Favre, a Swiss engineer from the Geneva district, seems to have contracted an illness that remained unidentified. He gave the appearance of growing old before his time. He developed a stoop and his hair whitened. He began to experience spells of dizziness.

On 18 July 1879, Louis was in the tunnel with another engineer when he experienced serious internal pains. He died there, an old man at the age of 53. Whenever I think of the Gotthard Rail tunnel, I think of the tragedy of Louis Favre.

The Gotthard tunnellers, working from both ends, met in the bowels of Swiss rock in 1880. The opening was in 1882, three years after Louis' death.

Simplon is deeper and longer. At its deepest, the tunnel is 7,000 feet (2,134 metres) below the mountain surface. I was challenged to think a bit when I first travelled through it. Wasn't that more than a mile of rock above me? That's an awful lot of rock! I took encouragement from the fact that trains had been running through the tunnel successfully for many years. Those engineers must have known their jobs. These days, I love Simplon. The romance of the vision, the endurance, the determination that Simplon represents is with me all the way through beneath that mile-plus of rock. I was thrilled to be travelling through it the first time. The chill in the knowledge of that mountain of rock above added to my very alive imagination.

Hydraulic drills were used in the tunnelling and explosives played their part. It was not unusual for between 200 and 300 hollow drill cutters per day to be used up. I can scarcely credit how the supply of drill cutters was kept up.

The saying, 'There's light at the end of the tunnel', is generally meant as encouragement for those in adversity. The American poet and wit Robert Lowell didn't quite see it that way. He said, 'If we see light at the end of the tunnel, it's the light of the oncoming train.' Depends on how you look at it, doesn't it? But in Simplon today, the light of the oncoming train is unlikely to be seen because a slightly longer tunnel was opened in 1922, sixteen years after the first, running approximately parallel to the original, so that Simplon has two impressive portals at each end, with one tunnel for southbound trains, one for northbound.

The original tunnel was opened in 1906 on 10 May in a joint ceremony by the Italian king, Vittorio Emmanuele III, and the National Council of Switzerland president, Hugo von Kager. As is usual on such occasions, the tunnel was opened by people who had nothing to do with its building. Still, it isn't difficult to imagine the solemnity mixed with celebration at Brig, where the opening ceremony took place.

Simplon has had its significant moments. For example, the first time I travelled through in the southbound tunnel, I had no idea (fortunately) that there were explosives there which were not removed until 2001. It is perhaps as well that I did not know. I can't for one moment believe I would have been comfortable in a train in a tunnel containing explosives. I would have considered that rather more than my ticket entitled me to.

Why were they there? The retreating German army in the later stages of the Second World War decided to blow up the tunnels. The work of Italian partisans and some Austrian deserters frustrated the German plan. How different train journeys into Italy would have been, at least for a while, had the plan succeeded.

In 2011, there was a serious fire in the tunnel, causing it to be closed for some days and provide a reminder to people like me who spend a good deal of time on trains that there can still be dangers for the unlucky in rail travel.

While today, we travel in comfort and smoothness through this massive engineering achievement, it will be so much more than a dark interlude if we remember that deep under Alpine rock, we are entering a history of mountain tunnelling which cost the lives of 67 men from accidents but was the engineering wonder of its age—and remains an engineering wonder of any age.

Simplon also takes us into the world of great luxury train travel. The American humourist and journalist, Robert Benchley, once said, 'In America, there are two classes of travel—first class and with children.' Perhaps he was right when seen in the light of a train he never lived to experience—the modern Venice Simplon-Orient-Express, which is very first class and devoid of child passengers.

The initial Orient Express, the Rolls Royce of travel, did not use Simplon for the best of reasons—the tunnel had not yet been cut. Its original route in 1876 was from Paris to Vienna. Later, it took in other destinations. However, the opening of Simplon in 1906 allowed a rival service to be commenced. This was called the "Direct Orient Express", and set its own standard of luxury, running from Paris Gare de Lyon through Switzerland and Simplon into Italy. Its destinations also included Austria.

The early Orient expresses consisted of luxurious cars of the *Compagnie Internationale des Wagons-Lits et des Grands Express Européens* (International Company of Sleeping Cars and Grand European Expresses), founded by the Belgian Georges Nagelmackers, much to the chagrin of the American entrepreneur, George Mortimer Pullman, who never really succeeded in penetrating the European railway market beyond Great Britain, and that due to an invitation from the Midland Railway Company of Derby. Pullman cars from the late 19th century onwards dominated British luxury rail travel, but on the Continent Nagelmackers' Wagons-Lits held the field. It was absolutely a journey for the rich and famous.

The first Simplon-Orient-Express ran in April 1919 and was routed to avoid Austria and Germany, both countries being decidedly non-U in the post Great War years. The decision was fortuitous. Lausanne and Simplon to Venice is one of the great scenic journeys of the world, and you can take it on more moderately priced scheduled everyday train services.

Turn now, though, to that sparkling, sumptuous, modern train, generally thought to be for the very rich, though my wife Ruth and I, who are far from rich or famous, have ridden in it on a number of occasions. It's a matter of what you choose to spend your money on. The Venice Simplon-Orient-Express has no direct connections with its famous forerunner. The modern VS-O-E is primarily the brainchild of James Sherwood, a visionary determined to see 'Orient Express' luxury on the rails again.

On 25 May 1982, the 'new' Venice Simplon-Orient-Express made its initial journey from London's Victoria Station to Venice's *Santa Lucia* via the wondrous piece of engineering called Simplon. Alas, in 1985 it was rerouted and now runs not through Simplon but via Innsbruck, entering Italy through the Dolomites, finding its way to Venice via Bolzano and the Veneto region. However, if you have a sum to spend which is generous with noughts, or you have a tight budget and choose to spend your cash on fine train journeys, you can still travel in style from London or Paris to Venice on the VS-O-E. The luxury and friendly train crew make it more than a train journey. It's an experience. But if you have no desire to travel on the Orient Express, shed no tears. You will have a rich journey on your Inter-City or other express train simply because your imagination will do for you here in the black tube what no VS-O-E luxury could ever do. Allow yourself to be transported!

The VS-O-E's route via the Dolomites happens to suit me because I can enjoy both routes. I've enjoyed the journey via the Dolomites three times in that luxury train (twice to Venice, once from that fine city), while I have been able to enjoy the Simplon route many times in more moderately-priced trains. I've had the best of both worlds. Some of my most precious photographs are of my wife Ruth looking radiant and deeply happy at the tables of the VS-O-E's three restaurant cars. Perhaps it is an affectation, but I'm very fond of wearing my Orient Express cufflinks and tie bar—oh, and one of three Orient Express ties. It's just too wonderful an experience not to wear the reminders of it.

Entering the light of day once through the tunnel, you find yourself in rugged Alpine Italy. Before long, after drinking in the beauty of snow-covered peaks, you will arrive at Domodossola, which reminds me that there are occasions when train travel introduces any traveller who is not entirely introverted to delightful people.

I offer you an example. While travelling on a train with my daughter from Lausanne into northern Italy some years ago, I enjoyed the company of a middle-aged couple from Milan. They were, of course, as Milanese, models of elegant dressing.

Surprisingly, I can't remember the husband's name, but the signora's I could never forget, Adelaide. Why can't I forget it? Because Adelaide in South Australia is the nearest large city to my current home.

Inevitably, we found ourselves talking about railways, and I praised the French passion for making sure that their trains run exactly to time. 'Yes,' he agreed, 'a French train is timed perfectly, but in Italy the timetables are'—and here he gave the characteristic Italian shrug of the shoulders with a slight raising of the eyebrows—'*piu approssimativi*,' more approximate. Absolutely.

Italy is at its heart more approximate. And more welcoming because of it. It does not stand on ceremony, and Enrico (I have to allow him a name) and Adelaide shared their love of their country with us with a warmth that left us in no doubt of their pleasure at sharing themselves as well. My memories of Italy are populated with many such outgoing, life-loving people.

I cannot imagine that the Genesis writer who wrote the Garden of Eden story could have seen a lovelier place than the northern limits of Italy, but his misfortune was that he never saw the Italian peninsula. Still, Babylon might have passed muster, though it couldn't possibly rival the Italian Alps, hanging gardens or not.

The first time that I made this journey was during a very wintry January. Under a blanket of snow, Domodossola is entrancing. The mountains at this point are rugged and inhospitable, and the snow added a majesty that Solomon in all his glory would have envied. Without its white covering, the town of Domodossola is relatively undistinguished, but its setting, wondrous in the cold of winter, is one of grandeur at any time of day. A lover of winter, I enjoy the pinching grip of the cold on my skin—something I miss in my warm, adopted home of Australia. Here in the Italian Alps it can be enjoyed with greedy satisfaction!

I am captivated by mountains and in this, I think, I am among a great company. Why do mountains transport us? It must be to do with the everyday world of manipulation. Most of us live in environments which we have shaped by erecting buildings to our taste (or not to our taste), laying out gardens to our own design, building roads and railways for convenience of communication, all of which and more I have no argument with; after all, I could not enjoy the mountains of Italy without the convenience of roads and railways.

Even so, the mountains themselves speak to me of a world largely untouched by the hand of Man, and of solidity and strength infinitely greater than ourselves. Or is it the remoteness and transcendence that seem to characterise mountains? So much of life is lived cheek by jowl that solitude becomes one of the most precious of all commodities. For whatever reason, mountains for me are gateways into deeper spirituality. So many of my memories of deep contemplation of life and of my own being are in the settings of remote trout streams in Australia's Snowy Mountains where, with fly rod in my hand, solitude among lofty places has led me into deeper things.

Before long, the great expanse of *Lago Maggiore* opens out. When I first saw it, it shimmered in winter sunlight and left me in no doubt that I was looking at a treasure of Italy.

At its most northerly point, it lies in Switzerland, but by far the greater part of its area resides in Italy. Shaped like a mirror-image of Italy itself, it provides one of the great panoramas of Europe. Sixty-four kilometres (40 miles) long and five kilometres (3 miles) at its widest, its three jewels are the Borromean Islands. (There are four, but one of them, *l'Isolina*, is hardly large enough for a mention. Forget I've mentioned it).

I had been well prepared for my first view of the lake. 'Wait until we get to Stresa,' said the man on the train, 'then you'll see something!' As the train drew into the station from the north, I certainly did see something. Stretching away to the east, the wonderfully blue waters were bordered on the farther shore by white-capped mountains which seemed to have been painted especially to contrast with the deep ultramarine of Maggiore. The islands of *Isola Bella* (Beautiful Island), *Isola dei Pescatori* (Island of the fishermen) and, farther away, *Isola Madre* (Mother Island), looked irresistibly seductive.

How I longed to leave the train for a few hours then and there to explore them, but I had a seat booked on a train from Milan to Venice, where I had to be that evening. Years afterwards, those islands were to become magical places for me, and for Ruth who spent some days on *Isola dei Pescatori* with me and fell immediately in love with the island and the lake.

Lago Maggiore has an Eden character which excites my spirit. It can't be denied that it lies far from the rivers Pishon, Gihon, Tigris and Euphrates of Genesis, but the *Ticino*, which feeds it from the Swiss Alps and drains it into the great Po Valley, can have few equals for beauty. The story tells us that in Eden, the Lord God caused every tree which is pleasing to the eyes to spring up. Here on the banks of *Lago Maggiore* the profusion of flowers and blossoms is breathtaking. The variety is dazzling, but perhaps especially, in their seasons, bougainvillea, camellias, azaleas, verbena, magnolias, cannas, oleanders, rhododendrons and orange and lemon blossom spread an exquisite mantle over the shores.

Verbena are especially important, having been around the lake for at least a couple of millennia, for they caused the Romans to name it Verbanus, which adds another dimension to my thinking about that remarkable, ancient people. Their military, legal and civil engineering genius is well complemented by their love of verbena! I have to say that I like the Roman name better than the modern one. Lake Verbena conjures up in my mind a faithful picture of the beautiful stretch of water I know and love.

The islands, collectively the Borromean group, are named after the Borromeo family. Sforza, Visconti and Ambrose may be more famous south of the lake, but don't underestimate the honour in which the Borromeos are remembered here.

The first of two outstanding members of the family was Carlo, who was born in 1538 at Arona, a town at the southern end of the lake, set against the backdrop of a steep hillside. He must have been quite a man, because on the outskirts of Arona there is the *Colosso di San Carlone*, a huge, copper statue of the man in question. He stands on a granite pedestal, itself 12 metres (40 feet) high. Carlo himself boasts a height of 23 metres (75 feet). Given that I had to climb a flight of steps even to get to the base of the pedestal, the effect of sheer size was overwhelming. Carlo gazes down upon us, seemingly from heaven itself, with a wise and compassionate expression.

Dressed in ecclesiastical robes, he appears as if he will crush the pedestal. It is surely the most powerful statue in Italy in terms of size and commanding presence. Those who are so inclined can pay an entrance fee and make the difficult climb to the top, there to enjoy one of the great views of Piemonte (Piedmont) and, more distantly, Lombardia (Lombardy). Such is the design of the statue that you can see the view through Carlo's eyes, because the eye-sockets form windows through which you can peer.

The statue, finished in sheets of hammered copper, was built between 1614 and 1698, and is simply the commanding feature of the southern end of the lake.

Perhaps surprising to some, the statue is noted far from its Lago Maggiore home, on a plaque at the foot of New York's Statue of Liberty, The French designer of the Statue of Liberty, Frédéric Auguste Bartholdi, visited Arona in 1869 specifically to study the Colossus' structure. I wonder how many visitors to the Statue of Liberty see the plaque?

I noticed a family talking close by the statue, and since they appeared to be local, I asked the man I took to be the husband and father what kind of person gets a colossus such as this erected in his memory. *Era un uomo grande*! He replied. 'He was a very big man!'

'You mean he was a physically large man?' I asked, this perhaps giving some justification for the size of the statue.

'No. He had a great heart and a great mind!' Indeed he had. Carlo Borromeo was a man of compassion and great breadth and depth of intellect. At the age of 12, he became an abbot; next he studied law at Pavia, becoming a doctor of law at the age of 21. The following year, 1560, saw him rise to the rank of Cardinal, with the appointment of Archbishop of Milan. He was still only 22 and must have been the envy of older clergy.

The cynical will say that his meteoric rise was due to the not insignificant fact that the Pope of the day, Pius IV, was his uncle. Be that as it may, no-one could have argued against his abilities. His influence throughout much of Europe, especially the Netherlands, Switzerland and Portugal, was considerable, and in the government of the Church his uncle did very little without consulting Carlo. Perhaps it was because Pius was himself a lawyer from Bologna that he had an especial regard for his nephew.

Pius' reliance upon Carlo was never more obvious than at the Council of Trent, held in the northern Italian cities of Trento (Trent) and Bologna, which met variously from 1545 until its final convening in 1563. It dealt with what the Catholic Church viewed as the threat of the Protestant Reformation and its outcome was the reaffirmation of almost every important Roman Catholic doctrine together with denunciation of Protestant positions. It made clear the authority of the Pope, and Carlo was, at the age of 25, a huge influence in its proceedings. While Carlo Borromeo did much to bolster the authority of the Pope, Pius could be said to have done a great deal to undermine it, being the father of three illegitimate children.

As Archbishop of Milan Carlo was a powerful influence for order and service. In the see of Ambrose he tightened up on the discipline of the clergy and founded many important services, including hospitals, schools, libraries and theological seminaries. But he is best known and loved around Lago Maggiore and in Milan for his heroic work in 1576 during a terrible outbreak of the Plague. When it broke out, he was away from Milan on pastoral work in the country areas of the diocese.

Upon hearing of the scourge, he returned immediately to the city and spent his days bringing whatever spiritual and practical help he could to the dying. He placed his life at risk daily in compassion for the suffering. For me, that is the mark of a man who can truly claim to be great, though Carlo would never have made such a claim. When I am in Milan, I am aware that in these streets a man of love once walked and served selflessly. There is a Greek word, *agape*, the love which is living for the wellbeing of others, that describes Carlo Borromeo perfectly.

He died in 1584 at the age of 46. Almost certainly it was a premature death brought on by exhaustion and by the growing viciousness of accusations made against him by those whose vested interests were at stake.

As is frequently the case with men such as Carlo, people quickly began to claim that miracles were taking place at his tomb, so spoiling and clouding the memory of a fine man. In any event he was elevated to the Catholic Church's official list of saints in 1610.

As I walk the streets of Stresa, Arona and Milan and visit the Borromean islands I see at every turn the large Cardinal-Archbishop whose intellect was relied upon by a Pope, and whose influence traversed Europe, but who will always for me be a pastor, who loved and served his flock selflessly.

There was another fine member of the Borromeo clan. Count Federico Borromeo was Carlo's nephew. Born in Milan in 1564 he also became a Cardinal and Archbishop of that city.

In academic circles, Federico is most celebrated as the founder of the great Ambrosian Library in Milan. But like Carlo, he was a man of compassion, and that is how I think of him above all. Plague again struck Milan in 1630. As his uncle had done 54 years earlier, Federico gave himself unreservedly to the relief of the sick in that ravaged city, risking his life daily, his efforts being no less heroic than those of his illustrious relative. So selflessly did he throw himself into the work that Manzoni, in his novel *I Promessi Sposi*, besides describing vividly the dreadful spread and devastation of the 1630 plague, writes of Federico Borromeo's devoted work among the sick.

The islands were for centuries Borromeo possessions. Each is a fascinating small world of its own. Isola Bella is the most touristy—but ignore the tourist trinkets offered for sale and you will discover the essence of an island which holds an important place in the history of this part of Piemonte, for here is the 17th century Borromeo Palace. And the essence is Borromeo.

Before you step ashore from the ferry, you recognise that a great deal of the island is occupied by the palace and its terraced garden, built in the 17th century by Count Vitaliano Borromeo, though another Borromeo, Carlo III, commenced the work. A small fishing village occupies the remainder. It is influenced by the Baroque style. Its two wings are beautifully balanced as they tower above the walkways below. The most powerful effect, however, lies in the way in which it has been built into its setting. Its impressive regularity of line, its white stone and burnt Sienna pitched roofs stand in fine contrast to the irregularity of the island and the deep blue of the water.

Vitaliano employed a very capable man named Angelo Crivelli to design both the palace and garden. Crivelli was, I think, a man who knew how to use what was available, in this case hardly more than a rock projecting from the water, with a flattish bit of terrain at its most northerly point. There, on the flatter end of the island, he put the palace, while transforming the rock into one of the most satisfying terraced gardens one could hope to see.

As I wandered through the palace, it was easy to reflect upon the comfortable living of the later Borromeos, but above all I was conscious of the family tradition of compassionate service that Vitaliano must always have been aware of when occupying this paradise in the lake. The Ghosts of Carlo and Federico, though in the flesh they never lived on Isola Bella, can never have been far away. I feel in one sense sorry for Vitaliano—the examples he had to live up to were daunting, and while he never came near to their achievements, in reality it would have been nearly impossible to do so. His home was and is one of comfortable and impressive living spaces. La Sala del Trono, or the Count's room, is especially impressive, particularly for its tasteful gilt.

The palace was erected, therefore, by a lesser Borromeo, but one who had an eye for fine architecture and for a fine garden, though completion of the latter was the work of a later Borromeo, Carlo IV. I took a lot of time strolling through what in effect is a garden constructed like a building. The terraces are carefully built at differing levels with an impressive symmetry. Something of this is seen from the traghetto—the ferry—as you cruise to the landing-point.

In fact, the effect of the terracing is seen most effectively from the water. But the tranquillity of the garden can be appreciated only by being in it. I counted nine terraces from the top to the bottom of the structure, a worrying exercise since I am told there are ten on this garden which stretches from the majestic structure of the palace at the northern end of the island to the white twin towers at the southern extremity. My mistake, I am sure.

The garden is the glory of the island. As I sat looking down from the top at the beautifully tended flower gardens, I wondered why it is that gardens play so important a part in the pleasure of the human species. For everywhere I go, I see lovely gardens—here on Isola Bella, the Luxembourg Gardens in Paris, the Boboli Gardens in Florence, Kew Gardens in London, Monet's exquisite pair of gardens at Giverny, the almost overwhelming beauty and scale of the gardens at Versailles, the wonderful gardens at the chateaux of Angers, Villandry, Amboise, Azay-Le-Rideau, Chenonceau and so many more. Where humans settle in significant numbers, they build gardens.

As one who loves gardens, there seems to me to be something mystical about them. There is a melding of the natural world with human ordering, a creating of something beautiful using the life in the seed already created for us; to put it another way, we have, perhaps, a sense of wonder in working with the beauty of the natural order and the life within it that we cannot create. That mystical melding is certainly present for me in the fine garden of Isola Bella.

These and others were the thoughts which took over my mind as I gazed at this wonderfully orderly garden of the Borromeos with its neat flowerbeds, smooth lawns, colourful borders, shady shrubs and trees, and its special adornment—glorious white peacocks which lazily wander over the grassed areas, unconcerned with the passing parade of those of the human species.

Yes, life in the palace and gardens of Isola Bella (named after Carlo III's wife, Isabella) was gracious. I think I would have found it more than tolerable.

A ticket bought at the imbarcadero (ferry terminal) at Stresa will take you to Isola Bella, Isola Madre and Isola dei Pescatori. Isola Madre, the farthest of the three from Stresa, is also part of Borromeo history, having a 17th century villa which they used as a kind of holiday home; however, it was no holiday 'shack'— the Borromeos required comfort and inspiration during their recreation periods, as witnessed by the fine art collection and fine furnishings which adorn the villa.

Isola dei Pescatori delights me most of all. The smallest, it is also, for me, the most charming. The island consists primarily of a fishing community whose boats are found tied up next to the landing stage and in the tiny marina during the day. In contrast to the lofty rock of Isola Bella, it is low and flat. Narrower than its larger neighbour, it also runs north and south. At its most northerly point, you can sit under trees and gaze across the water towards Switzerland, an especially sublime pastime at sunset when the lake can take on the most wonderful colours. On the southern extremity stands the Albergo-Ristorante

Verbana, a hotel for which I have a great love. It is, of course, beautifully and appropriately named.

There are more majestic hotels on the lakeside road in Stresa, but if I can go to my hotel each night by boat, and wake in the morning not to the sound of motor vehicles, but of water lapping under my window, then give me the latter always. A part of the hotel consists of an old two-storey cottage with some rooms looking out over the moorings of the fishing boats. My memory is filled with images of indescribable beauty as, especially in the mornings, I have looked out of my first-floor bedroom window in that old cottage over the blue waters to Stresa Lido and the hills of Piemonte.

Almost always, I would wait at the window until a train from Simplon went silently (to me) past, and I would follow it until it disappeared behind the buildings of Stresa to enter the station. A man in love with trains cannot ever let an opportunity pass! Only then would I leave the lovely picture framed by my window and head for the shower and breakfast.

What of the trains?

My mind easily goes back to my boyhood when, as a primary-school lad, I went daily to the station that was built for the Midland Railway. Every train that went through on that busy line captivated me, but none so much as the great expresses. The platform shuddered as they raced through in clouds of smoke and steam with a deafening roar. And the smell of the smoke and oil. How wonderful!

So, at Stresa and everywhere else, I cannot see a train without wondering where its passengers have come from, and where they are going. What adventures have they enjoyed? What special experiences are they anticipating? Trains always seem to me to be carriers of dreams. So, from my bedroom window I look across the blue waters at trains heading for Milan or Simplon and Switzerland, and I wonder. For to travel on a train is always, for me, to experience an adventure. The trains pass, and in them adventurers breathe and pre-live their experiences.

Isola dei Pescatori is host to the fishermen who, in their canopied boats of deep blue, fish for the huge trout of the lake. Often I have looked into the waters lapping the island's shores and been amazed by the size and number of the fish before my eyes. As a fly-fisherman, it has been difficult to prevent a twitch in my right arm. The blue boats venture out onto the lake late in the evening, returning usually a little before dawn. During the late afternoon you can watch many of the fishermen coiling ropes and doing many maintenance jobs to get their boats into order ready for the night's fishing. To do so is to watch part of the life of the lake close-up before you. Men are doing what they have done all their lives as they practise their trade.

Standing a couple of feet from the water late one afternoon I asked the middle-aged, roughly-shaven man—who looked exactly as I have always imagined the 'Big Fisherman' Peter of the Gospels to be—what time he expected to go fishing. Confirming my conviction that fishermen say as little as possible, he replied, *dieci ore*. Ten o'clock was still six hours away, but I planned to watch his departure from my bedroom window, just above the beached boats. 'This lake is half fish and half water,' he said. *Che cosa pensa?* What did I think? I thought he was going to get a bumper catch and that he always made a bumper catch. And there would certainly be no lack of a market with the long line of multi-storey hotels over the water at Stresa.

Understanding that fishermen are never in danger of becoming garrulous, I wandered off to the little marina just a couple of hundred yards away to contemplate how Catholicism is deeply embedded into the life of Italy, and especially into the existence of those who earn their living on the waters.

At the entrance to the marina, where more blue fishing vessels are moored, there stands a charming small statue of the Virgin Mary. She watches these men of the lake go out into the deep waters and she watches over them as they return. Stone she may be, but I can imagine a kindly light appearing in her eyes and slight suggestion of a smile moving her lips as those men whose lives are intimately connected with the water look at her and cross themselves on their outward and homeward journeys. Loquacious they might not be, but their actions and devotion speak volumes.

They return in the early morning hours, before most people of the lake are awake. They don't leave their boats until everything is tidied, ship-shape and Pescatori fashion.

The islands are irresistible gems in a deep blue lake, but on the northern end of Stresa lies another opportunity to enjoy a feast for the eyes. There at Stresa Lido stands the station at the lower end of the cable-car (*funivia*) ride to Monte Mottarone. The bright red cars invite you to enjoy a remarkable journey. Leaving the blistering heat of Stresa one fine May morning, I found myself, twenty minutes or so later, in the cold snows of Mottarone with a vista of the snow-clad, rugged ridges of the Monte Rosa Group running away to the west, and to the north the mountains of Switzerland glistened in the distance.

The scenery is truly spectacular. However, there is something else for the eye which searches keenly. A few minutes' walk from the Mottarone Funivia station, like a wild primula not seen until you are close to treading upon it, is the little chapel of Santa Maria delle Neve—Saint Mary of the Snows. To call it diminutive would not convey the picture at all; it is truly tiny. If more than a dozen people were sitting within it, you would call the occupants a crowd. I sat for a while on the hard seats and quickly became aware of how cold it is to be immobile within that stone building. It is plain and yet at the same time beautiful in its simplicity.

At that moment, cold or not, I would not have swapped Santa Maria delle Neve for London's St Paul's. Nevertheless, I remained convinced that worshippers in that little church must be devoted indeed to spend, perhaps, an hour almost immobile during a celebration of the Mass.

The journey down in the cable-car invites undisciplined camera use. The lake is far below, with all the Borromean islands in view and appearing rather farther apart than they really are. The lake's long finger stretching into Switzerland and its resort of Locarno appears as an artist's spilled ultramarine, running wantonly in a stream through seemingly sheer-sided mountains.

It is not difficult to think of Hemingway's fictional deserter Lieutenant Frederic Henry and his pregnant lover Catherine fleeing wartime Italy for Switzerland along that great arm of the lake which stretches away before your eyes from the descending cable car. As I descend and gaze at the magnificence before my eyes, I can very easily see myself rowing that glorious stretch of water, allowing, perhaps, the mountain scenery to distract me from the task of propelling the boat, because it truly is an Eden among the mountains.

The town of Stresa seems to have more hotels than any town of comparable size, and for the most part they lie alongside the road which follows the lake shore. It is also an important conference centre, boasting a number of important venues, including perhaps the major one, the Palazzo dei Congressi.

In 1935, Stresa was host to a conference in which Italy, France and Great Britain participated, attempting unsuccessfully to find a solution to Hitler's decision to rearm Germany, in defiance of the Treaty of Versailles. And yes, Mussolini was the Prime Minister of Italy at that time. How did he manage his amazing backflip so soon afterwards in allying his country with Nazi Germany? Italians, who have the healthiest scepticism concerning politicians, wouldn't be amazed by that at all.

I feel as though I am experiencing an important, if little-known, piece of movie-footage of European history when I walk through Stresa. Had a solution been found in 1935 in this lovely lakeside town, what misery Europe would have been spared. Perhaps given that a way of peace could not be found by Lago Maggiore, it wouldn't have been found anywhere. A certain Galilean said, 'Blessed are the peacemakers.' If the best efforts are made and still there is failure, then perhaps blessed also are those who at least try to make peace.

The conference was held in the Borromeo Palace on lovely Isola Bella, a setting of peace if ever there was one.

Away from the hotels, the conference centres and the Imbarcadero, you find colourful streets (brightly coloured cloths on outside tables and vast pots of bright flowers seem to be found in even the tiniest lanes) and charming cafés.

The cafés are for the most part welcoming places. It never ceases to amaze me that in a town so invaded by tourists, the waiters always seem able to sound and look welcoming and give the impression that there can be no higher calling for a man than to attend to the customer's every need.

Prego? he asks with a smile to melt the strongest sales resistance.

Un bicchiere di vino rosso, per favore. You must have a glass of red wine, otherwise why come to Italy?

Italiano o francese…forse australiano? Lei e australiano?

'Yes, I am Australian,' I reply, 'and English.' That confuses him so much that his expression clearly indicates he has decided not to follow it up. I am touched by his theatrically confidential tone as he tells me that he has only a few bottles, but there is a very fine Australian red if I would like it. I am tempted, if only because I don't want to appear ungrateful for his solicitous offer of wine he thinks I would like. But I am in Italy, and I want to drink only Italian wine. I want to be as immersed in all things Italian as I possibly can be.

Vino italiano, per favore—un bichiere di vino locale, senz' altro. Remarkably quickly, the glass of local purple liquid appears, accompanied by the inevitable broad smile, eyes sparkling. Actually, it isn't all that local, because Stresa is not a wine producer, but it's local enough—a Piemonte Dolcetto from Alba. And it is good. Fruity, and young, the age at which Dolcetto ought to be drunk. It's so good that the glass empties more rapidly than perhaps it ought.

The waiter somehow has remained totally invisible to me, while carefully keeping his eye on my drinking. I know that because he appears at the table as if he has suddenly materialised before me.

'You would like another, signore?'

'I would very much like another.'

By now, I am thoroughly relaxed and arguing to myself that I do not have to do any driving, so I order a third. Have the edges of the tablecloths become less defined? I'm not sure, but the girls have grown more beautiful, the voices more tuneful in their talking and the gardens I see not so far away more verdant. The voices of a group of girls at a nearby table have become strangely mellifluous. I decide that three is enough. The same smile is there as I leave.

Grazie, signore!

I can't help thinking that in Australia, once they have taken my money, they lose all interest in me. I step onto the footpath with a feeling of deep contentment.

Was Stresa always as attractive as I find it today? I don't know, but I suspect that the lake at least has always had its charm. At least, one who found it so was the religious philosopher Antonio Rosmini-Serbati, who in 1787 was born in a part of Austria which has subsequently found itself within Italy, and who chose to reside in Stresa where, at the age of 58, he died. His portrait by Hayaz in the Brera, Milan, reveals an aristocratic, sensitive face in which intelligence is unmistakably seen.

At an intellectual level, his life's aim seems to have been to unify Catholic theology with the social and political movements of his day. He was ever concerned with the dignity of the human person, but unhappily his writings for a time fell under the critical microscope of Rome, two of them being placed on the infamous 'Index of Forbidden Books'. However, all's well that ends well and in time all his books were declared acceptable in official Catholic eyes by the Church.

He would have rejoiced in at least some of the achievements of Garibaldi, Mancini, Cavour and Vittorio Emanuele, had he lived long enough to see the declaration of the Italian State in 1861. Sadly, her had left this life 16 years earlier. He was a nationalist who approved of the aspirations of the *Risorgimento*, the movement for a united Italy. However, he had no time for the anti-clerical elements in the movement and would have been deeply distressed by the isolation of the Pope when Italy was formed without Rome, and when the papal armies were defeated nine years later to complete the task of unification.

The Pope of the day, Pius IX, had understandably opposed the movement to deprive the Church of its authority in Rome and its states in the Italian peninsula. This is not the place to discuss the complexities of the unification movement;

however, it should be pointed out here that Rome and the papal army had to be defeated before Rome came into the new Italy. Rome was captured on 20 September 1870.

However, these are not the things the people of Stresa remember Rosmini-Serbati for. They see him not as the man who operated on an intellectual level, but one who operated from compassion as the founder of the Institute of Charity 'up the road' at Domodossola. Known as the Rosminians, their Institute has an educational thrust, but also, and perhaps more importantly, it majors upon charitable work.

Certainly, it is the latter that the people of Stresa think of when they bring Rosmini-Serbati to mind. And they can understand easily the desire he had to enjoy the tranquillity of Lago Maggiore and the charm of Stresa. I think Rosmini-Serbati and I, at least in our love of Lago Maggiore and the need for compassion in the community, are kindred spirits.

To descend from the important to the trivial, there are, of course, the obligatory souvenir shops in the town but turn a blind eye to them and seek out a more engaging Stresa and you will not be disappointed. Remember that you are in Borromeo country and the whole scene of Lago Maggiore, its islands and its lakeside towns will take on rich hues indeed. Whenever I depart the shores of Lago Maggiore, I have a deep sense of sadness that I must move on from Eden. Unlike Adam, I am not confronted by a flaming sword turning every way, so I know I shall return.

Chapter 2

High Culture, High Church and High Fashion

During my younger days, when the name Milan was mentioned, my thoughts always turned to football. AC Milan (*Il Milan*) and Inter Milan (*L'Inter*) dominated the Italian football scene. While other clubs have asserted their ascendancy in the ensuing years, it remains true that there is no more intimidating place for a visiting team to play than at the San Siro stadium, the home of football in Milan.

There is no denying that football is close to the pulse of Milan (Milano), but as my love for Italy grew, so did my understanding that this great city of the north is richer by far than any mere kicking of a ball around a green rectangle could make it.

To begin with, it has a proud history. If the people of Lombardy, of which Milan is the capital, appear to be physically different from many Italians of the south, it may well be because they come, by and large, from Lombard stock. Their blue eyes, fair skins and comparative tallness certainly allow our imaginations to see their ancestors as the *Longobards* who came down from more northerly European climes in search of warmer and more fertile lands. Their name indicates that the males wore long beards, a fact which makes it easy for me to see them as formidable-looking foes.

They were certainly successful in establishing themselves along most of the valley of the River Po, that most watered, most fertile territory of the Italian peninsula. In fact, they managed to build a Lombard empire in Italy which extended from north to south by the beginning of the 7th century—or perhaps it would be more accurate to say two empires because the northern territories were separated from those of the centre and south by a narrow strip of Byzantine possessions. I find it tantalising to wonder how the history of the country might have changed had those two Lombard empires ever joined to form a Lombard Italy. Might it have been powerful enough to resist all other incursions? So near, so far.

How did it happen? Italy could legitimately complain that it had been deserted. It had long lived under the protection of the Roman legions and perhaps would continue to have done so for some time longer than was the case, but for the appearance on the Roman throne of one Constantine. For a while, there were two contenders, Maxentius and Constantine. The year AD 312 was fateful for Italy because in that year at Milvan Bridge over the Tiber, Constantine defeated his rival and became the undisputed emperor. He claimed that his victory was linked to a vision he received in which a cross appeared before him with the words, 'In this sign conquer'. Genuine, or a clever piece of political opportunism?

The growth of Christianity had left the Empire in need of a unifying force, and it seems likely to me that Constantine saw the ideal opportunity to use Christianity for that purpose. Be that as it may, in time he granted Christianity legitimacy, which was not the exciting news that Christians at the time might have considered it to be.

More to the point, it was this Constantine who deserted Rome, and therefore the Italian peninsula, by transferring his seat of power from the old imperial city to Byzantium, which he promptly renamed Constantinople. With him went much of the army, though Constantinople established an administrative centre at Ravenna in Italy's northeast. The Ravenna administrators managed to hold only isolated parts of Italy against the invading Germanic peoples, including the Goths and the Lombards. Constantine had left the country virtually defenceless. The one great success of Ravenna, however, was holding that thin line across north-central Italy which kept the two Lombard empires separated.

The Lombards, then, were the people who settled the area around Milan and much more of Italy besides.

They invaded Italy in AD 568, making their capital at Pavia. For two centuries, they were dominant until being subdued by that most remarkable of Franks, Charlemagne, in AD 774. Thus, the crown of Lombardy was now worn not by a Longobard, but by the man destined to become the first 'Emperor of the West'. It was one crown among many that the Frankish king could select from his wardrobe. The Lombards were part of the East German tribal grouping known as the Suevi and they first come to our notice in AD 5 when, while living in the area of the River Elbe, they were defeated by a Roman force commanded by Tiberius during the reign of the Emperor Augustus.

They seem to have been, as many other Germanic peoples were, a migratory tribe. At some time during the 4th or 5th century AD, they settled in the valley of the Danube and by the middle of the 6th had found their way to Pannonia, the ancient name of a central European area south of the Danube. Demonstrating their tenacity and toughness they crossed the Julian Alps under the leadership of one of their most famous and able kings, Alboin, to make their conquest of northern Italy.

Lombardy became their long-term home where they flourished under an interesting system of government in which their kings were elected. During their time in the Danube they had become Christian, but to the Pope's chagrin the Arian form of the faith, not the Catholic. Thus, they were Christian but anti-Catholic, holding views of Christ which were wholly unacceptable to the Pope. However, around about 600, in Lombardy, they accepted orthodox Christianity. This might be thought to have ended the rift with Rome. Not so. The Longobards were becoming increasingly powerful and no small threat to successive Popes.

It was to Rome's relief, therefore, that when Liutprand, the most aggressive and competent of all Lombard rulers, died in 743, the Frank Pepin responded to a request from the Pope Gregory III to deal with his Germanic problem—a problem which was spreading throughout the Italian peninsula. Pepin began the conquest. His son Charlemagne completed it.

What have the Lombards left in Milan and Lombardy? That most enduring of all legacies, language. As in all of Italy, a dialect is spoken in the region; in this case the dialect is heavily peppered with Germanic words. You will have no trouble speaking Italian in Lombardy, nor will it present any difficulties wherever in Italy you speak it. But if you sit at a table in a café where the locals eat you might not always understand what they are saying if, as is their wont, they break into local dialect.

Milan, then, still carries the flavour of its Lombard past, but it carries the texture of a modern city. In fact, Milan is comfortably Italy's wealthiest city financially and among the richest culturally. You can still hear it said in this proud city that Milan is the moral capital of Italy and ought to have been the actual first city at the country's 19th-century unification. This is *Campanilismo* at its most obvious.

Campanilismo, or parochialism, refers to the sound of the local church bell. The *campanile*, or church bell-tower, is viewed as the centre of the parish. *Campanilismo* in Milan is not without a rich mix of historical substance, important values and the mix of qualities which make up the cosmopolitan capital of Lombardy. Another example of Milanese *Campanilismo* is the fact that its most noted poet, Carlo Porta, who lived in the late 18th and early 19th centuries, chose to write in the Milanese dialect because it was in that tongue that his fellow citizens had in the past expressed their love of Milan and their best hopes for its future.

Milan is not, however, locked into its past. It is a vibrant contemporary conurbation. For one thing, it is the fashion capital of Italy, and these days a serious rival to Paris. There is a good reason for that. Fashion shows, as they are manifested in Paris, are extraordinary events where bland (in my eyes) young women parade along a catwalk wearing what to me, a non-expert in fashion, are silly clothes, but seem to capture the imagination of devotees and certainly the newspaper headlines.

Milan, where fashion parades are now part of the local culture, emphasises a more restrained style. Even so, those who want to be seen to be someone occupy seats close to the catwalk, thus ensuring that the cameras capturing the models also ensnare them. And of course, the parades are money centres. The rich pay extraordinary prices for what some would see as the pieces of nonsense displayed in Paris, and for the generally more wearable items which make up the Milan collections. Do they ever wear them, once purchased? I am no position to say, but if the evidence of the outfits draped over the bodies of well-known film actresses at Oscar ceremonies are indicators, then certainly some wear them, if only once.

Italy can claim the exception *par excellence* in that most beautiful, most elegant of women, Gina Lollobrigida. You simply cannot imagine that she has ever appeared in public clothed in anything less than outfits which enhanced and were enhanced by her beauty. The paradox of her birthplace, Subiaco, forever associated with that rigorous, plain-dressed eschewer of all personal show, St Benedict, is a nice one. However, it is extraordinary to me that the women who can afford to pay for the expensive dresses of the collections are the wearers most likely to give them one outing only.

Fashion is part of the flavour of Milan, and in the Quadrilatero, the streets between Via della Spiga and Via Monte Napoleone, the window-shoppers can enjoy Giorgio Armani, Versace, Valentino, Gucci, among many others; for the more wealthy, a king's ransom will purchase something to take home. The

Quadrilatero is Milan's equivalent of Rome's Via Condotti—good to look, and perhaps dream.

The focus of the city is Piazza del Duomo, at the eastern side of which stands the extraordinary cathedral, a simply massive Gothic structure whose western façade stands in majestic dominance, its major portal facing the centre of the piazza. It is the largest church in Italy (the larger St Peter's basilica is in the Vatican State, technically not Italy) and the third largest in the world.

Milan's cathedral is fortunate in its piazza, which is large enough to enable the church to be viewed from any angle without close buildings obscuring the overall view. It makes the cathedral a very photographable building; given that it's among the most striking Gothic churches in Europe, that is fortunate indeed. I can still remember my first view of it. Walking into Piazza del Duomo from the western side I literally stopped in my tracks. The huge and magnificent building before me seemed too wonderful to be real. It had the feel of a film set about it. I felt that if I walked behind that great western façade with its array of spires, I would find nothing but scaffolding and a movie-set crew telling me to keep clear of the scenery.

What confronted me was the extraordinary sight of a multi-levelled façade with at least a dozen major pinnacles visible amongst a greater number of minor examples, six sets of soaring, slender buttresses, five portals, and in the mainly Gothic structure, elements of Renaissance and neo-classical architecture. There are altogether some 135 pinnacles or spires, and it isn't difficult when viewing the cathedral from, say, the south-west corner, to envisage the whole thing as a huge birthday cake for one who has left the century a long way behind.

How is it that this beautiful building, built on the site of an ancient church, contains elements which dilute its Gothic integrity? The simple answer is that 500 years elapsed between its beginning and its completion, an extraordinary length of time even by European cathedral-building standards. It was founded in 1386 by Gian Galeazzo Visconti, a famous name in Milan, and one who had an eye for the sumptuous. His remains, surprisingly, do not rest in the cathedral, but in the Certosa, or monastery, of Pavia, which he also founded.

There seems to me to be an extraordinary irony that the completion of the façade, as recently as 1809, was on the orders of one of Europe's great destroyers, Napoleon Bonaparte, yet at the same time there might just be an aptness to it in a strange way because the overall design of the cathedral is the work of another Frenchman, Nicolas de Bonaventure. Having said that, it has to be admitted that French nationalist though he was, Bonaparte was descended from an ancient Italian family (the name was originally Buonaparte). His Italian roots can be traced as far back as the time of the founding of the cathedral whose completion he ordered.

Sitting outside to eat a sandwich before entering that wonderful edifice, I found myself before long joined by another luncher, though in her case the repast was a plastic container of pasta and salad. We soon fell into conversation, and I discovered that her name was Anna and she was a lifetime resident of Milan. I guessed her to be, perhaps, fifty or so. Still trim and dressed with the style you would expect of Milanese, even one sitting *al fresco* with her plastic container of lunch, she had a sparkle in her eyes.

'Do you come to this church on Sundays?' I asked her.

'Yes, I've been coming here since I was a *bambina* in my mother's arms. I was married in this church and my two daughters were baptised here.'

'Are they grown up now?'

'*Si*, Antonetta is 18 and Bettina is 16.'

'Do they come to the church on Sundays, too?'

'Antonetta does. She's a fine young woman and I'm sure the saints bless her every day. Bettina? She would seduce the saints if she could! No, she doesn't come very much. She's interested in more earthly things, even on Sundays!'

With the intriguing mental picture of 16-years-old Bettina seducing as many saints as she could lay hands on, I went into the cathedral.

The impact upon entering compares with the first view of the exterior. The sense of size and space is overwhelming. With a length of more than 150 metres it seems to go on forever, with rows of great Gothic arches giving the impression of being in a giant bowling alley. I was surprised by its severity. My experience of Roman Catholic churches is largely of generously ornate interior decoration, but Milan is in some ways more English in its internals while being thoroughly un-English in its externals. It seems to represent a confluence of cultural streams. I walked through the nave, with two aisles each side, and my gaze ran up the pillars which take the eye soaring to the *trompe l'oeuil* ceiling so far above me. I found the severity, which enabled me to appreciate the architecture for its own sake, immensely appealing. However, the cathedral does not lack colour, there being some superb 15th-century stained glass to be enjoyed and the three bays of the apse contain wonderful tracery.

To complete the picture of the extraordinary size, it should be noted that the external height of the dome is 65.6 metres, or 215 feet. That in itself is a fact which speaks of magnificence.

For me, the most important interior features of the cathedral are the tomb of St Carlo Borromeo and the mausoleum of Gian Giacomo de' Medici, and in each case because of the family influence in their respective parts of Italy. The Borromeo family has already been mentioned. Carlo, whose tomb is in the crypt, has an appropriate final resting-place, having been bishop of Milan. He died in 1584. The de' Medici clan will find prominence in a later chapter.

Milan is not without its religious relic, as is the case with so many of the great Roman Catholic churches of Europe. There was, it seems, no shortage of monarchs and ecclesiastics in Europe ready to accept, and if necessary, pay big money, for relics of items from the Holy Land, especially if they were purported to have some association with the Cross. Hence, Milan's *duomo* has its item—a nail which, it is claimed, comes from the cross upon which Jesus was crucified, and which is displayed in the cathedral each September. At other times of the year, it is kept above the high altar. You draw your own conclusions.

I found the roof walk well worth taking. The entrance to the walk is outside the church on its northern side. As I walked the roof, I drank in again the glory of Gothic, with its feast of pinnacles, flying buttresses, and the great central spire topped with the gilded statue of the Virgin Mary. It was an exhilarating conclusion to a walk through the cathedral.

On the northern side of the Piazza del Duomo lies the Galleria Vittorio Emanuele II, known simply as the Galleria. It is the place of style, the magnet for Milan's smart set who stroll through it, meet for coffee, and simply enjoy its high-ceilinged elegance and the imposing central octagon with its striking mosaics. And there are the big brand-named shops whose display windows are works of art in themselves.

It was while I was drinking coffee in *Savini* and looking across at the Prada store that I had my first intimation of the symbolism of the Galleria for Milanese. The cafe was crowded. I found a seat at a table where a man who could have been in his forties was sitting. Like most Milanese he was dressed to look his best, a dark-blue suit looking as if he had paid a thousand dollars for it, his shoes, I noticed, polished with a shine that was not achieved in two minutes of quick brushing. I wonder how much he did pay for that suit?

His name, I discovered, was Marcello, and soon we fell into conversation. I commented upon the sheer style of the Galleria, to which he replied, 'Yes, the Galleria is style more than it is anything else, and for us in Milan, it is an important statement. You see, we Milanese pride ourselves on being the style centre of Italy. In fact, we believe we are the style centre of Europe. We take style in clothing and style in furnishings, even style in machines and other practical things, very seriously. You might argue that we are more style than substance, but we like to think that is not the case. After all, we have become the wealthiest city in the whole of the country, and you don't do that just on style. But yes, the Galleria is our most important style statement, and we like visitors to appreciate its elegance.'

I appreciated its elegance, and after coffee, I walked through its four arms again, drinking in its atmosphere and its style.

At the northern end of the Galleria lies Piazza della Scala, and of course the La Scala opera house itself, or Teatro alla Scala. Opened in 1778, it was badly damaged during the Second World War. It has now been restored to its rather uninteresting exterior and more compelling interior. Next door is the La Scala museum which can be visited from March to October. The exhibits depend for their interest upon the viewer's depth of immersion in music, and not a little upon his or her knowledge.

From the museum interior, you can enter the opera house. For me, that was the most important part of the visit, because it's there, in that wonderful auditorium, that the ghosts come to life. Strangely, it was not so much the great voices which excited my imagination, as the mental picture of the reopening of La Scala in 1946. I saw in my imagination the pride of the conductor, Arturo Toscanini, bowing to the audience, face aglow, at the conclusion of the inaugural concert in post-war La Scala. It has never been my privilege to be present at a live performance there, but inside the theatre it was not difficult to let my imagination run.

One delightful memory I have comes from walking through the opera house drinking in the details with my wife, Ruth. There were not too many other visitors on that day, and after most of the visitors had left and we could see no one around, we stepped into one of the auditorium's boxes, we looked down at the stage and thought, 'Why not?' We sang *Nessum Dorma* together. Yes, I know it is not a duet, but that day it was, and so, allowing for no audience being present, we can both say that we have sung at La Scala! Yes, there is no denying it, we *have* sung at La Scala.

Milan is not only for serious experiences, as perhaps our singing at La Scala indicates. We love to engage local people when we can. I recall an occasion of lunching at an outside table at a café on the north-western corner of Piazza del Duomo when we were served by a waiter who knew his trade supremely well yet was able still to engage in real personal connection, and not a little banter.

It is easy to be cynical about waiters who have developed lines for the tourists, but my experience is that if you refrain from engaging in the 'tourist stuff', you will find that a good conversation can start, to the extent that the busy waiter's duties will allow. It was not long before we began to discover something of his home life and his family, as we shared some of our personal information with him. That takes us over the dividing line between cultures and we learn cultural insights that tourist sights and tourist banter don't supply. Personal engagement makes travel exciting and immensely fulfilling.

The Basilica di Sant' Ambrogio, a mostly Romanesque church, lies not far from the centre of town. I have a special love for it, partly because of its architectural fascination, and partly because of its association with Ambrose, bishop *extraordinaire*. I walked westwards from Piazza del Duomo along Via Meravigli and Via Sant' Agnese to Piazza Sant' Ambrogio. As I was walking across the piazza to the church my mind was preoccupied with the man responsible for the basilica's existence.

Ambrose was the most famous of all bishops of Milan, and the man who became the city's patron saint. What kind of man was he? Born at Treves in Gaul, son of the city's Praetorian Prefect in AD 340, he packed more than seems possible into his 57 years. Connected with the powerful Roman aristocracy, he studied in that city, was trained as a lawyer, and practised at the Roman Bar. He was appointed Governor of Liguria (which at that time included Milan) and Aemilia by Probus, the leading Roman noble.

In 374, Auxentius, the Arian bishop of Milan, died, and Ambrose, to his great surprise, found the populace clamouring for his appointment as Auxentius' successor. He accepted the transformation from a governor to a bishop reluctantly, but once in charge of the see proved to be a tough, uncompromising defender of the Church Catholic. His predecessor had embraced Arianism, a form of Christianity which had its origins in the teaching of one Arius in Alexandria, and which was regarded as heretical by the bishop of Rome.

Ambrose also was implacably opposed to the Arian form of the faith. His elevation to the see of Milan was as extraordinary as Thomas Becket's appointment to the see of Canterbury. The latter had to be ordained with great alacrity in time to be consecrated twenty-four hours later. Ambrose, upon accepting the see of Milan, had not even been baptised.

He proved to be an unusually effective preacher, his mellifluous speech attracting great congregations. I see this man in my imagination as one with a commanding presence, determined to make his new calling one which counted not only in the city of Milan, but in the western part of the Empire as he settled to the task of suppressing Arianism.

In that enterprise, he achieved considerable success. When he died in 397, Arianism did not die with him, but it was seriously weakened in its influence in Italy and western Europe generally. I see him also as a man of great determination and leadership with a gift for articulating an argument with great persuasion.

He is remembered as a pastoral saint whose care for his people was without reserve. Some parts of his ministry stand out as major achievements: his introduction of eastern hymnody into the Milan musical tradition, his hymn-writing (four of his hymns survive today), the naming of the Milan collection of plainsong (though he is not known to have written any of it) becoming known as Ambrosian Chant, his confrontation with the Roman nobility who wished to retain allegiance to the Roman cult, his humiliation of an emperor and his contribution to church orthodoxy in his fight against Arianism.

The Ambrosian Chant is still sung in Milan, where the Gregorian form, from which the Ambrosian differs in many ways, clearly takes second place. Unfortunately, we can't be certain of the original form of the music, since the earliest Ambrosian manuscripts extant are from the 10th century.

His stand against the forces of the nobility which sought to reinstate in the Senate-house the practices of the old, pre-Christian, religion was unyielding. During Ambrose's time Milan was the centre of government of the Empire in the west, Constantine having moved the seat of Empire to Byzantium, and renamed it Constantinople. Rome had become the pre-eminent see of the Catholic Church, though no bishop had yet claimed the title of Pope. The best part of a century was to pass before, in approximately AD 450, Leo the Great made that claim and insisted upon receiving the appellation.

The Senate-house contained an altar and statue to the goddess Victory. The statue had been brought there from Tarentum (the modern Taranto in Calabria). She was a winged maiden holding a laurel wreath in her hand. Standing upon the globe she was a commanding presence in the Senate. The altar had a chequered history. Constantius, erstwhile Eastern Emperor, but from 350, sole Emperor, removed the altar, but Julian his successor reinstated it. What was its role? In the Senate-house, it represented the old Roman cult and was therefore a strong anti-Christian Church statement. The senators habitually offered incense on it, and when taking oaths placed a hand upon it, rather as the custom developed in the western world of placing a hand on the Bible when making an oath.

In 381, Gratian, who had briefly been the sole Emperor, removed the altar again from the Senate, and it is possible that he also removed the statue. Representatives came from Rome to Milan to plead for the old cult. The leading figure was one Symmachus whose arguments were in vain. Gratian continued his reforms not only by keeping the altar out of the Senate, but by confiscating all monies associated with the Temple of Victory and abolishing the privileges of its officials.

On Gratian's death (383), the child Valentinian II became Emperor, which meant that his mother Justina was the real wielder of power. Symmachus again brought a deputation to Milan, where he addressed the young Emperor, depicting the Roman state speaking in the first-person, pleading to be able to follow her 'holy religion' which had so prospered her in the past. Here, Ambrose came into the picture, warning Valentinian not to act without the agreement of Theodosius, who was by now Emperor in the East. He poured scorn on the cult's need for money to support vestal virgins while 'thousands' of Christian women offered themselves freely to a life of virginity. He carried the day and the altar remained suppressed.

The altar had a brief resurrection when Valentinian was murdered in 392, but shortly afterwards when Theodosius, who supported Ambrose's position, became sole Emperor through battle, it was removed for the last time from the Senate. Ambrose had won.

Earlier, he had been instrumental in encouraging Gratian to refuse the title of Pontifex Maximus, the appellation which described the reality of his position of Head of the State Religion. Gratian gave up not only the title, but the reality, and there was no ambiguity about the fact that the Church had its Head within its own ranks. For Ambrose, there could be no validity in the Emperor being Head of the Church. The Church was not a State possession, nor was it a branch of the State. It must have its own head from within its own ranks. The separation of Church and State was fundamental for Ambrose.

His determination and stiff backbone were shown in an incident concerning the Emperor Theodosius. Perhaps this was the pinnacle of Ambrose's demonstration of statesmanship and pastoral concern in the same incident. An unruly mob in Thessalonica had murdered an imperial commander, and Theodosius ordered the killing of all those thought to be guilty. On his command, seven thousand Thessalonians were butchered by the army.

Ambrose was furious at the brutality of it and refused no less a man than his Emperor entry to the cathedral. It was not the current cathedral, dedicated to *Santa Maria Nascente* (St Mary of the Nativity), but the first cathedral, completed in AD 355.

Ambrose could be a man of steel when he knew it necessary to be so, and this was an occasion when he determined that even the Emperor should know that no man is above the law of God. Theodosius, rebuked by the bishop of Milan, remained banned from the cathedral until he made public penance. Humbled, he was again allowed to worship in the sanctuary.

I contemplated the exceptional life of this man as I gazed at his bones, there to be viewed in a reliquary in the basilica. Deeply reflective shaper of liturgy, committed pastor, statesman, champion of orthodox Christianity and implacable confronter of an emperor. The Church has known few like him. Somewhat sceptical of the claims regarding relics in churches all over Europe, I have no difficulty in accepting that the bones in the Basilica of Sant' Ambrogio are those of Ambrose. He founded the church and was very much a man of Milan.

Even so, Ambrose's as they almost certainly are, they are simply bones. It seems to me that one who contributed so much to the Church and to Milan should at least have warranted a decent burial. Veneration seems to have denied him that.

These are the thoughts that occupy my mind when I am in the church of Sant' Ambrogio. The man adds glittering pages to the history of the city.

Not far from the Basilica di Sant' Ambrogio is the church of Santa Maria delle Grazie, perhaps in itself not an overly compelling edifice to visit, though the main portal, early Renaissance in a Gothic structure, has unusual elegance. However, Santa Maria delle Grazie has one irresistible attraction—Leonardo's mural of *The Last Supper*.

Queues can be quite long to get in to view what many regard as the artist's greatest work, so I should have guessed that something was wrong when I first approached the church. The pavement outside was deserted. It was a warm afternoon and to my cost I discovered that the refectory, which contains *The Last Supper*, is open only during the morning and the evening. These days, you can book online a time of viewing (but it is only for 15 minutes).

Returning after my own supper, I joined the queue in the Piazza Santa Maria outside the refectory entrance marked *Cenacolo* and in time found myself gazing upon the remarkable picture. It is struggling to survive. Leonardo did not paint it in the true fresco style by working on the wet plaster but worked *a tempera* on the dry wall, some time before 1499. The process enabled the painting to be modified as the artist worked. That cannot be done when working on wet plaster. The deterioration began early, some of the paint having peeled off by the middle of the 16th century. Some restoration was done during the 18th and 19th centuries and more modern restoration continues today, but the task is remarkably difficult and there is not an excess of confidence concerning the painting's future.

Leonardo concentrated upon the moment when Jesus tells his disciples that one of them will betray him. The tenseness and confusion of the moment are captured in the faces and gestures of the disciples. The shock they must have felt is well-mirrored, for this was almost certainly a Passover meal, though theologians are not united on that point, and Passover was a time of thanksgiving for deliverance. The last thing any of them would have expected at the meal was a note of doom. I find it easy to slip into their shocked psyches as I gaze upon the picture.

The painting tells us something about Leonardo, for the figure of Jesus is unfinished. The artist, it seems, did not see himself as a person spiritually and morally acceptable enough to complete the depiction of the Christ. Is it possible that Leonardo places himself in the shoes of Judas? I think so, just as I am convinced that he is inviting us to see ourselves in the Judas role.

There is one other undeniable, it seems to me, indicator in the accounts of *The Last Supper*. Judas is the Greek form of Judah. An analogy of the rejection of Jesus (the Greek form of Joshua) by his own people? Could it perhaps be that the Gospel writers had something like this in mind?

The painting, still unhappily deteriorating, is a wonderful accomplishment and needs many visits. Alas, Italy is not on my doorstep, so my viewings have to be far apart, but to see *The Last Supper* is always a profound spiritual experience.

To the northwest of Santa Maria delle Grazie lies the Castello Sforzesco, built on a site associated with the great Visconti and Sforza families. The *castello*, or palace, is surprisingly severe from the outside, given that it was built by Francesco Sforza, a member of a noble family who liked to make a stylish splash in the city. It is built on the plan of a series of courtyards, and my first impression was the huge scale of the layout. The arcaded Cortile della Rocchetta is the most gracious of the courtyards giving, as the whole castello does, an unmistakable impression of space.

The interior is as beautiful as the exterior is plain. It contains some important collections, including furniture, antiques, coins, sculpture (including Michelangelo's unfinished *Rondanini, Pietà* and paintings).

The Visconti family were the builders of the first fortress on the site. The family appears in the area as early as 1078 when Ottone, prominent in the First Crusade, is recorded as being the Viscount of Milan. Two centuries later another Ottone in the family became archbishop of Milan in 1262. Many powerful Visconti followed, but the one most proudly remembered in Milan is Gian Galleazzo who, in 1378, became ruler of all the family's territorial possessions. He founded the cathedral of Milan, the city's most loved structure, and the Certosa (monastery) at Pavia together with the bridge over the Ticino river which provides access to the town.

He was an ambitious man whose vision was to bring the whole of the Italian peninsula under the control of the Visconti. While he fell well short of such an achievement, he did bring Visconti rule to much of northern Italy, including parts of Tuscany and a number of cities between Milan and the Adriatic.

Such a man was Gian Galleazzo, and such a family was the Visconti.

The present *castello* was built after the fall of the Visconti from power in the mid-15th century. If the Sforza, who can be traced to the 14th century, were not as old a family as the Visconti, they were no less ambitious. The family name comes from one Muzio Attendelo, who died in 1424. Because of his extraordinary strength he was nicknamed 'Sforza'. An adventurer, he became a *condottiere* (a mercenary captain). He served a succession of masters and gained considerable wealth from his activities.

The Sforza family also included a Gian Galeazzo, whose life was lived out ineffectually in the 15th century. Confounding the name "Sforza", he was weak in health and far from being strong-minded. His father, Galeazzo Maria, however, was both sturdy in health and strong in mind and character. Probably the most notable of the Sforzas, he was a well-respected patron of the arts and a capable ruler. He was anxious for the Emperor to lift his domains from the status of a duchy to that of a kingdom. His concerns for the welfare of his territories was genuine, and among other achievements he introduced rice-growing into his lands.

Great names are etched into the proud history of Milan. For me, the city is the place of the Visconti, the Sforzas, Ambrose, the Borromeos and, though he was not a Milanese, Leonardo—the men who contributed more than any others to making Milan a proud city. Oh, and of course, the football! The players might be cardboard heroes compared with those famous names from the city's illustrious past, but don't say that to the supporters who flock to the San Siro every weekend during the football season. For them, 'L'Inter' and 'Il Milan' each put eleven heroic men on the field each time they play.

Chapter 3
Shakespeare, Learning and a Useful Saint

The Po is a remarkable river occupying a wide valley in its lower reaches. It almost cuts Italy in half, rising beyond Turin and making its way to its multi-coursed delta and the Adriatic, giving Italy great, fertile river flats. The journey from Milan to Venice does not follow the river; in fact, it keeps to the north of it, though many streams are crossed which run into it. Town after town *en route* owes no small part of its prosperity to Italy's longest and, usually, most benevolent river—usually benevolent, but just occasionally appearing not to be so when it decides to flood its plain. It's the flooding, of course, which feeds the soil.

One of the towns that benefits from its relatively close proximity to the Po valley is Verona, a town of elegance and intense literary and historical interest. How well acquainted with Verona Shakespeare was, I do not know, but his ghost certainly walks the streets. The *Two Gentlemen of Verona* and *Romeo and Juliet* have given the city a lasting romantic aura.

The former might well have been Shakespeare's first staged play; if so, it can be seen as nothing less than extraordinary, in view of the elegance of the verse and the accomplished storytelling. Entering Verona for the first time, I fancied I saw Proteus and Valentine heading westwards for Milan, followed some way behind by a boy who looked remarkably feminine! Julia's words, close to the play's end, came easily to mind:

It is the lesser blot, modesty finds,
Women to change their shapes than men their minds.

I wonder whether the playwright would have used those words in today's climate of cosmetic surgery, when the aim is the very reverse of looking boy-like. Even so, the romantic power of the story of Proteus and Julia, and of Valentine and the idealised Silvia, makes suspension of disbelief very easy.

One of the first places I made for in Verona is the house which, it is claimed, is the setting for Romeo and Juliet—*la Casa di Giulietta*. It is found via a walk along Via Cappello, the city's major retail thoroughfare, to number 23. I arrived at the house by entering through its courtyard. I would like to say that in the first few seconds I noticed the first-floor balcony at the front of the dwelling. Alas, no.

The first object which caught my eye was the bronze statue of Juliet, her right breast shining in the sunlight, due to the prurient habit of male tourists who like to say when they return to their homelands that they have stroked so intimate a part of Shakespeare's heroine. I hope that it was just the blinding glare of the sun on that scene which caught my attention rather than some murky Freudian weakness hiding from my consciousness.

Why did I make for Juliet's house? It is, of course, a piece of fiction, just as Juliet and her beau, Romeo, were fictional. Yet the story is so compellingly romantic. I easily found myself reliving the tortured love of Romeo of Montague (*Motecchi*) and Juliet of Capulet (*Cappello*), lovers kept apart by their feuding families. Who, possessed of warm blood, could not identify with these two whose plight is succinctly put by the Chorus?

Being held a foe, he may not have access
To breathe such vows as lovers us'd to swear;
And she, as much in love, her means much less
To meet her new-beloved anywhere.

And then, to show the intensity of their love, Shakespeare adds the lines which glue me to the story:

But passion lends them power, time means, to meet,
Tempering extremity with extreme sweet.

In those lines, he surely has the sympathy of all star-crossed lovers. Who, deeply in love, will not go to any lengths to win his beloved? The tragic ending of the affair, with the suicides of both because he cannot live without her, and she without him, simply adds to the romantic heart of the tale.

I gazed up at the balcony, took my mind in memory through the play, and was thankful for the magic of romantic love.

Leaving Verona's house of Juliet, invented no doubt for people like me, I made my way along Via Stella to Piazza Bra, over which towers the Roman Arena. Being a hot day, my first requirement was a seat under a canopy with a cup of coffee, and since there are very few places in Europe more pleasant for coffee drinking than Piazza Bra, I made for one of the outside tables facing the Arena, under a yellow sunshade. Piazza Bra gets its riot of colour from the sunshades, over every table, each one a brilliant hue at the time of my most recent visit.

My cappuccino came quickly to the table, served by a master of the serving art, the Italian waiter. As I might already have said, there is none like him anywhere outside Italy. Dressed impeccably in black, with a perfectly tailored white shirt, he placed my coffee carefully on the table with such practised skill that there was never the slightest possibility of even a suggestion of liquid escaping down the side of the cup.

Grazie.
Prego.
As always in Italy, it was delicious.

I sat gazing at the massive structure of the Arena, and while contemplating the wonder of its survival, I heard a voice from the table next to me.

Buongiorno, Signore. L'Arena e molto grande, e molto vecchia. Che cosa pensa?

What did I think? Yes, of course, it was extraordinarily large and very, very old, but that didn't say even the half of it.

'Yes, it certainly is big and very old. I think it was built in AD 30. That makes it about the time of the Crucifixion of Christ. I find it fascinating to think that here in Verona Rome was building one of the many symbols of its power, quite unaware of the influence yet to be of the carpenter's son they had crucified at Jerusalem.'

'Ah, yes. Rome really only understood one kind of power. But Rome brought values and civilised living as the other side of the coin which also contains its brutality.'

I realised that I was speaking with a Veronese for whom history was a living influence at the heart of things.

'Yes,' I replied, 'here in Verona, there seem to be more monuments to Rome's civilised activities than anywhere else in the north of Italy. They are everywhere. The theatre is one important example.'

'Yes, the theatre is important,' he said, 'because in a Roman town of any size, they built a theatre for drama as quickly as they could. If you have travelled in Europe very much, you will have seen so many of them—in Orange, and Arles in France, in Spoleto, in Taormina (following in the footsteps of Greek builders), in Gubbio, in Fiesole—they are just a few. I could go on for a very long time with examples.'

'And in the country of my birth, too,' I contributed, 'there are examples. The one that I know best in England is St Albans, a little north of London, where there are the remains of a small theatre which was part of the Roman town of Veralamium. You can see from what remains that it was a very attractive theatre. You are right. The Romans were a cultured people, as well as being capable of great cruelty.'

'You have been into the Arena this morning?'

'No, I've spent the morning in Via Cappello.'

'Ah, you have been shopping!'

Shamefacedly, I had to admit, 'No. I've been to *la Casa di Giulietta*.'

I realised that I had quite deliberately said that I'd been to Via Cappello in an attempt to disguise the fact that I'd been to the tourist attraction of 'Juliet's house'. The worst kind of snobbery, I suppose, is the hypocritical kind. I was uncomfortable with the self-revelation.

'*La Casa di Giulietta?* How interesting it is that an Englishman has given us our chance to set up our little tourist trap!' (I felt even more uncomfortable!) 'I know, of course, that the original story was written by Luigi da Porto from Vicenza, so it's quite a local story, but it's Shakespeare who has made it into a magnet for Verona. I suppose you have helped the *seno di Giulietta* to shine?' At least, I could be honest there.

'No, that's not the kind of thing that appeals to me.' Now I had moved from hypocrisy to pomposity.

It seemed not to worry him, and we shifted our conversation to literature as we discussed the merits of *The Two Gentlemen of Verona* and *Romeo and Juliet* and the power of Shakespeare's story-telling. Alfredo (as I discovered him to be) remarked in passing that if Romeo and Juliet did exist, they were in Verona around the time of Alberto della Scala, who ruled the city at the beginning of the 14th century. Given that Shakespeare was born in the 16th century and given also that the period of della Scala supremacy in Verona was characterised by a plague of vicious family feuds, I could see no reason to argue with his point of view.

We progressed to Italian literature.

'You will know,' Alfredo said, 'that the Scaligeri family, though they came to power in a very calculating, ruthless way, were benign rulers who brought a high degree of stability to Verona. They were interested in literary matters and in 1301 were glad to have Dante Alleghieri here in the city. I'm proud to say that Dante seems to have liked Verona.'

'Is it too much to say that Dante has in Italian literature the same kind of place as Shakespeare has in English?' I asked him.

'They are different,' he replied. 'Shakespeare's written more, and you might say that he was more nationalistic than Dante, but they were alike in some ways too. *Per esempio*, Dante and Shakespeare were both masters of their languages and of the art of drama.'

'They also both had massive influences upon the development of their national tongues, too,' I said.

'Yes, the development of an Italian national language was greatly influenced by *The Divine Comedy*.'

'There is an intriguing question that comes to mind when I think of Dante,' I said. 'A significant part of the *Divine Comedy* was inspired by the Val d'Enfer near Les Baux de Provence, and Dante spoke Provençal fluently. I wonder if Italian would have developed very differently if he had written the Divine Comedy in Provençal?'

'I'll give my opinion on that in two ways. First of all, it would have developed differently. *The Divine Comedy* put the Tuscan dialect at the centre of the Italian language stage. Almost certainly Tuscan would have been less influential, and that would have been bad. Tuscan has given elegance to modern Italian. But the second thing is that a language understood and spoken by all Italians had to happen. For a long time, thinkers in Italy saw the problems of small Italian states.

'Years before the *Risorgimento*, true Italian patriots were looking for a one-country Italy. Cavour, Vittorio Emanuele, Garibaldi and Mazzini were really putting into action a dream that went back a long way. Verdi, our great musical nationalist was doing the same thing. And yes, the *Risorgimento* had a wonderful uniting force in the language which Dante influenced so strongly. I feel proud that he had at least a brief association with Verona.'

It was time to end my *al fresco* coffee interlude and I thanked Alfredo for his company and the pleasure of the conversation. Leaving him, I walked towards the massive symbol of a unified Italy of 2,000 years ago, the huge 1st century monument which has the distinction of being the third largest arena ever built by the Romans, the only larger being the Colosseum *(Il colosseo)* in Rome, and the amphitheatre at Capua, 18 miles north of Naples.

Francis Bacon once wrote, 'Antiquities are history defaced, or some remnants of history which have casually escaped the shipwreck of time.' In what sense, I wonder, is the Arena at Verona 'history defaced'? In one sense, the defacing is visual, for that great structure, wholly Roman, stands in tandem with Piazza Bra, and all around it is modern Verona. It exists as it has existed for 2,000 years, but it exists out of its context. No toga-clad Latin-speakers enter through its portals. These days the visitors are mostly tourists, and I admit that my own feeling when first I entered the huge edifice was the uneasy sense of being a voyeur from another time. It was, I think, the guilt-tinged sensation I would get were I accidentally to walk, unannounced, into a lady's dressing room.

Here, in the great oval arena (perfectly shaped and proportioned with axes of 505 feet and 404 feet respectively), I was gazing at rows of terraces all focussed upon the central flat campus below where some of the Empire's most popular entertainments took place. I was conscious that the terrace upon which I sat as I contemplated the life of the arena so many centuries ago was where Romans sat or stood engrossed in the action, and at times applauding— cheering—often with deafening enthusiasm.

I was in a cultural icon of the life of Roman citizens, but they had all gone with the departure of their civilisation. Not even their ghosts were discernible in that great open place. More recently the arena has been used for operatic and other dramatic performances, and while in one sense that might be 'history defaced', in another it seems not out of joint with the cultural strains of the more sensitive Romans. Had they lived long enough to experience *musica lirica* I have no doubt they would have enjoyed it. Certainly, they were admirers of staged drama, as the proliferation of their own theatres across the Roman world confirms.

Verona's arena has certainly 'casually escaped the shipwreck of time'. So many other Roman structures in Europe have not survived the scavengers for building materials. Rome, and especially the Roman Forum, provide many examples. Noble families were quite ready to plunder Roman monuments in order to build their own palaces. But the majestic Arena at Verona, with its two levels of huge stone arches, has survived to remind us of the considerable building expertise of Rome. Somehow, I think that Tiberius, Emperor during its building, would be pleased to see it today standing head-and-shoulders above its surroundings in Verona.

The Teatro Romano was also built in the 1st century AD. It has suffered the ravages of the centuries, the stage area being virtually non-existent. But the wide arc of terracing is still there, and there is enough of the structure to enable imagination to complete the task of seeing the crowds and the plays. Ancient buildings lack clues to what sometimes we really want to know. Were there local actors and actresses who got their first 'break' in this theatre and went on to enjoy successful acting careers? How good it would be to know their stories, but maybe that is another way in which ancient monuments are 'history defaced'. The really interesting secrets of Verona's Roman theatre are never to be revealed. But that doesn't stop the wondering.

Piazza Erbe is a place for people-watching. The name comes from the fact that this is the location of the old herb market, but today is a market which sells a wonderful variety of food. It's an easy walk along Via Mazzini from Piazza Bra.

Taking time is the key to enjoying Piazza Erbe. The numerous stalls are shaded and pressed by a mass of people. Everyone, it seems, goes to the market in Verona. Business is brisk as every imaginable delight to the taste buds is sold. Browsing, I became fascinated by the variety of mushrooms at one of the stalls. Being a mushroom lover, I asked the elderly man behind the stall which *funghi* I should buy to get the best taste. No hesitation. 'Porcini'. I bought a bag of porcini, knowing that I'd have to pay the price required for the best mushrooms. I spent an hour or two wandering, enjoying the wonderful smells which always pervade a market which sells food, and admiring the way in which Italians are so very careful in selecting the food they buy.

Eastwards towards Venice lies the city of Padua, another part of Italy in which Shakespeare placed an unforgettable character, Katharine the Shrew.

Padua, or Padova, is a city of great charm, with arcaded streets and wonderful open spaces.

My first visit to Padua was a gala occasion. It was one May 8 and the whole town was celebrating VE Day. Sky divers were landing with pinpoint accuracy on the Prato della Valle, the beautiful public garden in the centre of town, accompanied by coloured 'smoke', and everywhere there were (presumably retired) soldiers of the Alpine Group, with their wonderful red feathers in their hats. In some cases, they were in the local equivalent of jeeps—and how grand they looked! Bands were playing everywhere I went and I have never seen a whole town celebrate with the enthusiasm Padovans put into it that day. Wine was flowing freely, and by mid-afternoon the singing was beginning to be more fervent than tuneful! No-one in Padua that day could have doubted the ability of Italians to celebrate.

I found my way to the Basilica di Sant' Antonio. For the most part built between 1232 and 1307, it reflects the architectural influences of the transition period from Romanesque to Gothic. Its imposing façade, both Romanesque and Gothic, with four major arches and one minor arch above the main portal, takes the eye up to the roof, with its spires of clear Gothic character mingling with seven Byzantine domes, an effect which is entirely pleasing.

In fact, the Basilica di Sant' Antonio has at least one thing in common with the great church in Assisi which commemorates St Francis. In Assisi, they commemorated *Il Poverello* with a richly-decorated church, just as, in Padua, they commemorated St Anthony, a man who rejected the world's riches and modelled himself on Francis, with one of the most sumptuous churches in Italy.

Inside this wonderful church, magnificent stained glass abounds as a celebration of human artistry. The high altar features a feast of works of Donatello, including his depictions of the miracles of Sant' Antonio. The north transept contains the remains of the saint himself, a fact which makes that part of the church irresistible to a person interested in Church history and whose imagination is alive and well. My strongly developed scepticism concerning relics has no place in Il Santo, as the basilica is popularly known, and for much the same reason that I have no quarrel with the claim of the basilica di Sant'Ambrogio to contain Ambrose's bones. The church in Padua which bears his name was commenced in the year following his death, and for me that is sufficient reason for not doubting the authenticity of the remains.

Anthony is my kind of saint. He seems first of all to have been a traveller with a great thirst for life. It's also clear that he had a considerable love of language and was known throughout Italy as an unusually fine preacher. Now the patron saint of Padua and of Portugal, Anthony was born in Lisbon in 1195, the son of a noble. At the age of 14, he entered the Augustinian order, in itself an astounding fact, but in his mid-twenties he joined the Franciscans.

He found his way into Italy in an entirely unplanned way. He was on his way to Africa on a journey with a missionary purpose when his vessel was wrecked on the coast of Sicily. From there he wandered through Italy, building his preaching reputation. He was so powerful a speaker that at the conclusion of sermons he invariably received applause. He found himself, by his eloquence, in his own century's equivalent of the limelight. Such an experience would hardly be expected by even the best of preachers today, though they might not be reluctant to receive it were it possible. Such was the near-adulation given to this travelling, life-celebrating, word-loving, faith-living preacher of the Church.

He was a staunch advocate for the Franciscans and a fine teacher as well as preacher, teaching theology and preaching in Toulouse, Padua, Bologna and Montpellier. The Portuguese Franciscan, teacher and preacher in France and Italy, was clearly a linguist. We can of course, assume that he was perfectly at home also with Latin.

Legends concerning his ministry are legion, and here scepticism is perfectly legitimate. However, legends do say something about their subjects, and given that one of them tells of even fish being affected by the eloquence of his speech, there is no doubt that the impact he made as a preacher was dramatic. In fact, legend after legend attests to his power of speech.

The Church honoured him as a servant of great eminence and there was widespread mourning when, in 1231, in only his 36th year, he died in the convent of Ara Coeli in the vicinity of Padua. In the following year, he was canonised by Pope Gregory IX. How tragic that a man of such abilities was given only 36 years of life.

He is regarded as a very helpful saint in assisting the careless to locate lost items. Now I think that makes him very useful! Having said that, I must admit that I have never invoked his aid when I have mislaid my car keys or my wallet, but that does not mean that I won't, in a future weak moment, do so. Saint Anthony is the helper of those seeking lost items; I am Anthony too, but I am a mis-layer of items rather than a helper of those who do so. If I were to call on him, he would be seriously overworked.

Heading out of the town centre northwards towards the railway station at a brisk walk I came to my objective, the *Cappella degli Scrovegni* on the edge of a parklands area by the river. Once a great palazzo existed here, but since 1820 only the chapel, built by Enrico Scrovegni, remains. Enrico, it seems, erected the chapel in 1303 as a kind of bribing of God. His father was a moneylender, and whether or not he charged exorbitant interest rates I do not know.

But apparently for Enrico, a devout Catholic, it was danger enough that his dad was in the money-lending business and he feared that his parent might be destined to hell. Perhaps he was unduly conscious of the line in the fifteenth Psalm which tells that the man who can dwell on God's holy hill is he 'who does not lend his money at interest'. That might suggest that an awful lot of people in the finance industry, on Scrovegni's estimate, have some thinking to do!

Dante's *Divine Comedy* was not completed until 18 years after the building of Scrovegni's chapel, but it seems that the latter's mind was tortured by the same horrifying pictures that *Inferno* describes of everlasting tortures too appalling to dwell on. *The Divine Comedy* was written in three parts, *Inferno, Purgatorio* and *Paradiso*. Metaphorically, it represents the soul's journey to God.

To say the least of it, *Inferno,* said to have been inspired by the *Val d'infer* at Beaux de Provence, appears in Dante's writing as a horrifying part of the journey. It is the place where Christians see sin for what it really is and have to face the reality of poetic justice as a major theme of *Inferno*. Scrovegni, it seems, saw only the terrifying in it, and hence his need for provide the means for building a House of God. The construction of the chapel, then, was Scrovegni's attempt to persuade God to spare his father from an unthinkable fate. Bribery it might be, but perhaps bribery nourished from the soil of compassion is not entirely sinful in the mind of the Divine.

Whether the bribe was efficacious or not, the chapel's interior is a feast of beauty, focused in the feast of frescoes by Giotto depicting scenes from the life of Christ. Giotto, it appears, was not insensitive to the motives of Scrovegni, because one of his scenes is an exposition of the Last Judgment, a matter very much in the mind of the chapel's builder. As I looked long at the picture, more and more my eyes dwelt upon the detail of Enrico offering the chapel to the Virgin Mary. Giotto highlighted the bribe!

On the same theme, the lower row of pictures on the southern side of the chapel depicts the virtues and vices which presumably are to be taken into consideration at the Last Judgment. I did not see usury there, but perhaps I missed it. The chapel, with its blue, curved ceiling, its simple mosaic floor, and every wall frescoed, is a lovely place of quiet and peace.

Padua is home to an ancient university, founded in 1222 by imperial decree. That does not make it the oldest in Italy. Bologna, the oldest university in Europe, was founded in the 11th century, and there is evidence that there was important academic teaching in that city as early as the 5th century. Even so, Padua's seat of learning antedates Cambridge (1284), though Oxford (1167) precedes it.

The university at Padua is not without its claims to fame. Celebrated students have included the poet Tasso, derided in his home town of Sorrento during his lifetime but now claimed as a local celebrity, the Florentine Dante and Petrarch of Arezzo. It even had Galileo among its professors as a teacher of physics. Oh, and those who feel smug about modern enlightened views of women and education might care to note that in 1678, Padua graduated its first female student, one Elena Piscopia.

The medical faculty of the university was originally housed in the main university building, the Palazzo del Bo. I can't help feeling that it should have been the veterinary faculty, because the palazzo takes its name from an erstwhile tavern which carried the epithet of Il Bo, The Ox. The palazzo is open daily, and well worth a visit.

I found myself feeling strangely excited when I walked through the timber-built anatomy theatre, constructed in 1594, knowing that Padua was not only the host to a medical school famous throughout Europe during the middle ages, but the anatomy theatre around me was the oldest such structure in the world. I would like also to have rejoiced in the knowledge that here a very famous man taught, but he lived from 1523 to 1562, therefore before the appearance of the theatre. His name was Gabriello Fallopio and he was teacher of anatomy in the Padua medical faculty.

Fallopio should be much better known than he is. Born in Modena, he had an ecclesiastical background, becoming a canon of the cathedral in that city. His major medical studies were undertaken at Ferrara where he became, as he was later to be at Pisa and Padua, teacher of anatomy. The Fallopian tubes take his name. Fallopio, or Gabriel Fallopius as he is sometimes known in medical circles, taught and researched during the great age of medical discovery in Padua, and made important findings in the areas of the nervous system and the female reproductive system. He was the anatomist who named the placenta, the ovarian tubes, the vagina, the clitoris, the cochlea, the palate and a number of muscles of the head. His writings and research were extensive, covering a multitude of medical subjects.

Other great men at Padua during its extraordinary period of medical discovery were Vesalius, dissector, medical writer and producer of fine anatomical sketches whose book, *De Humani Corporis Fabrica*, published in

1543, had a massive impact in European medical circles, a man who gave up anatomy during a strange attack of depression and resigned his chair in 1546; Realdo Colombo who succeeded Vesalius and added greatly to the store of knowledge of eyes and lungs; Geronimo Fabrizio, one of the greatest anatomists of all who occupied the chair at Padua for half a century; and Adrian van der Spiegel, a Belgian, that is, from the area which became, in 1830, the modern state of Belgium (as was Vesalius), who died in 1625, but not before making important discoveries concerning the muscles of the spinal column.

Padua held, undisputed, the position of the leading centre for anatomy studies in the world until the passing of Spiegel. It was a golden age for the city, and one which Paduans still recall with pride.

In that ancient wooden anatomy theatre, thoughts of Fabrizio and Spiegel ran through my mind at a racing pace, as I saw them in imagination dissecting, making notes, explaining carefully to enraptured students who no doubt for the rest of their medical careers boasted that they studied under Fabrizio or Spiegel.

The University of Padua is a place where momentous discoveries were made and great teachers held their students spellbound.

At Bologna, to the southwest, is the most famous university of them all. Its foundation date is not certain but is believed to be 1088. It has operated continuously since its foundation.

One of the more interesting facts of the university's past is that though it is the oldest university in Europe, there was no building it could call its own during the early years of its existence. The *professori* were required to conduct their lectures in their own homes, and I wonder if they were paid a special supplement for providing the venue for their classes? I suspect not. But it must have been very cosy, and certainly class sizes can't have been very great.

Today, we might gain a good deal by having in our own academic institutions the kind of intimacy which must have existed at those lectures in Bologna before the university had its own building. The tertiary classes I attended were in halls of 30 or 40 students, a different, more distant experience altogether, and therefore without a great deal of interaction with the lecturer. The students at Bologna did much better, I think.

In 1520, the university gained a temporary home in a building owned by the Church, but in 1562 its own palazzo was built by St Carlo Borromeo (that man again!), who at that time bore the title of Cardinal Legate, though not, of course, saint. The authorisation for constructing the building came from Pope Pius IV.

The ancient Bologna—*Bononia*—was an important road junction. Roads from Venice to Rome and the south crossed the Via Emilia, and that famous Roman road still runs through the centre of Bologna. That centre is, above all, elegant. My first sight of it left an indelible impression of porticoed streets and fashionable shops, tasteful architecture and well-heeled shoppers.

The focal point of the city centre is Piazza Maggiore, around which are clustered the fountain of Neptune (*Nettuno*), the church of San Petronio and, just slightly off the piazza, the Palazzo Archiginnasio, which now houses part of the university. The Fontana di Nettuno is a magisterial piece of work. Designed by Tommaso Laureti, it is both huge and masterly in its execution. Neptune looked down on me from a great height, looking every inch the epitome of masculinity. Other bronze figures are by Giambologna, complementing the main statue and producing a work of wonderful balance.

Standing in Piazza Maggiore for the first time I had an overwhelming sense of the ugliness of the exterior of San Petronio. My difficulty is that the façade looking out onto the piazza has an acceptable enough lower level, featuring quite attractive pilasters, but to my eyes is overpowered by the upper level which I still think looks like the functional, featureless wall of a barn. Since then I have come to appreciate the other aspects of the building, and especially its fine brickwork. Its interior attracts only admiration. The Gothic arches and pillars taking the eye up to simple but elegant vaulting are together magnificent.

A wonderful series of over twenty chapels are housed off the side aisles, and to appreciate them takes time. I found myself thinking of great ecclesiastical decision-making when I recalled, while walking through the nave, that for a while in 1547 the Council of Trent was accommodated in the building rather than the church of Santa Maria Maggiore, where most of the sessions were held during the 1545 to 1563 life of the council. It was known as the *Concilium Tridentinum* and was the 19th ecumenical council of the Church.

It had as its major purpose the Church's response to the Protestant Reformation. It was presided over successively by Popes Paul III, Julius III and Pius IV. Its major sessions during the late period of its work were attended by more than 250 participants, hardly a good number for effective decision-making. It concluded with 17 teaching decrees which dealt with Catholic religious positions challenged by the Protestants. They were the products of 25 sessions held over the life of the Council. There were many Church developments stemming from the Council, including the Vulgate being proclaimed the official

Church canon of scripture, and the promulgation of the Tridentine Creed (*Tridentum* was Trent's Latin name). There would be just over 300 years before a further ecumenical council was called, namely the First Vatican Council in 1869.

San Petriono is the largest church in Bologna, a striking reality given the fact that it was never completed according to the plans for the building. It was intended that it should be over 700 feet in length, but the diversion of monies to the Palazzo Archiginnasio close by meant that in its final form it is 384 feet in length, just above half the intended distance, with a width of 157 feet, compared with the intended breadth of 460 feet across the transepts. Given the size of the church as it stands, it's hard to visualise what it would have looked like if its intended gigantic proportions had been translated into reality. If my arithmetic is somewhere near sound that makes the present building between one 6th and one 7th the ground floor area it was intended to be. Anyone looking at the huge building today would find it hard to imagine it six times the size it is.

Just as *Bononia* of Roman days was a junction of some importance, so is modern Bologna, but the junction is rail—in fact, the most important rail junction in Italy. If all roads lead to Rome, all railways lead to Bologna. I enjoy the view of Bologna from the train, as much as anything because I simply can't resist that means of travel.

As my train pulls into the station, I am always looking for something very specific—a hole in the wall of the station buildings. I soon manage to pick it out and give myself to thoughts of the many people who lost their lives in a 1980s terrorist bomb attack which devastated the station. The Bolognese were very sensible in their reaction to the attack. Besides expressing their grief by recording in the station the names of all those who died, they left the hole in the wall just as the bomb left it—jagged brickwork edges—as a memorial to the dead and an indictment of the terrorists. How wise they were.

My leaving Bologna is usually by train. I think of the wonderful academic history of the city; I think of the culinary delights of its restaurants; I think of its cool, tasteful porticoes; I think of the fashion-conscious Bolognese; and I think of the fine defiance of terrorism represented by that hole in the wall.

Chapter 4
The Most Serene Republic

One of my visits to Venice was with my younger son, Richard, a much-travelled young man who has Down Syndrome. Recently, I asked him, 'Richard, what did you enjoy most about Venice?'

Quick as a flash, he replied, 'The water-buses!'

Now Richard is someone who retains impressions vividly and who fell in love with Venice at first sight. I think it likely that his mental picture of water-travel is one shared by most people who have been fortunate enough to spend time in the City of St Mark.

I add to that the delight on the face of Ruth, my second wife, when she first saw Venice. We had just arrived on the Venice Simplon-Orient-Express and walked the short distance from Santa Lucia station to the water-taxi quay and boarded the walnut-timbered, ultra-comfortable taxi on the Grand Canal. As we proceeded along the canal towards Piazzale Roma, her eyes lit up in sheer wonder of all that was around her. I understood the thrill in her eyes. It was my experience, too, when, many years earlier, I had first seen Venice and the Grand Canal, though on that first occasion, my transport was not in a comfortable water taxi, but aboard a vaporetto (a water bus).

Other friends have shared with me their own memories of the compelling city in the lagoon. Among their recollections are 'People, people, people in St Mark's Square and pigeons, pigeons, pigeons'; 'St Mark's Basilica with those wonderful domes'; 'The gondolas and men with straw hats standing up to row them'; 'No roads, cars'; 'The funny-shaped Rialto Bridge'; 'Palaces everywhere'; 'Lots of shopping'.

They are all vivid pictures of Venice but let me return to Richard's. The diesel motor sound of the vaporetto, the bump of the vessel against the pontoon of the 'bus stop' (*la fermata dello vaporetto*), the clunk of the mooring line falling around the bollard and the slam of the sliding tubular-steel gate meeting its end-stop are auditory impressions which live long in the memory. The crush of passengers alighting and coming on board, and the bustling traffic of the major canals are the tonal values on the vaporetti canvas.

The vaporetti form the public transport system. It's important to travel on them the moment you arrive in the city. That means 'catching a bus' on the Grand Canal.

For that purpose, there is one way of travelling into Venice which beats all others. You can travel to the city in many ways. A number of cruise ships berth there, disgorging their passengers directly onto the wharf at the passenger terminal. You might enter the city by coach, in which case you will be set down in Piazzale Roma, from there to find your way either to your nearby hotel or to the Grand Canal via the 'back-streets'. Flights from London Gatwick land at the airport on the mainland from where you can take the vaporetto to the islands, and that is a very pleasant way to make your entry.

On the cruise out to the city on the vaporetto from Venice's Marco Polo airport, you begin to see before you what surely must be an apparition, because you will swear that you are looking at buildings ahead of you which are rising directly out of the water! Perhaps, if you blink an eye, they will disappear! Certainly, that first impression is unforgettable. But the way that beats all others, for me, is arrival by train.

I have arrived in Venice by coach, and I have flown into the airport, but for my money, arrival by train at Santa Lucia station after crossing the causeway from Mestre is the method of entering the city above all others. I have done it far more often that way than any other, mostly by scheduled state trains, twice on the Venice Simplon-Orient-Express. The train brings you over the Austrian-built causeway from the mainland into Santa Lucia station.

You feel you are there before you get there. The water is all around you, the gentle hum of the wheels of the train generate a kind of electricity within, and ahead the buildings of Venice, coming slowly into view, seem to rise directly out of the water, as indeed they do, for their foundations on larch poles are driven deeply into the mud below. The magic of Venice is with you even in the anticipatory journey over the causeway.

As you leave the station concourse you find yourself, once outside the building, at the top of a flight of steps which descend to the Grand Canal and one of the most thrilling views in any city. When I first did it, many years ago now, I had to pinch myself to be sure that it was not a dream. It was like no other city

I had ever seen. The canal before me was alive with activity of vessels of more kinds than I could count. And everywhere, there were mooring poles!

My prior imaginary picture was a city of canals, certainly, though I thought of it as a metropolis where canals had been deliberately cut, a concept as far from the truth as it could have been. But now, gazing at the magnificent spectacle before me, it was as obvious as obvious could be that Venice was a city that existed by water. Canals were the everyday life of Venetians as roads are the everyday life of other cities. Watercraft were and are the vehicles by which Venetians move if they have too far to go for walking. It was clear to me on that first sighting of Venice on the steps of Santa Lucia station that a wholly different way of life was before me to explore. I have never lost my fascination in exploring the Venetian way.

If it's a sunny day, the water glints from the surface of the Grand Canal and is reflected on the hulls of the many vessels which carry out their business upon its waters, the vaporetti, the water-taxis, the private vessels; sometimes you see a police launch or a fire-fighting unit; I have even watched a McDonald's boat unloading supplies at Rialto and Richard, our son with Down Syndrome, who at that time worked at McDonald's, was delighted with the picture of it I brought home with me (he was not with me in Venice on that occasion). And, of course, you don't have to look far over the water to spot a gondola or two.

Any conveyance that moves must move on water in Venice. And everywhere along the sides of the canal are those wonderful barber's-pole-like mooring posts. The architecture of the buildings lining the waterway provides a visual feast. If it looks like a film set, and I confess that it does, you must put that thought out of your mind quickly. This is a real city which has occupied the lagoon for many, many centuries (the first doge, or duke, was elected in 697). You are in an ancient city which was once among the most powerful city-states of Europe.

Descending the steps, upon which sit many visitors to the city, especially young people in animated conversation and couples looking dreamily alternately at the Grand Canal and into each other's adoring eyes, you walk to the *biglietteria*, the ticket office for the vaporetti. You can buy a single-trip ticket to get to your hotel or, a better deal, a three-day ticket which gives you unlimited use of the vaporetti during that time. You'll be surprised how often you use those bustling craft. However, to use them effectively you will need a vaporetti route map showing the locations and names of the stops as well as the names of the 'streets' in the city.

The major 'bus route' is the one which follows the Grand Canal, a circular line (Number One) which takes in Santa Lucia Station, the Rialto Bridge, and St Mark's with, of course, many stops between. One of the realities of the vaporetti is that they are always crowded. But that's part of the fun, which leads me to say that my own immediate mental picture, when I think of Venice, is an impression of people—people milling around St Mark's Square, multitudes squeezing themselves into the glass-sales shops on the outlying island of Murano, a two-way press of humanity spending big in the Mercerie, the dog-leg shopping "street" which runs from St Mark's to Rialto.

And just about everywhere else in the major tourist areas, there are people, people, people. But back to the vaporetti. Once you have struggled onto the waterbus with your suitcase, your airline cabin-baggage, your camera (unless you are relying on your smartphone) and probably a couple of carrier bags as well, your adventure on the Grand Canal begins.

There is something peculiarly Venetian about the swish of the bow-wave and the sound of the diesel motor as you make your way along the canal, feasting your eyes on the extraordinary number and architectural variety of palaces lining the waterway. Along the canal, the vaporetto moves from one side to the other, calling at the many stops which are necessary for the smooth transportation of tourists, visitors and Venetians alike. All stops include a pontoon with a predominantly yellowish-orange waiting room, and it is to the pontoons that the 'buses' tie up. You will quickly find yourself admiring the consummate skill of the man at the vaporetto controls. It all seems to happen effortlessly, although not without its bumps and grinds.

Given that once out of Santa Lucia station the water-bus is your first experience of the crowds, you'll also be impressed by the obvious fact that Venetians are talkers. They are distinguished from the tourists in many ways, not the least in that they are mostly dressed elegantly. But they are also different from the other passengers on the vaporetti because they talk, and talk, and talk! The tourists generally don't, though there are clusters of exceptions. You can't help picking up the equally obvious reality that the locals are going about their business and are animated, while the tourists look subdued by comparison, perhaps because they are occupied with the activity of photographing almost everything on the Grand Canal and the buildings lining it.

The fact is that Venetians are animated people. In Venice, once I have been awake for an hour or so, I hear the clacking sounds of feet on the pavement below the window and the enthusiastic conversation of locals on their early way to work. One of my favourite hotels in Venice is the 'Scandinavia' in Campo Santa Maria Formosa, a beautiful open space between St Mark's and Rialto where during the mornings a fruit and vegetable market trades.

I remember vividly the second time that I stayed in that very comfortable hostelry. My late wife Annie was with me, and on our first morning, we woke early. Below our window people were walking to work, their shoes making that 'clacking' sound on the pavement. Annie turned to me and said, excitedly, 'Just listen to that chatter!'

Chiachiarare (a wonderful word meaning to chatter) is one of the loves of Venetians, and the vaporetto is where you first experience this wonderful side of the locals.

Eventually, you pass under the Rialto Bridge, as distinctive as Florence's Ponte Vecchio but a good deal neater. The vaporetto pulls in to allow a major contingent of visitors to pour ashore to find their hotels in the Rialto district. If you are travelling on to St Mark's square, you have to stand well clear of the departing passengers because once caught in the stream it is like being carried along by a major current. Whatever your intention, you will find yourself on the pontoon being pushed shorewards, to see, as you turn your eyes back, the vaporetto with your bags heading back into the centre of the canal to continue its journey along that great, inverted 'S' waterway which winds, serpent-like, through the city.

Assuming you were wise enough to stand clear of the departing crowd and are still on board the vessel, you continue towards your destination, and in due course leave the Grand Canal by its majestic exit guarded by the wonderful baroque church of Santa Maria della Salute and the old Customs House, the latter a reminder that Venice was once an independent republic, *La Republica Serenissima*. The whole Venetian lagoon opens out before you and you see vaporetti criss-crossing it as they service the islands of the Giudecca, San Giorgio Maggiore, Burano, Murano, San Michele and Torcello. The water, being open yet shallow is rougher here, but still there are gondole with their striped-shirted, straw hatted gondoliers sculling them with great skill.

The Doge's Palace grows in size to your left, the *Piazzetta* (little piazza) which leads into St Mark's (*La Piazza di San* Marco) opens out, the lofty *campanile* (bell tower) soars commandingly above you, and in a few minutes you arrive at the *San Zaccaria* vaporetto stop outside the 'Savoia e Jolanda' Hotel, another of my favourites, in *Riva Degli Scavoni*. The Riva, with its hump-backed bridges, its milling people, its fine hotels, the La Pieta church (forever associated with Vivaldi) and trinket-selling stalls all add to the cosmopolitan ambience of this most scenic of all Venetian promenades.

Yet the vaporetto experience is only one part of the life of this unique city. Over forty years ago, one Truman Capote wrote, 'Venice is like eating an entire box of chocolate liqueurs in one go.' His words are true only if you spend just one day on the islands, racing from one place to another before continuing your journeyings to other parts of Italy. In that case, everything in Venice will merge with everything else and what seemed delectable in the consuming will end with a mood of mental nausea.

But spend time exploring and this ancient, miraculous city will offer you such a range of experiences that each one will stand out as special and discrete. I eat my Venetian chocolates one at a time, slowly, mindfully, reflecting upon the flavours and textures. Venice is too good for gulping.

Venice is a miracle that, by any stretch of the imagination, should never have been. No-one would build such a city today—unless, of course, a developer with unlimited money to spend saw some tourist potential.

To determine what Venice is about needs a discerning eye. The masses of tourists who descend upon St Mark's 'Square' (there is no right-angle in it) and pack the Rialto Bridge create an almost entirely holiday-making atmosphere. It is easy to believe that Venice is just a quaint city of waterways and gondole where you can feed the pigeons and be serenaded off-key by a gondolier. In that case, half a day in Venice will suffice. But begin to discover the treasures of this extraordinary place and you will be compelled, as I have been, to come back again and again and stay as long as possible on the islands.

Note carefully the words *on the islands*. There are many places to stay on the mainland (*terra firma*) so that Venice is just a few minutes away over the causeway by which the Austrians during their hated occupation ended the remoteness of the islands of the Rialto in the lagoon. There are places to stay on the Lido, the sandy 'resort' separating Venice from the Adriatic where, forgetting why they are in Italy, many scantily-clad visitors sunbathe on the beaches just as they do at home. Have none of it. Stay on the islands.

There are in excess of 130 of them, and once there were more, though you might be quite unaware of the multi-islands reality of Venice, because each small island, joined by hump-backed bridges to its neighbours, seems to be part of one whole, larger island. Not so. At the time of the first settlement in the Venetian lagoon, all that existed above the water were these many small mud islands. Centuries ago some of the people of the Veneto region fled to them to escape invading tribes who were spreading terror before them (I sometimes think that the modern Venetians must feel like fleeing Venice to escape the invading hordes of tourists).

Eventually, the city replaced the fishing settlements that first existed on these inhospitable mud-banks of the lagoon. The buildings upon them today disguise the fact that the small canals are simply the water between the islands.

The Grand Canal is different from its smaller sisters. Deeper than all the associated canals, it is formed from the bed of the Brenta river, which runs into the Venetian lagoon and now provides the trunk waterway for the movement of people and goods in Venice. There is surely no thoroughfare in the world to match Venice's 'high street' for elegance.

There is one major canal which runs off the Grand Canal. Though its name might not be known by the many tourists whose hotels are located nearby, they are certainly aware of its existence. Not long after they leave Santa Lucia station on the vaporetto, heading for Rialto, they see the Cannaregio Canal opening out to the left. A number of vaporetto services use it. Running from Santa Lucia station to the Cannaregio Canal is a walkway called Lista di Spagna, the promenade where tourist hotels exist cheek-by-jowl. Because this is the principal tourist hotel 'street', it is lined also with stalls selling souvenirs.

From the station to the Cannaregio Canal, you are in a sea of people, many of them haggling over souvenirs, including replica football shirts bearing the names of famous players of Europe, especially, of course, Italians. No-where else will you see as many people walking around with Bonucci, Rossi, Totti or some other famous footballing name on their backs. And the postcards! No-one needs to take a single photograph in Venice.

There is no location in all the islands that is not already on postcard, and they are all on sale in Lista di Spagna. It's a promenade of noise, where stallholders call out to passers-by just to be sure that they see the stall and all that it has to offer. As the Mercerie is the expensive shopping precinct, Lista di Spagna is the cheap souvenir area. As the Mercerie is dignified, having shops where prices are fixed, Lista di Spagna is noisy, brash, and an arena where bargaining is at least attempted. While the Mercerie does a great deal of its trade via credit cards, Lista di Spagna is a place of cash turnover. Hungry shoppers in the Mercerie will often look for a restaurant; buyers in Lista di Spagna are more likely to be eating ice cream and be wearing the garb which might be frowned on in Venice's more expensive eating places.

A nice touch to Lista di Spagna is that it is neatly terminated at each end by Santa Lucia. You are not in Venice long before you notice that every second gondolier propelling his boat beneath the hump-back bridges of the smaller canals is 'serenading' the occupants of the craft with 'Santa Lucia', usually none too musically. And because you had probably heard references to St Mark before coming to Venice, you begin to wonder why the gondoliers sing of Santa Lucia rather than San Marco (not that I am aware of any song having ever been written about St Mark).

At the time of writing, Venice claims to have the relics of both. The remains of Santa Lucia, if the remains of Santa Lucia they are, repose in the church of San Geremia which stands at the Cannaregio Canal end of Lista di Spagna. It's a pleasant church in a prime position in its own campo. (At this point, note that there is only one piazza in Venice, St Mark's. There is the Piazzetta which connects St Mark's with the lagoon. Other open spaces are known as campi (singular campo). If it is very small it might be a campiello.) San Geremia's campo has aspects facing onto both the Grand and Cannaregio canals. The word 'campo' means 'field' and there surely can be no other city so grassless with so many fields! Tourists from Lista di Spagna pass the church of San Geremia every day as they cross the Ponte delle Guglie (Ponte is bridge) to explore the district of Cannaregio. Its impressive dome and tall campanile dominate the junction of the two canals.

The remains of the saint were not always there. Once they were housed at the railway station end of Lista di Spagna where at that time the church of Santa Lucia stood, but since demolished to allow the railway over the causeway to enter Venice and take the saint's name for its terminus. Therefore, her remains have graced both ends of the 'tourist strip'. Some years ago those remains were stolen from the church of San Geremia, but to the relief of the parish priest recovered and restored to their place of repose.

As you pass the church with its elegant cupola and tall campanile, you might care to enter it and pay your respects to the ancient and venerable lady who was martyred at Syracuse in Sicily during the bloody persecutions of Christians by the emperor Diocletian. According to a legend, which almost certainly has no truth to it, Lucia was martyred because, having taken a vow of virginity, she refused to marry. It's a standard legend which comes from a time when martyred women were elevated to the status of virgins, indicating that special sanctity was ascribed to virginity during the early centuries of the Christian Church.

We do know that she was martyred, a 4th/5th century inscription at Syracuse providing reliable evidence of it. Almost certainly her martyrdom was due to her refusal to resile from her Christian commitment rather than to her vow of virginity. It was the former that bothered Diocletian when he found it in the Christians who resisted his will. Lucia means 'light', a lovely name, I think, for a saint. In refusing to abandon her Christian faith, she made her own costly contribution to the continuance of the message of the Galilean who is known in the Church as 'the Light of the world'.

Across the bridge over the Cannaregio Canal, the main entrance to Venice before the construction of the causeway, a delightful walk continues to Rialto, but before taking it you should turn left to follow the Canal for a short distance, about a hundred metres, until you see on your right a doorway above which on the lintel are obviously Hebrew characters. Turn under that arch and in a few minutes, you will enter Campo Gheto Nuovo (the Veneziano 'gheto' rather than the Italian ghetto is used), a place of dark memories. The saint of Light across the canal could not prevent the darkness which descended over this place, so close by, during the Second World War. This, and the street you walk through to get to it, comprise almost the whole of the Ghetto.

Don't ignore that street which links the doorway on the Cannaregio Canal with Campo Gheto Nuovo, because this street, a dog-leg with its knee formed by the Campiello delle Scuole (the little field of the schools) is Gheto Vecchio (old ghetto). It is grim, if only because so many of the ground-floor-level windows have steel bars across them, dark reminders of the fear experienced simply by being Jewish at various times in European history. To live in the *chazer* (Jewish slang in Venice for the Ghetto) was sometimes a melancholic experience, and always one in which the Jewish heritage and cultural bonding were important in keeping hope for better times alive.

Walking through the Gheto Vecchio should be a slow amble, even though the street is short. It is the only way to absorb the Hebrew ambience of the place. As you enter the Ghetto from Fondamenta di Cannaregio you will see on each side of the doorway, if you look carefully, markings which are the remains of the gates which once were closed each night, locking in Venice's Jewish population. Those gate-markings are a sombre link with the 16th century 'enclosure' of Jewish peoples in Italy.

In 1516, the Venetian Ghetto was established, the first in Italy. It is now over 500 years old. It was not until 1797 that the Ghetto was declared by the French to be a free area, and the gates were removed. Until then all the Jews had to return to the Ghetto at sunset where guards kept a vigilant eye on things to ensure that no-one left the area until sunrise. And who paid the guards? The Jews themselves were required to foot the bill! The two small windows through which the guards kept a careful watch are still there, now bricked in, but visible.

Those hard days are remembered in a plaque, dating from 1704, on the wall to your left as you enter the Ghetto from Fondamenta di Cannaregio. Though barely legible now, it declares that any Jew converted (to Christianity) is forbidden to have anything to do with the Ghetto. It also declares that swearing is not allowed. Penalties are set out for transgressing those requirements and rewards are indicated for those who make accusations against Jews which result in prosecutions. There were certainly Venetians and Venetians.

As you walk slowly through Gheto Vecchio, look for Hebrew characters at the sides and on the lintels of the doors. As you approach Campiello delle Scuole, you enter the area of the synagogues (called 'schools' here). Immediately on your left is the Spanish School while ahead of you on the other side of the campiello is the Yeshivah Luzzatto (kind of Jewish-studies college), and right next to it the Levantine School. Those who pass by preoccupied and unseeing miss the superb carved doors of the schools.

In the Gheto Nuovo (New Ghetto) are the Italian, Canton and German schools, each distinctly different from the others, illustrating the fact that there are many Hebrew traditions of synagogue worship and culture. A tour of the synagogues operates in the Ghetto, with explanations from very informed guides. There is no possibility of understanding the rich admixture of Jewish traditions which make up the culture of the Ghetto without making a careful study of the synagogues which remain as colourful, often brilliantly so, pieces of living history.

The wrought iron entrance to the Spanish School, its interior of red wall-hangings and chandeliers, the more sombre yet more classically elegant interior of the Italian school where Corinthian columns contrast with those of the Doric order on the building's facade, the strange mixture of styles of the exterior of the Canton School with its domed gazebo-like structure on the top, the whole building being tucked away in a nook in the south-east corner of the campo, are just some elements in the rich mix of the wonderful synagogues of the Ghetto.

There is one other essential place to visit in the ghetto if you are a student of culture—the Museum of Jewish Art. It is located next to the German School on the eastern side of Campo Ghetto Nuovo.

Sometimes a person or group of persons appears in a place at the right time, fired by a great vision. The Museum of Jewish Art is in place today because two such men were around when it mattered. At the end of the Second World War, the reduced number of Jews of Venice bore terrible internal scars after the ravages suffered by their community under fascism and national socialism. Venetian Jewry needed the kind of vision which would remind them of the rich past, and the future of hope that such a past supplied.

Rabbi Polacco and Rabbi Toaff set about creating a Jewish Museum in the Ghetto which could provide an exposition of the heritage which was so powerful a source of pride to every informed Jew. The establishment of the Museum of Jewish Art is their accomplishment, both in its concept and its birth. As I have walked through that museum and enjoyed a major contribution to my education, I have been grateful to Rabbis Polacco and Toaff, and thankful for their vision.

Strangely, I had visited the Ghetto a number of times before I realised that the museum was there. Its entrance, next to the German School, hardly demands attention. In a way, there is an appropriateness to its out-of-your-face presence, both because everything in the Ghetto is low-key and because for anything to impose itself would almost defile an area whose reticence expresses a history where prominence and survival were incompatible.

When I did discover it, I wasted no time in making my way inside, where I discovered a collection of art and artifacts which exceeded even 'Solomon in all his glory'. As with all museums it turned out to be a rich educational experience as I learned many Hebrew words for the sacred vessels and items used in the synagogue, and gazed upon often intricately made exhibits from many places in world Jewry—items such as plaques to adorn the *Sepher* (scroll of the Law), mantles and covers for the same scroll of the Torah, terminals (*rimonim*) for its ends, curtains beautiful beyond description, crowns which in some cases were stunning in their design, seven- and nine-branch candelabra (*Menorah* and

Chanukah respectively), a gorgeous wedding canopy, a number of marriage contracts, and so much more.

One of the loveliest items for me, which compelled me to gaze upon it for a very long time, is a *parocheth* (a sacred curtain) that seemed to my eyes to be embroidered work on a velvet-like cloth. It depicts the Jews in the desert, a beautifully balanced piece of work that illustrates the descent of the manna and rows of striped, tall tents. The whole experience for me was a glimpse into a culture, a religion and a community whose origins are found in Abraham, and whose manifestations in the Museum of Jewish Art show the richness of millennia of development. I left the museum feeling that in some deep, yet indefinable way, I was a changed person through the experience. Certainly, I have always seen Jewish history in a much more personal way, and I hope more informed way, since.

This small area gave the word 'ghetto' to the world. It was originally 'Geto' or 'Getto' (the 'g' being pronounced as the 'j' in jam), and remained so while the area was chiefly populated by Italian and Spanish (Sephardic) Jews. However, the arrival of German (Ashkenazic) Jews gradually brought about a harder pronunciation, necessitating the addition of an 'h' after the 'g'. The area was so-called because it was once the location of Venice's new iron foundry. The name 'geto', meaning 'foundry' in Venetian, is related to the verb 'gettare', to cast. The campo became the focal point for Jewish settlement in Venice and has remained so to this day.

A book of this kind is not the place for a detailed history of the Jews in Italy, but it is worth noting that it is an ancient story. As early as the second century BC ambassadors of Judas Maccabaeus, a heroic name in Jewish history, arrived in Rome, an event which led to a steady stream of Jews finding their way to Rome from Judaea. The conquest of Jerusalem in AD 70 was the watershed which increased the flow of Judaeans to the centre of Empire, so that by the end of the 1st century AD a Jewish community had been established in Rome.

When did the Jews arrive in Venice? Were there Jewish people on the islands in the first centuries of Venetian settlement in the lagoon? We know that they were close by because archaeological remains attest to the presence of Jewish people in the Veneto region, the mainland in the direct vicinity of Venice, as early as the 4th and 5th centuries BC. In time, the Jewish community established and developed a rich culture in the city of Venice.

There are three ghettos which comprise what we call the Ghetto of Venice—Gheto Vecchio, Gheto Nuovo, both already mentioned, and Gheto Nuovissimo. The last named means the 'Most Recent Ghetto' and is entered by leaving Campo Gheto Nuovo by the eastern portal. Gheto Nuovissimo was added to the Ghetto in 1633, and if you follow the alley running from the bridge over the small canal immediately outside the campo, you will find that it too ends in a gateway which once contained gates closed at night by the guards to lock the Jews in. Look carefully at the jambs and you will see where the gates once hung.

As I wander through all three of the Ghetto areas, I find my mind filled with the most vivid pictures. I see the men and women of Jewry herded like animals into what really was a human pound. I feel their yearnings for the freedom which governments all over Europe denied them. I see men of the Middle Ages in the long frock-coats and turban-like hats so characteristic of the Levantine Jews who settled in Venice; I see Jewish pedlars in their gathered, knee-length trousers, tight-waisted jackets and near-stovepipe hats; I can see in my mind the long, flowing robes of the German Jews and their pointed hats with brims looking for all the world like upside down basins giving a head covering looking remarkably like the 'witches hats' put on the roads in Australia to divert traffic. It is a colourful mix of life I see in my imagination as I walk through the Ghetto (or ghettos) in the City of St Mark, but I also see the indignities, the sufferings, the struggles, and the binding effect of an ancient faith.

But let me take you back to the first impressions of the campo. You will be impressed, I am sure, as I was when I first entered it, by the silence of Campo Ghetto Nuovo. I remember vividly sitting on a seat in the middle of the day soaking in my first impressions. The impact of listening to paper being blown across the campo is with me still. That is perhaps inevitable with memories set in such a place where one of the worst monsters of Europe's long story had so devastating an influence.

On the western side of the campo, an oddly-shaped space with no side running parallel to any other, attached to a crude brick wall erected to confine the Jewish population, are five *bas reliefs* of the herding of Jews onto trains to commence their journeys to the Nazi death camps. They are the work of one A. Blatas and were placed there in 1979. They are salutary and disturbing, a reminder to all who stand before them of the need to be vigilant. I am reminded each time I see them of the need to keep an eye on myself, for we humans are so prone to be swept up in movements—especially nationalistic ones with heroic slogans. Hitler's slogans were many, and none more horrifying than 'the final solution' to 'the Jewish problem'. To the right of the *bas reliefs* is the inscription:

The city of Venice remembers the Venetian Jews who were deported to the Nazi concentration camps on December 5th, 1943 and August 17th, 1944.
Il Sindaco (Mayor) Mario Rigo.

The inscription is also in Italian and French, where the words are far more graphic—*nei campi di sterminio Nazisti* and *dans les camps d'extermination Nazis*, respectively.

On the northern wall is a simple memorial which reminds us that 246 Hebrew citizens of Venice were taken by Fascism and National Socialism, and their names and ages are carved on plain boards. The youngest I have been able to find are a girl and a boy, each two years old, and the oldest a man of eighty-eight. Returning to the western wall, there is an inscription of a speech from the French commander of the liberating forces at the end of the Second World War which demands some focused contemplation:

'Men, women, children, masses for the gas chambers

Advancing toward horror beneath the whip of the executioner,

Your sad holocaust is engraved in history

And nothing shall purge your deaths from our memories

For our memories are your only grave.'

When I first read it, I found that statement deeply moving, and selected a name from those on the timber boards, one whom I shall call Leah; I do not feel free to publish her real name. She was seven when she was taken to Auschwitz. I never knew her, as I never knew any of the others. I do not know what she looked like, but I do know that an evil man, head of an evil regime, assisted by men who no doubt claimed that they were 'just following orders', took her life from her when she was a little girl who should have had many years before her. She was herded to a dreadful death. I often think of how frightened she must have been.

I am not Jewish, but I remember Leah at the time of every important Jewish feast. I imagine the husband, the children and the grandchildren she might have had, for she would be in her late eighties now, had she lived. I can do no more than provide a grave for her.

To refuse to remember those dark days is to allow them to happen again and so I visit the ghetto each time I find myself in Venice. I go there during the daytime, but return in the evening, for a different purpose. I make my way to a bar in the campo on the southern side. It has some outside tables. I go inside to order a glass of red wine, then take a seat outside. The waiter brings me my wine with the utmost courtesy, and with just a few words always leaves me feeling very welcome.

As I sip my wine, I utter a quiet *Shalom* to the spirits of those who never returned from the concentration camps to Venice. I watch families arriving and taking their seats for an hour or two's conviviality at the end of the day. They talk to one another, often in an animated way, and as I watch them, I rejoice that the 'final' solution was no solution at all, because there was no problem to solve, save that of Nazi brutality. Jewish life goes on, despite the worst efforts of a demented man of power.

Sitting at my table, facing into the campo, I speak for a few minutes with a man at the adjacent table—he has very warmly greeted me. He wants to know why I am here at a bar in Campo Gheto Nuovo when he is pretty sure that I am not Jewish.

'I come here to remember,' I say, 'to remember and to remind myself of the dreadful things we are all capable of, and the need to be vigilant—vigilant of others, but also vigilant of myself.'

'You see events like the holocaust always as human possibilities?'

'Yes, and I think there are more than enough examples to support my view—and not just persecuting emperors bent on killing Christians and crazed regimes determined to exterminate Jews, but in our own day tyrants in Africa and in Europe have practised their own form of mass genocide.'

'But the holocaust was a special case, surely,' he says, 'because it was Hitler's great plan to remove Jews not only from a country but from a whole continent. If he'd had the chance, he would have removed us from the whole world.'

'Yes, I've no doubt he would have done.' I'd like to say, 'Fortunately, he was not able to,' but as one who did not suffer as Jewish people did, it seems insensitive to speak of good fortune at all in a place where so much suffering has been experienced.

'Sensitive or insensitive,' he says, seeming to read my mind, 'it is true. He would have done. It's fortunate that his power to exterminate a race was confined to one continent. And he failed to exterminate us, though his brutes took so many of us.'

I look at him carefully, trying to judge whether I have the right to ask a question that I really want him to answer. I take a chance on it.

'What impact does it have on your faith?'

'Oh, God, you mean? Do you know that when the Jews were being herded into the gas chambers, they sang Psalms? Some were quoting scriptures from the Bible about God's help and his unfailing love. But the Psalms—they were the important things. Jews singing Psalms as they walked to their deaths. Where was God in all that? What help was he to any of them? They were still exterminated. No, I don't believe any more that there is a God. But I do believe that our religious practices are good—they build our identity and they provide coherence for us. They bind us to our history and lift our eyes to a future. But God? I doubt if there is a God, and I'll tell him so when I see him!'

Having listened to that wonderfully typical Jewish conclusion, it's about time to go. Feeling immensely blessed by the brief conversation, I lift my almost empty glass. We toast, first in Hebrew, *Lo Haim!*, then in English, *To Life!*

Leaving the Gheto Nuovissimo by its eastern portal, you are able to re-join the major 'street' which runs from the Cannaregio Canal to Rialto. This is a wonderful walk I delight in every time I visit Venice. Small shops, the odd gelateria here and there, the small 'back alleys' to investigate with their diminutive canals to walk beside before coming back to the route to Rialto—all are filled with the specifically Venetian ambience that you never forget.

On the way to Rialto, it is important to make a small diversion northwards to visit the very special church of the Madonna dell' Orto, so called because in the 15th century a statue of the Virgin Mary was found in a vegetable garden (Orto) close by. The church had been built in the previous century and dedicated to St Christopher, the patron saint of travellers, the establishment of the sanctuary and its dedication apparently being greatly appreciated by the ferrymen who had to traverse the lagoon daily in all its vagaries of weather.

St Christopher's statue still stands above the ornate portal at the centre of the intricately decorated façade of this superb Gothic building. It's possible to argue that the portal compromises the Gothic because a fine semi-circular arch overlooks the door. Above that lovely arch, however, is a pointed one formed by beautifully flowing lines which complete the columns flanking the door.

Why is the church special? Apart from its Italian Gothic splendour, it is associated with Tintoretto, Venice's Mannerist master of the late Renaissance. Tintoretto (1518-94), whose real name was Jacopo Robusti, received his nickname because he was the son of a silk dyer (tentore). Hence his name means "little tinter". He was a parishioner of the church and must have known Venice better than almost any of its citizens because he was born in Cannaregio, lived in it and died in it, leaving the city of Venice only once in his lifetime. Venice, and especially Cannaregio, were his theatre of life. Most of his best-known works are still in Venice and there is an appropriateness to that, given his commitment to his home city.

He was apprenticed to Titian, and it was surely the shortest apprenticeship any painter ever had. After ten days, Titian sent him packing because he didn't approve of the young man's drawing methods. I like to chuckle over the fact that Tintoretto became famous for his draughtsmanship. He seems not to have let the incident get in the way of learning, even though he was deeply distressed by the termination of the arrangement. He studied Titian's work very carefully and is said to have been deeply affected by the draughtsmanship of Michelangelo and Titian's use of colour.

Tintoretto died on 31 May 1594 and was buried in the church of the Madonna dell' Orto next to his daughter Marietta whom he outlived by four years. (In 1550, he had married Faustina de' Vescovi, the daughter of a banker in the city—a useful marriage for an artist!)

Inside the church, whose interior is relatively plain, but grand in its spaciousness, you can find on the right-hand wall as you face the chancel Tintoretto's 'Last Judgement', a graphic representation not designed to bring peace of mind. On the other wall is a painting that has a habit of making a bid for freedom. It is Bellini's 'Madonna With Child'. It has been stolen from the church three times. The statue of the Madonna is to be found in the chapel of San Mauro, within the church.

As you leave the church, there is a small bridge just ahead of you that crosses the Rio Madonna dell' Orto. Stand on that bridge and look back to gain the best view of the church, beautifully balanced, even though the campanile with its lovely semi-circular dome is offset.

Then continue over the bridge into Campo dei Mori. At the end of the campo, turn left. The third building on your left, 3399 Fondamenta dei Mori, was Tintoretto's residence for the last twenty years of his life.

Return to the walk to Rialto, which becomes Strada Nova. Just before you arrive at the Ca' d'Oro, the finest Venetian Gothic palazzo in the city, you pass on your left a long 'street' which runs to Fondamente Nuove, where you can find the very convenient vaporetto stop for visiting the outlying islands of San Michele, Murano, Burano and Torcello. In the area of that 'street' a few years ago, I had one of my most pleasant unplanned interludes in Venice. Walking from the Fondamente Nuove vaporetto stop towards the Grand Canal, I saw some outside tables behind which was a board with the words, 'Trattoria Antica Adelaide'.

The 'Old' Adelaide Trattoria in Venice where 'modern' is 500 years old? But there it was. How could I refuse to stop for refreshment? Sure enough, having felt neither thirsty nor hungry I succumbed to the name, went inside and ordered a red wine to drink at one of the outside tables accompanied by a *prosciutto* and *formaggio panino*. My ham and cheese roll was so light that I was barely conscious of its mass, only of its exquisite taste. And the wine seemed all the more seductive for drinking it in that amazing 'Venetian outpost' of Adelaide.

I took my time over the wine and the roll, musing on the extraordinary manifestation of a trattoria called Adelaide in so un-South Australian a place. But then everything in Venice, including its very existence, is amazing. The city of St Mark has never known what it is to be ordinary. I whiled away the best part of an hour occupied in the wonderful pastime of people watching, before deciding to continue my meanderings. Before leaving, however, I went back inside the trattoria determined to discover, if I could, how it came by its name. Was the woman behind the counter the proprietor, a waitress? I decided to ask her anyway.

'*Per favore, signora—un momento, se possibile.*'

Hoping that it was indeed possible that she could have a moment to spare, I responded to her 'Yes?' in the most direct way.

'*Abito ad Adelaide.*'

Her eyes rose in amazement.

'You really live in Adelaide?'

'Yes, and I had to come to ask you why you called the trattoria "Adelaide".'

'Well,' she said, 'I saw Adelaide on television, and it looked very nice.'

'It is a nice city,' I replied, 'and it's a very pleasant place to live.'

'You have many Italians there?'

'Yes, a fairly large number. A lot of Italians migrated to Australia after the War and quite a few came to Adelaide.'

'You have places like this to eat?'

'Yes, restaurants with outside tables are becoming very popular in Adelaide, and there are also many Italian restaurants. One of them is called the "Venezia".'

At this, she threw her hands up in delight.

'In Venice, my trattoria is called "Adelaide". In Adelaide, there is one called "Venice". That is beautiful, that is perfect!'

And that was the beautiful moment to move on. I thanked her for a lovely hour at her trattoria and for making the name of Adelaide known in Venice.

'*Grazie per La Venezia ad Adelaide!*'

I wasn't sure why she thanked me for that. After all, I hadn't named the 'Venezia'; I had only eaten there. But not wishing to quibble, I accepted her warmth gratefully and continued on my way.

A few years later, on another visit, I decided to call again at the 'Trattoria Antica Adelaide'. Sadly, it was not to be found. I asked a lady walking by what had happened. '*E chiuso,*' she replied. Learning that it had closed, I felt glad that I'd photographed it when I had the chance. I still have my memento of Adelaide's temporary presence in Venice.

Rialto is a place of bustle. In Shakespeare's 'Merchant of Venice', Shylock the Jew complains to Antonio that the latter reproves him in Rialto for his moneylending trade, yet the lucrative business of Venice could never have been carried on without the availability of funds on loan, and funds can only be on loan at interest. Shakespeare is surely reflecting the anti-Semitism of Venice and of wider Europe of the day when he depicts Rialto as the hub of Venetian business prosperity, but a hub where Gentiles are welcome and Jews tolerated for their usefulness.

Moneylending takes place in other areas of Venice today, but Rialto retains the air of a business centre. The area's focus is Campo San Bartolomeo, a charming open space liberally supplied with cafes and bars, all well patronised during the evenings. The moment you enter the campo you notice the fine statue of the Venetian playwright Carlo Goldoni, sculpted by Antonio del Zotto. It's appropriate that his statue is here because Goldoni (1707–1793) showed over and over again in his works an admiration for Venice's merchant class. Having studied law at the University of Padua, he found the stage a good deal more attractive than a law practice and completed an output of 120 plays.

He was a refreshing influence in Venice which, during his time, was still enamoured of the *Commedia dell'Arte*, where actors wore masks to identify their characters. Goldoni would have none of that. He wanted real people on the stage without masks so that they really had to learn well their trade of acting in order to portray characters effectively. It also meant that audiences could learn to appreciate the actors and actresses and become fine judges of their dramatic abilities.

Goldoni's most famous play is *La Locandiera* (The Female Innkeeper). It's a wonderful presentation of a vain woman, Mirandolina, consumed by her need to be adored. Mirandolinas can still be found in Venice, no doubt, but some of them perhaps are brief visitors to the islands.

You have to cross the Rialto Bridge to get to the Rialto markets. It's among the most recognisable bridges in the world and is approximately at the centre of the city with its rounded arches on the walkway and its balustraded side stairways used by those who just want to look up and down the Grand Canal. Between the arches is a fascinating retail centre. It's a bridge of jewellers where some surprisingly well-priced cameos of good quality can be bought.

In fact, at different times I have bought fine cameos there, one for my late wife Ann, one for my wife Ruth. At the height of the season, the bridge is packed with tourists during the daytime, but come back at night when many of the visitors have left the islands and you'll have much more room to move, and you can gaze down from the bridge at the lights of the vessels plying the canal. It is a very special sight and one to share, if possible, with someone you love at your side!

Once the only bridge which traversed the Grand Canal, the present structure is a stone construction. One of its predecessors, a wooden bridge, caused an embarrassing 15th century moment during the fashionable wedding of the Marchese di Ferrara. Packed with spectators eagerly viewing the proceedings, it decided that enough was enough and collapsed into the canal. Not quite what the modish nobleman was looking for on his wedding day.

In 1854, the new Accademia Bridge provided a second crossing over the Grand Canal. Those today who have business in Venice or who are visitors have reason to be pleased that it was built, because it is the nearest bridge to St Mark's to cross the canal, and is therefore much used. It's at a very convenient spot, close to the Peggy Gugenheim collection, the church of Santa Maria della Salute and the Accademia gallery.

Having crossed the Rialto Bridge, you come first to the fruit and vegetable stalls. On one of my earlier visits to Venice, I was somewhat taken aback while making my usual lunch purchase of one large yellow apple. Having selected an especially large, delicious looking *mela*, I looked up ready to pay. I was put completely off my stride to find myself looking across the stall at a truly lovely young Venetian woman wearing a white head-dress and a bridal gown, her hand reaching across to receive my money!

Having no idea what to say to disguise my confusion, I must have looked totally nonplussed. 'It's okay,' she said, 'I've just got married. I work here at this stall and we've come back for some wedding photographs of me serving.'

After I'd paid for my apple, the groom walked up to the stall, selected some fruit and paid his new wife while the cameras flashed. Top marks for very special wedding photographs.

Just a little way past the fruit and vegetable market are the stalls of the fresh fish sellers. Always they are smiling, always they are ready for some quick, joking comment. There is an obvious *camaraderie* existing between these 'fishmongers' and their regular Venetian customers.

While on that side of the canal, it's important to walk through the labyrinth of small streets to the church of Santa Maria Gloriosa dei Frari. Within this church, above the altar, is Titian's 'Assumption of the Virgin', one of the greatest artworks in Venice. There are two Titians in the church, the other being 'Madonna di Ca' Pesaro', a smaller work and less dramatic than 'Assumption'. The colour in the work is brilliant and the drama compelling. All the action is vertical, but balanced by three horizontal bands of figures. It is a truly magnificent painting and I shall always remember as one of the finest evenings of my life the experience of sitting in the front row of seats set out in the nave listing to a Vivaldi concert while gazing at Titian's 'Assumption'. How could such a Venetian evening be bettered?

The church also has some works by Giovanni Bellini and Donatello, and the neo-classical pyramid-shaped tomb of Canova. Monteverdi's tomb is in a small chapel in the left transept and the impressive monument to Titian is found on the right, after entering the church through the main portal, though the normal entrance is via a small door on the eastern side of the building.

Returning to the Rialto Bridge the walk continues to St Mark's Square. It's possible to use one of two shopping streets, the main one being in fact three, the Mercerie which find their way by doglegs to St Mark's. These three streets joined as one are the expensive shopping arcades of Venice and are best used for window-shopping unless you have a well-filled wallet or a card with a large credit limit. There are some especially fine glass boutiques whose windows I love gazing at. Venetian glass is certainly eye-catching and fine in quality, though some question whether the quality is as fine as it was when Venice ruled the glass trade of Europe.

Whether that is so or not, the quality is still fine, though it's probably wise to shop in the mercerie or Calle delle Rasse, to have the best chance of the glass being genuinely Murano, unless of course you intend to visit that island for your purchases. I usually admire the glass in the Mercerie, but buy it on the island of Murano simply because the furnaces and glass-blowers are there and it tends therefore to be available at a better price. Besides, it's nice to buy Murano glass on Murano.

The other, less direct way to walk to St Mark's is via a secondary shopping street, Salizzada San Lio. Taking this route allows you to visit one of the most charming campi in the city—Campo Santa Maria Formosa. Every morning in this lovely 'square' there is a fruit and flower market where I have often selected my lunch for the day. It's also a campo to return to in the evening to relax at an outside table with a glass of red wine, there to muse on the day you have enjoyed in Venice.

On the edge of the campo, there is one of the best *pizzerie*—if not the best—in the city. Once buy a slice of pizza there (it's placed on a paper napkin for you to take away and eat while you walk) and you will know that there is pizza and there is pizza. I maintain that the pizza I buy in Australia is by Italian standards hardly pizza at all. In Campo Santa Maria Formosa, at my favourite *pizzeria* in all the world, I buy a piece of ambrosia.

Its crust is hardly to be called a crust. It is soft and filled with taste while the toppings are simple—usually no more than three or four items—and the whole thing is wonderfully digestible and leaves a glorious taste in the mouth. Not surprisingly, there are always customers in large numbers waiting to buy the pizza of their choice. Many a time I have done so and wandered off to drive my taste buds insane as I walked through the *salizzada*.

Use of the word *salizzada* prompts me to say that you need to understand the local terms in order to find your way around Venice most effectively. *Salizzada* is only one of the words which describes a street in this magical city, and it's given to the main thoroughfare in the parish (Venice is divided into six parishes or *sestiere*). Two words, *riva* and *fondamenta*, both mean a street bounded on one side by water. Both *calle* and *rugo* mean an ordinary street while a *rughetta* is a short street running off a *calle* or *rugo*. A *ramo* is also a short street and often a *cul-de-sac*.

One of the more interesting words is *rioterra*, which is a street formed by a filled-in canal, an example of which is Rioterra di Stia near the Frari church. *Corte* and *sottoportico* both mean a passage while *sacca* is an open space where a canal enters the Venetian lagoon. Strangely, a *sacca* can be either land or water, an example of the latter being Sacca della Misericordia not far from the vaporetto stop for the outlying islands of Murano and Burano. *Rio* is the word for a canal.

Piazza is a large open space, St Mark's being the only example; a *piazzetta* is simply a small *piazza*, while a *campo* is an even smaller public space, but still larger than a *campiello*.

Armed with this knowledge of terms, the map of Venice begins to make some sense. Without it, the 'streets' seem merely a jumble of names having no rhyme or reason.

The walk from Rialto to San Marco (St Mark's), whether via the Mercerie or Salizzada San Lio, is liberally dotted with structures which were vital to the history of Venice, but are noticed by very few tourists—well-heads. Consistent with the Venetian propensity for elegance, many of the well-heads are works of art, though they have the most practical of purposes, namely to supply potable water. For centuries, Venice gained its drinking water by conserving the run-off from the roofs of the buildings. It was channelled to the centre of the nearest campo where it was filtered in an underground sand-trap and entered the central well-chamber ready for drawing. The observant will see evidence of the channels running to the well in many of the campi.

Arrival at St Mark's brings you into the *piazza* where pigeons exceed even the vast numbers of humans to be found there. Mostly the humans are tourists, of course, while the pigeons are native Venetians whose ability to find a meal on demand is rivalled only by their brothers and sisters in London's Trafalgar Square. Still, the tourists love them, though I can't imagine why, and are never happier than when a friend photographs a friend whose head is the temporary perch for a pigeon.

St Mark's, or *Piazza di San Marco*, is the number one assembly point for the thousands of daily visitors to the city and there is a wonderful atmosphere of life and buzz and fun. During the tourist season two or three small orchestras are usually playing outside the restaurants which have *al fresco* eating. The music entertaining the diners at Florian's on the lagoon side of the piazza is always classical. Florian's, after all, occupies the pride of place for prestige in San Marco, the eating and drinking venue which attracted so many of the great literary figures of the 19th century.

It isn't difficult to imagine Proust contemplating wasted time over a glass in Florian's, nor Dickens honing his nose for Venetian social injustice, in contrast to Byron, on an altogether less practical plane, musing on loftier things! Florian's was the meeting place for men of letters in Venice, and it has not forgotten its history. Elegance and *hauteur* have their place in this café of historical riches.

That the orchestra *en terrace* at Florian's is selective in its musical choices should not imply that the other groups in the *piazza* and the *piazzetta* are common or garden. Only fine musicians play in San Marco and the evening is the time to enjoy them. The *piazza* is not densely packed with people after dark and often I have enjoyed wandering it to listen first to one group, then to another, soaking up the atmosphere of this wonderful open space where once the amazing pageantry of the reign of the Doges took place. Like all successful civilisations, when Venice was at the height of her power she indulged in the pomp and circumstance which amounted to a powerful statement to visitors that, like Tarsus, this was "no mean city".

Seats for drinkers and diners are set up outside the cafés where, in the open, the orchestras are playing. But you don't have to sit. Many stand in groups to listen. Ruth and I decided that just to stand was not sufficient. A classical piece was being played that supported the dancing of a Viennese waltz, so we did just that. We danced the 3/4 dance that sent us in joyous circles to the music. Of course the dance had to end in a kiss when the music stopped. To our surprise, we heard loud applause and saw that a crowd had gathered around us. Another delightful memory of Venice.

The pageantry was more than matched by the architectural statements, principally the *Basilica di San Marco* (St Mark's Basilica) and the *Palazzo Ducale* (the Doge's Palace). Both buildings have been described *ad nauseum* in book after book about Venice, so I shall refrain from the indulgence of detail. However, it is important to recognise that the two buildings are the core of Venice's pride.

The basilica is the most important survival of Venice's Byzantine past. A magnificent building of look-at-me cupolas, it has to be viewed from three sides to appreciate its glorious exterior properly. First stand in the *Piazzetta dei Leoncini* (named after its two lions carved from red, granite-like Egyptian stone) whence the cupolas behind the façade are best seen, then stand well back at the narrow end of the main piazza to enjoy the wonderful panorama of rounded portals, the four bronze horses, and spires of the façade, behind which you can see the tops of the cupolas. Next you enter the courtyard of the Doge's Palace for yet another view of this extraordinary product of Byzantium, alias Constantinople. From every angle, it appears impossibly beautiful.

The bronze horses above the main portal are these days replicas, but exquisite nevertheless. The originals, after a brief spell atop the Carousel Arch in Paris, are now back in Venice, but must be seen in their museum setting inside the basilica. Napoleon took a fancy to them after the conquest of the island-state and no doubt, in removing them to his own capital, saw them as trophies of war well-suited to feeding the Bonaparte glory. However, given that they first saw the light of day in Constantinople and were, for Venice, trophies from the diverted fourth Crusade, Napoleon might have felt that their theft from Piazza San Marco was legitimate. Nor were they alone in being imports to the city.

The Tetrarchs (Diocletian's appointed four to administer Rome's Empire?), a 4th-century piece of sculpture from Egypt mounted on an external corner of St Mark's on the Piazzetta side, seem to have arrived in Venice in a cloud of mystery. Given that the bones of St Mark came to the city following their theft from Alexandria, a dark shadow seems to fall over the treasures of the basilica.

There are of course many more treasures inside the edifice, but I prefer to let my imagination run and try to picture the scene when a new Doge (duke) was elected. Here, in this great basilica, in all his finery, he was presented to *La Republica Serenissima*—the Most Serene Republic. Surrounded by nobles in their trappings, the Doge was feted by Venetians high and low, for in this man was focused all the power and glory of the City of St Mark. He was ruler and head of state of the most commercially successful city in Europe, and of one which had a fleet well able to protect its hegemony.

I imagine, as I walk through the basilica, men of power being received here, as they were in the Doge's Palace next door, ambassadors and heads of state from many parts of Europe and beyond. The man with the Doge's hat was an elected leader, the head of an immensely wealthy state and the envy of Europe.

I always come down to earth with a bump when the musty smell of the interior, caused perhaps by the aqua alta, 'high water', which from time to time has found its way in, reminds me that those days of Venetian grandeur have gone, to be replaced by the more mundane attentions of tourists. But the past cannot be changed. What Venice once was, lives on in its architectural wonders and in the minds of those who care to discover what those glory days were about.

'Next door' is the Doge's Palace (*Palazzo Ducale*). Whatever else can be said about this amazing edifice, it is a triumph of Venetian Gothic. Standing, watching a woman perhaps in her twenties photographing the façade, facing into the *Piazzetta*, I wait until her 'shot' is completed. As she holds her camera by her side her eyes remain on the pink edifice before her, and I wonder what impression it is making upon her. A little anxious that I might be misunderstood, I decide to ask her in English, 'What do you make of it?'

'Oh, 'ullo,' she says, betraying immediately that we are from the same city, 'Well, it's sor'er like a big decora'id cake, ain' it? The designs raand all dem winders makes it look like someone's bin pipin' icin' on it. But it looks pretty great, doan it?'

I agree that it looks pretty great, and to avoid giving the impression that I'm trying to pick her up, I keep the conversation brief and tell her that I hope she enjoys the rest of her time in Venice.

A big, decorated cake? I'd never thought of the Doge's Palace in that way, but following her comment, I walk around it with fresh eyes. She is right, it does look like a large, rectangular, iced cake. She is more perceptive than I. It is so easy to imagine a giant icing bag and nozzle at work around the pointed-arched windows and picking out the winged lion (the emblem of St Mark) design on the *Piazzetta* façade. The closely-spaced pointed arch decoration around the roof-line, looking for all the world like hundreds of Doge's hats lining up on parade, strengthens the impression of a piped border. The pink tinge to the brickwork adds to the confectionary picture.

The long succession of Doges who ruled from this palace from the mid-15th century, when it took its present form, would all have been greatly put out by such a suggestion. The palace was designed to add prestige to Venice and its rulers, not stimulate images of confectionary!

The first palace was built on the site in AD 814, and was more a castle in form than a ducal residence. The walls were battlemented with defensive towers at the corners, the whole being surrounded by a moat. These days the only water-boundary is the *Rio del Palazzo* on the side farthest from the *piazza*. That first palace had a short life—only just over a century and a half, being burnt down in

976. Its replacement was also damaged by fire, and in 1340 the palace was treated to a complete rebuild.

By now, Venice was supreme in the Adriatic and had a sufficiently large mainland empire to attract the name '*Serenissima*', so that the palace which now stood by the lagoon needed no defensive towers and was very much a building erected for prestige. The wall facing the Bacino (St Mark's Basin) was enlarged to allow the construction of the *Sala del Maggior Consiglio* (the Hall of the Great Council). This is the room which, perhaps more than any others, declares the prestige of *Serenissima* Venice.

This is the room where so many momentous decisions were made in the life of the city. 54 metres in length and 25 wide, approximately a thousand men of the great families assembled here to give assent to new laws. Upon the death of a Doge they would convene in the *Sala del Maggior Consiglio* to elect his replacement, in a complicated process designed to eliminate the possibility of electoral corruption. The man who received the Doge's hat became ruler of the most prestigious state in Europe and the most powerful in the Mediterranean. The city at the meeting point between Europe and the Silk Road seemed that it could only become richer. How paradoxical that an Italian, Cristoforo Colombo, should sow the seeds of Venetian decline in his discovery of the New World which in time would shift the focus of trade to the ports of western Europe.

The *Sala del Maggior Consiglio* is sumptuous. To look from one end towards the huge painting which provides the focal point at the other is to enjoy an artistic feast. Before an extensive fire in 1577 the hall was decorated with works by Pisanello, Titian, Carpaccio, Gentile da Fabriano and Giovanni Bellini. Now the major works are by Veronese and Tintoretto. What is the painting at the focal point? Tintoretto's *Paradiso* (Paradise).

Paradiso is the largest painting in the world, taking up almost the whole of the end wall and measuring 7 metres by 22. The little tinter certainly painted big. The painting depicts a vast throng of those who have made it to Paradise surrounding Christ and the Virgin Mary. If anything could put me off heaven, this painting would. The thought of being caught up in such a multitude generates pictures much closer to hell than to heaven in my mind. Even so, Tintoretto has produced an extraordinary work which complements superbly, in its dominant blue hues, the reds, pinks and yellows of the masterpieces which decorate the walls and ceiling—those of the latter surrounded by very heavy gilding.

A frieze around the upper part of the other walls depicts 75 of the first 76 Doges of the city. The one missing is Marin Falier, whose attempt to become absolute ruler of Venice resulted, in 1355, in his execution by beheading. So far as the nobles of Venice were concerned, that Doge never existed. The best-regulated systems of government can't change human nature.

My thoughts run wild in this place. The Doge was a man who carried immense prestige, yet it was not entirely a life to be envied. He was, for example, a virtual prisoner in Venice. The absence of the Doge from the *Serenissima* was unthinkable. *De facto*, he was the *Serenissima*. Moreover, he was the Head of State of the most powerful city-nation in the Mediterranean and Adriatic, a state which controlled the trade-routes from the Silk Road to western Europe, and sea-routes to Africa, the Levant and Spain.

Inevitably, it was a prestige and power which manifested itself in pageantry, elegance and confidence, glimpses of which are seen in artworks such as Canaletto's *Bacino di San Marco*, in which the basin is crowded with fine craft bearing not only finely-dressed passengers, but sumptuously-liveried boatmen. Tintoretto's portrait of Doge Alvise Mocenigo and especially Giovanni Bellini's painting of the best-known Doge of all, Leonardo Loredan, show glittering official costumes more magnificent than anything worn by the showiest of popes or the most self-conscious of monarchs. Perhaps Solomon in all his glory was not arrayed like one of these!

Bellini's depiction of a procession in the *Piazza di San Marco* half a millennium ago shows both pageantry and solemnity in the same brush strokes while the picture of the Doge and his Grand Council by Joseph Heinz reminds the viewer that the Head of State was not the only finely-arrayed notable in Venice; his Councillors too were clad as those who knew themselves to be the guardians of a great heritage and a city of massive influence. If the Doge was in effect the *Serenissima*, the Councillors were the ramparts around it. They dressed the part, they acted the part, they perpetuated pageantry fitting for the part.

There is a darker side to the Doge's Palace. Attached to it, across the *Ponte dei Sospiri* (Bridge of Sighs), are the prison cells, surely the most horrifying places of incarceration to be found anywhere. They are small, dark, stuffy and mostly windowless. The Bridge of Sighs is well-named; escape was close to impossible. One man, however, did achieve it, one Cassanova. Perhaps his motivation was considerably greater than that of other prisoners! Depressing though they are, the dungeons should be visited. They are reminders of what Venice was—a city which had its pitiless side too.

If there are dark sides and pitiless sides to Venice, there are also tragic sides. In 1630, the outbreak of plague which Manzoni describes in his *I Promessi Sposi* ('The Betrothed', a historical novel in three volumes, considered one of the great works of Italian literature) brought about the greatest slaughter in the history of the city—almost 46,500 souls. Plague was a dreaded visitor from time to time in every conurbation in Europe, but compared with even the worst of previous outbreaks the visitation upon Venice was appalling. San Clemente island was the quarantine enclosure of the *Serenissima*, and to that place were dispatched the servants of the visiting ambassador of Mantua, the Marchese di Strigis, whose city was already in the grip of the plague.

The unfortunate Marchese found himself indirectly responsible for the terrible plight of Venice, for one of his servants was already infected when the party was housed on San Clemente, a fact which was unknown to di Strigis. Luck was not with the *Serenissima*, for the infected servant passed the plague on to one of the construction workers engaged in building accommodation on San Clemente for the Marchese's party, accommodation designed to make the 40 days' quarantine as comfortable for them as possible. He, of course, carried it into the Venetian community. It's worth noting at this point that the quarantine is a concept which has come to us from Venice, the word *quaranta* meaning forty.

The stricken city was a place of the most dreadful suffering for 18 months, and when the plague passed it was felt that a great church should be built to express the *Serenissima*'s gratitude to God for its deliverance. The result was one of the greatest baroque churches in the world, *Santa Maria della Salute* (St Mary of Health). The church was built on the order of the Senate and the task of design given to Baldassare Longhena, a master of the baroque whose skill would be admired by every informed visitor to Venice. The wonder of the Salute is ample evidence of the genius of its architect.

I have photographed the Salute many times but never once even come close to emulating the magnificent view of the church found in Canaletto's wonderful painting of the entrance to the Grand Canal from the Doge's Palace, looking across the *Piazetta*. Its massive central dome seems to claim the canal as its own so that it lends an air of majesty to the waterway. From the same vantage point, the eye can run to the other domed votive church built to express gratitude for deliverance from the plague, Palladio's *Redentore* of 1576. Its full name is *La Chiesa del Santissimo Redentore*, in English, 'Church of the Most Holy Redeemer'. It is, as you would expect, a magnificent building, given Palladio's genius.

As you gaze across the canal at Longhena's masterpiece, *Santa Maria della Salute*, it is hard to accept that the huge Salute is built upon thousands of larch poles. Indeed, the very promenade upon which you stand is built on the same kind of foundation. All of Venice is.

Such unlikely foundations are the support upon which Venice rests because the mud islands were suitable for no other form of groundwork. Every building in Venice is built upon thousands of timber poles driven through the mud until they found solid ground. Over the years they have petrified. That method of building will probably never change in the *Serenissima*. When in the earlier part of the twentieth century, the *Campanile* (bell tower) in *Piazza di San Marco* collapsed it was rebuilt in the same way—upon a foundation of timber poles. The *Campanile* is Venice's most efficient lightening conductor! It has been struck many times, some of the strikes having caused extensive damage.

Two more of Venice's remarkable collection of notable churches need to be mentioned, *Santa Maria dei Miracoli* and *San Pietro di Castello*.

Santa Maria dei Miracoli, a little to the north-east of the Rialto Bridge, is tucked away in a comparatively unvisited area of Venice as though, shyly, it does not want to be noticed. Consequently, it is a church that can be enjoyed at some leisure, it rarely if ever being over-run with tourists. It stands in its own *campiello*, closed in to some extent by other buildings. That fact makes it difficult to find a place from which to view the whole church.

The best location to view the pretty façade is from a bridge fairly close to the left of the front of the building. Its rounded arches, coloured marble and delicate pilasters combine to provide a harmonious composition of sheer delight. The façade ascends to a semi-circular face rising from the full width of the top of the rectangular section, preparing the visitor for the barrel vault which characterises the interior.

The major interior feature, however, is the split-level formation of the space. The congregation sits at ground floor level, but the sanctuary is at a level considerable higher, the two being connected by a stairway.

The church is especially important because it is that rare building type in Europe, a church consistent throughout in its architectural style. It is Venetian Renaissance, built by Pietro Lombardo and completed in 1489.

Why does it carry the name of *Santa Maria dei Miracoli* (Saint Mary of Miracles)? The answer is that it was built to house an image by Zanino di Pietro, 'Virgin Mary and Child', believed to have miraculous powers. The image is displayed on the high altar.

The church is not large, has a single nave and is very popular among Venetians for weddings. The canal alongside the church enables the bride and groom to arrive at and depart from the church by gondola—in fact, a gondola of sumptuous decoration which would not have impressed the Doges favourably at all.

At the end of the *siestere* of Castello farthest from San Marco is the basilica of *San Pietro di Castello* in its quiet monastic grounds on its own island. To reach it from San Marco, one walks *Riva degli Schavoni* along the waterfront, then along the broad *Via Giuseppe Garibaldi* until a bridge is crossed onto the island. An immediate left turn provides a walk to the grassed area in front of the basilica. The cloisters of the old monastery are to the right of the church.

The basilica is important because from the ninth century until 1807 it was a cathedral, the archdiocesan seat of Venice. The present building is the result of work carried out in the 16th and 17th centuries. Most notable externally are the restored façade by Francesco Smeraldi with clear similarities with the style of Andrea Palladio, and the massive cupola at the crossing of the Latin cross design.

Internal points of importance are the high altar of polychrome marble, designed by Baldassare Longhena, the architect responsible for the magnificent Salute church, and an urn containing the remains of the first primate of Venice, Lorenzo Giustiniani. Longhena is also responsible for the impressive Vendramin chapel in the basilica's north transept.

The church is out of the way and so receives few visitors. It is an important part of the history of Venice. A serious student of the city will find it fascinating as, for that matter, most of the churches of Venice are.

Venice, then, is a cornucopia of riches. Its everyday life of the vaporetti, of municipal services, of retail trading, lives with great works of art, architecture making the Grand Canal one of the world's most elegant main 'streets', a city with a history of power and 1,100 years of Doge government and far more besides. For a serious student of culture and life, Venice is irresistible.

Chapter 5
Carnival Time

Venice can't be left without mention of *Carnevale*, the days when the *Serenissima* is at play. *Carnevale* is Venice having fun.

Perhaps you remember, as I do, those playful days of childhood when we dressed up and acted out rudimentary plays to an audience of other children. Anything would do for a pretend stage, any lengths of cloth or paper would do for pretend character clothing. And wasn't it fun?

In Venice at *Carnevale* time, *Piazza di San Marco* is the pretend stage, and the character clothing is often sumptuous, hired from companies on the islands, companies who know what is authentic, companies who know how to replicate as much of the historic dress of Venice as is practicable for revellers in the modern Venetian playground. The *piazza* (but not only the *piazza*) becomes a glittering spectacle of sumptuously dressed, fun-loving players in roles that in real life they would never enjoy. At *Carnevale* time, whether dressed in character or there simply to enjoy the colourful scene, have a great time!

My wife, Ruth, and I enjoyed *Carnevale*, or, to give it its full title, *Carnevale di Venezia*, together. I might better describe it by saying that we were taken by surprise by *Carnevale* together. We arrived in the *Serenissima* quite late and made our way to our hotel in the vicinity of the church of Santa Maria Gloriosa dei Frari and settled in for the night. The following morning, we boarded a vaporetto to the *San Zaccaria* stop near *Piazza di San Marco*.

We were a little surprised to find that at the stop after the one where we had boarded, Napoleon Bonaparte joined the passengers. Two stops later, a plague doctor came aboard. The penny dropped. We were in Venice during *Carnevale*!

How could I have missed knowing that, I who am well aware of the Church calendar? *Carnevale* means 'Farewell to meat' and the celebration ends on Shrove Tuesday, the day before the more culinarily spartan forty days of Lent, hence the name by which Shrove Tuesday is alternatively known, *Mardi Gras*, or Fat Tuesday (*Martedì Grasso* in Italian). Shrove Tuesday is therefore the last day of fat and meat eating before the season of Lent begins on Ash Wednesday. So why not party until Ash Wednesday comes?

They are the official matters of Lent, and while they are important background (it's good to know why a certain celebration is happening, and Venice is, of course, a deeply Catholic city), it's the happenings, the exuberance, the heightened senses, the bustle, the atmosphere of playing parts, that makes it the special time that it is.

The modern *Carnevale* in Venice was established in 1979, though there were antecedents and I have to say that reviving *Carnevale* was one of the best ideas to have its birth in the city.

As I recall my experience of *Carnevale*, I am still amazed that I was taken by surprise. It simply hadn't occurred to me when Ruth and I made our booking for another sojourn in Venice that Lent was just around the corner. Even when we had some difficulty in finding accommodation the penny didn't drop.

Our week of *Carnevale* was extraordinary. The atmosphere of Venice changes dramatically during the festival. St Mark's is a place of a great variety of activity, daytime and evenings. We enjoyed watching the celebrations from two places in particular. The first was the balcony by the horses over the entrance to the basilica. From there, we were able to look down upon many masked and character-dressed visitors, groups of musicians, giraffes, dinosaurs, acrobats and many other fascinating people.

We had bird's-eye views of winged lions carved from shrubs—real shrubs or artificial? We never found out, and we never got around to touching them. We watched an acrobatic woman in tights performing amazing stunts beneath a tethered balloon, sure that what she was doing was impossible for the human body, yet she was doing it. Well, it isn't difficult to believe in miracles in Venice during *Carnivale*. After all, Napoleon Bonaparte did board our vaporetto. That prepared us for anything.

The place of enjoying the pageantry, in a more passive way, was from a table in Florian's. It is the place to enjoy the heart of the proceedings. As we sipped our wine, we enjoyed watching one costumed character after another coming in and enjoying a refreshment break. The more relaxed look at the costumes showed us how intricate most of them were. And how fascinating it was to see that even in repose with a glass of wine, the costumed characters still took the trouble to sit elegantly and play the part of the Venetian nobleman or noblewoman. Well, how else would an aristocrat behave in Florian's?

It is, by any account, a remarkable coffee house. To give it its full title, *Caffè Florian* in *Piazza di San Marco*, established in 1720, shares with Paris' *Café Procope* the title of the oldest known continuously operating coffee house. There is, then, a special feel to drinking in Florian's. To drink in a coffee house which, in 2020 will have been operating continuously for three centuries, is one of the special experiences of Venice.

Opening on 29 December 1720, as *Alla Venezia Trionfante* ('Triumphant Venice'), its 300th anniversary is precise. It might be expected that something special will be happening at Florian's on that day. The original owner was Florian Francesconi, and hence it soon became known as Caffè Florian. I hoped I should be in Venice on 29 December 2020 which unfortunately did not happen because of COVID, I was not able to make it.

The sense of a special experience when drinking in Florian's is added to when it is remembered that this coffee house was at times the drinking place of such notables as Charles Dickens, Marcel Proust, Ernest Hemingway, Lord Byron, Charlie Chaplin, Jacques Chirac, Clark Gable, Helmut Kohl, Andy Warhol, Jean Cocteau and so many more who have attracted fame. Clearly, *Caffè Florian* has never sought to be the piazza-side café for *hoi polloi*. Yet you can drink there and enjoy their magnificent confections, providing you dress neatly and have a well filled wallet.

Florian's is *de facto* the hub for *Carnevale*. Every day of the celebration, and especially in the evenings, one superbly dressed participant after another, be he a duke for the week, be she a duchess for the week, be he or she a famous figure for the duration of *Carnevale*, or a plague doctor or a person-sized cat, enters Florian's for a few minutes drinking and rest from *pavane* (peacock) walking of *Piazza di San Marco*, pausing and posing for photographs, bowing and being gracious.

Florian's is also the place where the masks are removed for a few minutes, and the faces of the real people can be seen, those playing the game of pretend. It is the opportunity to exchange greetings with the playmates as well as to drink the fine coffee of the house.

The masks are part of the fascination of *Carnevale*, though it has to be admitted freely that many seen are not historically authentic. Many of the authentic masks are complemented by particular dress. One or two are worth mentioning here.

Since it is the most common outfit worn at *Carnevale*, the dress of the *Medico della Peste*, the Plague Doctor, might be the one to begin with. I like the plague doctor impersonators because there is something macabre about having fun with the memory of men who risked (and many lost) their lives in attempting to help sufferers from the dreadful disease that took huge numbers of Venetian lives. The mask is fun because of the bizarre feature of a long white beak with round holes cut for the eyes.

Those who want to be as close in their dress as possible to the plague doctors of those terrible times also wear the black hat, black cloak and white gloves that were part of the protective covering of those courageous doctors. A staff was carried by the *Medici della peste* in order to be able to turn or move sufferers without the need for physical contact. Today the festival nature of the mask is heightened by the wearers adding their own decorative variations.

The authentic mask is said to have been worn first by a 17th century French physician Charles de Lorme. Pleasant-smelling herbs were placed in the beak to keep away the odours associated with plague sufferers. In addition to the stage-playing of plague doctor revellers today, they remind us of days of great Venetian suffering.

There are more cheerful masks. My own favourite is the *Bauta*, a mask which speaks of democracy. It covers the whole face, so if you want to be part of *Carnevale*, you can have the great fun of being entirely anonymous. It's a mouthless mask with a square jawline, an important factor at meetings where it was important that everyone looked alike. The mask is tilted upwards slightly so that the wearer can talk, eat and drink while remaining anonymous (though voices, of course, can be identified by the skilled listener). The *Bauta*, in the days of its wearing in Venetian society, was usually worn with a tricorn and a red cape, so if you want to enjoy looking out for authentic masks and outfits during *Carnevale*, *Bauta* is one you can look out for.

What has the *Bauta* to do with democracy? In the 18th century, it was regulated by the authorities of Venice to ensure anonymity at political decision-making assemblies. All citizens of Venice had the right to be equal when engaged in decision-making processes and the *Bauta* provided that assurance. It was the means of providing a secret ballot. If you can pick out an authentic *Bauta* at *Carnevale*, let your mind run to its important place in Venetian democracy.

Similar in some ways to the *Bauta*, the *Volto* is full-faced and is usually worn with a tricorn and cloak. It is white, sometimes with minor markings and like the

96

Bauta is slightly upwards tilted for eating, drinking and speaking purposes. It seems to have been an especially popular mask for dancing at masked balls.

One of the masks most commonly seen at *Carnevale* is the *Columbina*, a half-mask held up to the face by a baton. Sometimes it is held in place by a ribbon, but it's more easily managed in its hand-held form. The eyes are expressive, as perhaps no other part of the face is expressive, so the half-mask allows for relationships to develop. Some forms of the *Columbina* are spectacular in their decoration. They are enhanced by feathers, silver, gold, crystals or almost anything else that is colourful, and sometimes by a mixture of all.

There are many other masks and outfits associated with Venice's past, and a good number are seen during the festivities before Lent. The wearing is encouraged by prizes offered for the best outfits and masks at *Carnevale*, and they are keenly sought after. One inevitable result of the prizes is that authenticity can take a back seat in the drive to be innovative or spectacular. But the festivities are supposed to be fun, so let's live with it, join in and enjoy it.

The annual celebration and fun part of the life of Venice is compelling. The sets are magnificent. *Piazza di San Marco* is transformed into something between a large playground and a circus big top or a huge theatre. It cannot be defined. It is unique and therefore it can only be described by alluding to what it is like, and yet not like. The unique has no likenesses.

The cynical might say that, like the Passion Play at Oberammergau, it is a money-spinner for the city, and yes, it certainly is. But that should never stop a traveller from visiting Venice at *Carnevale* and being caught up in the experience. It is joyful.

While the piazza is the major place of celebration, the area where most of the official entertainment takes place, evidence of *Carnevale* can be found in other parts of the city and the lagoon. Those who have spent good sums of money to hire costumes for our pleasure, visit other parts of the city and the outlying islands. Their costumes can be seen on Burano, Murano, Torcello, and even on the Lido. Dressed-for-the-part characters are seen on the vaporetti, in the markets, in the Mercerie, in fact, wherever you go in Venice.

Carnevale means 'farewell to meat'. But that comes at the end of the festival when Lent begins. In the meantime, as *Carnevale* proclaims by its celebratory spirit, let's eat, drink and be merry!

Venice is the Italian miracle on the Adriatic.

During *Carnevale*, there is an illusion of miracles. Or is it an illusion?

Chapter 6

A Different Riviera

Bathed in bright autumn sunlight, the Mediterranean is blue in the way that only this sea is able to be. It heaves its gentle swell against the shore, subtly changing its hues, white flecks picking out the surface movements. We have entered Italy at Ventimiglia, on the border with France. Between Bordigherra and San Remo, two of Italy's most popular beach resorts, the train, an inter-city, leaves the sea vista for a little while, threading its way through one of the many tunnels to be negotiated on this most scenic of lines from Nice to Genoa.

Already, we have passed through more tunnels than can be remembered, gazed over what seem to be countless glorious bays, spectacular cliffs and headlands, all the while enjoying the comfort of first-class European train travel.

The train's announcer, speaking very fast Italian, tells us that the next stop is Porto Maurizio, so we are already fifty kilometres into Italy. Very quickly afterwards, we pull into the station. A young woman, among the boarding passengers, has 'Richard' printed across the seat of her jeans. I find myself assuming that Richard appreciates that statement of exclusivity.

As we continue, Liguria's magnificent coastline passes by our window in this part of the Mediterranean also known as the Tyrrhenian Sea. My mind is filled with pictures of Etruscan traders and builders, those mysterious people whose chief influence was in the northern part of central Italy, who established the powerful Etruscan League of twelve cities and who were called by the Greeks Tyrrhenoi. Of them, more later.

Passing through Cervo San Bartolomeo, heading north-eastwards towards Savona, I gaze at a wonderful baroque church tower which soars above the town, surely making it clear that *La Chiesa Cattolica* lays claim to the place! The dominant position of the church is so characteristic of this country that I feel immediately at home in what I seem quite naturally to call *Italia mia*.

The train accelerates and the refreshment trolley arrives. I buy a *cappuccino* and a packet of *biscotti*. Forgetting myself for a moment, I say *Merci* (a few hours ago, we were in Nice) and immediately correct it to *Grazie*. 'Another shot,' says the smiling man selling refreshments. At €2.60 it's good value given that Italian railway coffee is the very best.

I strike up a fine conversation with an Italian lady bound for Switzerland who joined the train a stop or two ago. Heavily built, soft of complexion, kindly of look, she has grown up 'children'. The youngest, a male, 'lives in a film,' she says. Impractical, out of touch with reality, he wants to be a farmer.

How charming she is! I think she might be older than her appearance suggests. Speaking of how her children have caused her concern, she tells us, 'Once, my hair was green.' Looking a faded, brown, beneath the treatment, it is probably grey.

She tells me that one of her daughters is Marie Antoinette. I ask her if she has a good head on her shoulders. She chuckles in obvious enjoyment.

'Oh, the French!' she says. Marie Antoinette is a problem, but she doesn't elaborate.

'The first girl I fell in love with,' I tell her, 'was called Marie Antoinette. I was ten years old and so was she.'

'Just as well it was not this one,' she answers, 'she is *pericolosa.*' And clearly she means it. Marie Antoinette is dangerous.

Carla Theresa (we have agreed to use the *tu*, the Italian familiar 'you' that allows us to address each other by name) tells me, now that she knows I am going to the Cinque Terre, that my destination is 'very romantic' and I should walk the *Via dell' Amore*. She tells me that her 20-year-old is 'a very, very, very little boy.' I find myself wondering if he has the little boy's charm and sets hearts fluttering. As we progress towards Genoa, the journey is warmed by a conversation that can only take place between ships that pass and continue to their separate worlds.

After a break at Genova Piazza Principe, a lunch of *Capresi* and *caffè latte* and the necessary discovery of toilets, then stamp purchasing and postcard posting, I am on an Intercity, Genova to La Spezia Centrale. Soon I find myself in conversation with feisty Elisabetta.

She has been watching me writing in my journal. 'Are you a writer?' she asks from the other side of the table between us, her eyes registering intense interest in the strange behaviour of this man with the pen who alternately looks at the passing scene through the window and applies the writing instrument to paper, apparently absorbed in what he is writing.

'Oh, this is my journal. I'm writing my impressions of the journey.' We talk about many things, including Switzerland. She works in both Monaco and Switzerland where she also has a home. She tells us that she loves Berne, Zurich and Lucerne. She especially likes the 'little theatre' in Berne and is delighted that I know it. While she likes Lucerne, she is not too keen on the excessive rain. I can't help wondering if she is an actress. Interesting how we both wonder about the other. It's one of those travel occupations of the mind.

Perhaps in her late fifties, she has a slight build and the sharpest eyes. She is in love with everything and I enjoy seeing her childlike gaze of wonder as she looks through the window at all that is passing.

We are almost at Sestre Levante where she has to leave the train. She takes her bags to the carriage door at the far end, but she has forgotten her handbag. At least, I think it is hers but I'm not sure, so rather than pick it up, I go to the door and tell her that there is a black handbag in the seat next to the one where she was sitting. It is hers so she comes back to collect it and says to us, '*Molto stupida! Ha il mio passaporto.*' Getting up again, she makes sure that she, who is certainly not stupid, has all her belongings including her passport, but realises that the train has not yet stopped. 'If I get off here, I'll become an omelette!'

Sestre Levante now left behind, she has left the train and, sadly, I miss her sparky conversation and her enthusiasm for life.

La Spezia Centrale, as it turns out, occupies very little of my time. I walk quickly through the *sottopassagio* and up the stairs at the far end to find details of the next train to Corniglia. I find the information office.

'*A che ore parte il treno prossimo per Corniglia, per favore?*'

'The next train to Corniglia leaves,' the lady behind the counter tells me, 'at 5.22 from platform 6.'

It is now 5.20 and I am on platform one! Is it possible that I can just make it? Or just miss it? I run as fast as I can down the stairs into the *sottopassagio*. With my case, I run all out. Almost flying, it seems, I race up the steps to platform 6. I just manage to bundle my case into a first-class carriage. The train moves off. What you can do when you have to!

The train is a *locale* and the carriage, though not sumptuous on such a service, is very comfortable. After a brief journey (perhaps no more than ten or fifteen minutes, the longest part being La Spezia to Riomaggiore, then rapid-fire Riomaggiore-Manarola-Corniglia), I arrive at my destination. Standing on the platform at Corniglia station, I feel exhilarated.

I have planned for so long to be here in the Cinque Terre. Westwards lies the ocean, bounded by headlands at each end of the station; the sea is grey, reflecting an overcast sky, but I am bubbling with the joy of being here after my day's journeying from Nice. How different this small village station is from the bustle of Nice, a city extensive and busy enough to have the second-largest airport in France. But this is tiny Corniglia and from where I stand if I look in any direction other than the sea it has to be up.

I descend the stairs to the inevita*ble sottopassagio* and, struggling with a case far too big and certainly too heavy, make my way to the station exit. In the tiny ticket office, which doubles as an ice cream, chocolate and drinks kiosk, I ask the young woman behind the counter how I get up to the village. She points to the northern, far end of the station platform. 'That way, up the steps—about ten minutes.' I walk out of the little office and look to the end of the platform. Ten minutes? The steps zigzag upwards on what looks to be a near-vertical hillside to a height which seems more than a little daunting. Even without the case, ten minutes is surely absurd!

I decide upon an alternative course of action, perhaps the only practical one. Another newly alighted passenger, a lady, also needs to get to the village. She will sit on a seat outside the station with the cases while I walk up the road to find a more sensible means of reaching the village. She seems trustworthy to me. Risky? Perhaps, but those steps look formidable.

After five minutes of walking, I decide to continue to the village. The very steep, winding road was more than a little challenging, but the frequent glimpses of the ocean below add wings to lift my leaden feet. As houses begin to appear, so do drops of rain. Hoping that it will not be torrential, I trudge on to seeking the *Bar Matteo*, where one Signora Guelfi (what pictures of medieval conflict between popes and emperors flash into my mind at that name!) is to meet me. Coming to a small piazza, which is clearly the centre of the tiny village, I ask the first person I see where I can find the Bar Matteo.

He is the driver of a small green bus parked in the piazza and his knowledge makes it immediately clear that he is very local indeed, almost certainly a resident of Corniglia. He points to a narrow, ascending alley, dwarfed by tall stone buildings on each side. '*Il Bar Matteo e la—due cento metri.*' And approximately two hundred metres it turns out to be, after even more climbing.

The bar is on my left, and having announced to the lady behind the counter who I am, a very alert young woman appears. she takes charge immediately and calls a strapping man of, perhaps, 40 or so and asks him to drive me back to the station to pick up the cases and the woman she thinks is very likely the lady she is expecting as a guest today.

He turns out to be a real gem—a wonderful talker without a word of English (why should he have in remote Corniglia, a village not frequented by tourists?). He assures me that while it would rain that night, the following day would be *bella*. His enthusiasm for life and especially for his village is wonderful to listen to and experience. Soon the lady, whose name turns out to be Anita, and the cases are in the car (he has refused to allow me to help carry them) and we commence the ascent to the eagles' nest called Corniglia. His pride in the village is irrepressible. He tells us that it has 200 inhabitants, '*poco, ma buono*'—an understatement! Very quickly, we discover that while Corniglia is small, it is not just good, it is wonderful.

Having parked the car in the small *piazza*, he puts one of our bone-crushing suitcases on his right shoulder, picks up the other in his left hand, and begins a rapid ascent up the alley. Anita and I, carrying no more than our cabin bags need to put all our remaining energy into keeping up with him. We look at each other; I had thought myself to be fit! Not far beyond the *Bar Matteo*, we take a left turn and climb a long flight of steps, our 'porter' treating them as if he were walking over a very long billiard table. Then one more shorter but even steeper stone stairway and we are at our Cinque Terre accommodation.

Our Italian Hercules unlocks the *portone* (the outer door), then, turning to the right in the small hallway, unlocks the door to our respective rooms. Before leaving, he gives us our breakfast vouchers, takes the details of our passports and gives us registration forms. He talks excitedly of Corniglia while we complete the forms. He leaves us with a bow and a welcoming smile.

I open the shutters and discover that my room opens out onto a small balcony. I gaze out upon the sea—what a view it is! As Carla Theresa had said on the train, Corniglia is *molto romantico*.

That evening I decided upon pizza in the *pizzeria* a little downhill from the *Bar Matteo*—and a very good pizza at that. The man doing the cooking was jigging around to the mambo music being played. In conversation, I discovered that his football team is Boca Juniors, one of the more successful sides in Argentina. I couldn't remember the name of the infamous 'hand of God' man who had deceived the referee by handing the ball into the England net in a never-to-be-forgotten World Cup match, but I remembered that he played for Boca Juniors.

'*Come si chiama il gioccatore "La mano di Dio"?*' I asked him.

'*Maradonna,*' he replied, and I was satisfied. He was clearly pleased that Maradonna had succeeded in getting away with it.

I made our way back to my room at the very top of Corniglia, having started the day in France, enjoyed a journey through the spectacular coast of the Italian Riviera, and ended it talking to a man whose heart was in Argentina. Quite a journey!

I was in the Cinque Terre for the walking, and the walking was truly superb. I started at the gentle end, taking the local train from Corniglia to Riomaggiore, the southernmost of the villages and the nearest to La Spezia.

The day began with breakfast at *Bar Matteo*. I was joined by Anita, whom I had met at the station and discovered that we were staying in the same hostelry. After an animated conversation, we decided to be walking companions on the *Cinque Terre* trails. It was enjoyable at breakfast to observe the continual traffic of the locals as they came in, grabbed a croissant, and stood talking at the counter while they munched, talked and drank coffee, small, strong and black. Every breakfast in Corniglia was an immersion into village life for me, and I loved it.

Breakfast finished, we met at the doorway of *Bar Matteo*, and were soon descending the 365 steps to Corniglia station. Arriving at the station, I asked the lady in the ticket office-cum-kiosk how long we had to wait for the train.

'*A che ore parte il treno prossimo per Riomaggiore?*'
'*Dieci minuti.*'
'*Binario?*'
'*Binario uno.*'

Equipped with the knowledge that the next train was to depart in ten minutes from platform one, we awaited its arrival. A few minutes before it appeared, it was announced over the station PA that it would now stop at platform three. Sure enough, the Riomaggiore train arrived on time—at platform two. Ah well, Italy is Italy after all.

Alighting from the train at Riomaggiore, we found ourselves in a sardine-like crush on the station platform, due to a train scheduled to arrive before ours not having shown itself. An interesting altercation developed as a man on the platform who had probably been waiting for some time decided to blame the guard on our train for the non-arrival of his! As the train left, taking with it the object of his ire, he decided to transfer blame to a railway official over the tracks on the opposite platform. He was still shouting at him, ever more excitedly at a steadily increasing volume, as we left the station. This unexpected entertainment certainly took our minds off the less pleasant task of forcing our way through the apparently impenetrable mass of people between us and the exit.

In Cinque Terre terms, Riomaggiore is quite young, dating from the end of the 12th century, though there were smaller Greek settlements in the area five centuries earlier. Two rivers enter the sea at the village, the larger being the Rio Maggiore, the modern version of the older name, Rivus Major. The most dominant feature of Riomaggiore is the castle on Cerrico hill. The castle, built by a nobleman of Brugnato, approximately 30 km to the north and now separated from Riomaggiore by the Autostrada del Sole, is as old as the village it looks down upon. 'Modern' or not, Riomaggiore, with its green-shuttered mustard, ochre and grey-white houses, has its own charm.

Buying our walking ticket (the paths require expensive upkeep), we began the gentle stroll northwards along the *Via dell' Amore*. This involved a walk through a pedestrian tunnel, where we had the delightful experience of listening to two very fine-looking young buskers of extraordinary quality playing Antonio Vivaldi's 'L'Inverno' (Allegro) from 'Quattro Stagioni'—a Venetian moment in Liguria.

The young woman, full-lipped and sensuous, was playing the violin as if the instrument expressed her very soul; the young man, of broad forehead and wide-set, intelligent eyes was playing the accordion with incredible agility. Vikhor Maryna and Musliyenko Gennadiy, as later we discovered their names to be, were providing moving entertainment for the walkers in what are the surprisingly good acoustics of the tunnel. We couldn't move on before listening for a little while and buying their CD, so the experience lives on for us.

It didn't take us long to reach Manarola along the flat *Via dell'Amore*. The ease of the walk gave us a wonderful but false self-confidence for our conquest of the Cinque Terre. The path follows the sea at the base of the cliffs. The views are therefore of ocean-level seascapes, a perspective which gives a great depth to the panorama. Returning some years later, I found it closed. Temporary due to a rockfall? I did not know.

We enjoyed Manarola, where we decided to do a little exploring before continuing along the *Via dell' Amore* to Corniglia. Manarola sits mostly on a headland jutting into the Tyrrhenian Sea. It is colourful. The houses, which seem to cling to one another in a huddle to ensure they don't fall into the sea, are a riot of pastel colours—pinks, oranges, yellows, the occasional beige, even pale blues. Like Riomaggiore, it is young in local terms. It originated at the end of the 12th century, settled by people from higher up the mountainside who were themselves probably descended from Roman soldiers.

Manium Arula has become the lovely village of Manarola, sloping ever upwards from the sea. As temporary residents of Corniglia we were certainly not going to be daunted by the gentler climbs of Manarola. We followed what seemed to be the main road up the hill, coming to a small piazza with, on our left, the plain-exteriored but attractive-interiored church of San Lorenzo. We enjoyed its peaceful sanctuary, lit candles and spent some moments in silence in a side chapel. A sense of being in touch with the mystery of Life greater than I swept over me for those few minutes, an experience quite different from the exhilaration of life which it is so easy to be caught up in when confronted by scenes of great natural wonder.

On the other side of the *piazza*, we saw the entrance to *La Torretta*, a B&B which had been recommended to me some time before, though in the event I chose to stay at 'La Torre' in Corniglia. Even so, we decided to sticky-beak and wandered into the property, sitting for a moment or two in the outside breakfast area. We knew from what we saw that *La Torretta* was a fine guesthouse, and the view we took in was very special.

Descending to the lower end of the village we took the opportunity for enjoying a lunch of *capresi, vino bianco locale* and *acqua minerale* at an outside table. Returning to the *Via dell' Amore*, we walked the still gentle pathway to Corniglia.

How ancient is Corniglia? Perhaps it will never be possible to answer the question definitively. It seems at least safe to say that this isolated village high above the sea dates at least from Roman times. Does it take its name from Romans Cornelius and Cornelia, producers of wine locally? I want to believe it, but I suppose I can do no more than say it is at least possible that it takes its name from those two local worthies. In any case, there doesn't seem to be any other plausible explanation for the Corniglia moniker.

All our walking was not done on the same day, of course. We had so far done the easy sections! Our next day's assignment was to make the journey from Vernazza, the next village northwards, back to Corniglia. So off we went on another *locale* train after once more descending the steps to the station. More tunnels, more brief breaks with ocean views, more tunnels, then Vernazza, which is surely one of the most remarkable stations in the world. It is elevated above street level, but there are many stations on the globe above street level. In Vernazza's case, the line emerges from one tunnel onto the viaduct and disappears into the next. The portion between the tunnels is scarcely longer than one railway car, so that most of the passengers are in one or other of the tunnels when the train stops. My love for railways was wonderfully fed by Vernazza station!

Such is the quirky humour of life that you have to descend from the station viaduct before commencing the ascent on the pathway above the village. 'Let's take a look at the village first,' said Anita, and so we did, walking down to the picturesque small harbour through quite a wide, winding road from the station.

Vernazza, we discovered is 'touristy' in the way that Corniglia is not, there being stalls selling trinkets on the road to the harbour, and shops which have clearly targeted the tourist market. Never mind; the village remains beautiful and wears its age well. Its age? I am aware of no documenting of its origins, but under its Latin name Vulnetia it appears in recorded history at least as early as the 11th century. The fact that at the time it carried a Latin name suggests that it had been around a while before that.

As if jostling for position, the tall red, pink, yellow and brown centuries-old houses crowd in upon one another, squeezing the narrow *carruggi*, or alleyways, into the minimum width allowing the passage of people.

Quite soon, we arrived at the harbour, the heart of Vernazza. It is small, very pretty, and not well protected from the worst moods of the ocean. On our first visit to the village, the sea was exhibiting an angry disposition with huge waves crashing against the breakwater and sending spray 60 or so metres high in spectacular displays. A good deal of the spray was expending itself on the seaward walls of the tall houses at the limit of the harbour and the noise was thunderous. Inside the breakwater the harbour was in turmoil, the small moored boats being thrown around like the sea's playthings. It was spectacular.

The harbour *piazza* is lined with bars with outside tables and canopies, just inviting you to eat and drink. However, it was not the kind of day to sit outside and we wanted to commence our walk while there was plenty of daylight left, so we each settled for eating a banana and taking an apple for consuming on the walk.

Two important features of the village were built for quite different purposes. On the northern side of the harbour stands a church which can only be called huge for such a small community. A white building with Romanesque windows for two-thirds of its length (the rear, square-windowed, part of the building is clearly an add-on), it has a very tall octagonal tower which is the architectural gem of the village. The hemispherical dome leads the eye to a wholly satisfactory conclusion of the tower.

Beyond the southern end of the harbour lie the castle and connected defensive towers, built under the Genoese, who took control of Vernazza in 1276. The building, being at sea-level, needed powerful fortifications, especially since no reinforcements could be brought in from the landward side. Until comparatively recently all the five villages were approachable only by sea. In that respect, Vernazza is very different from less vulnerable Corniglia perched high above the water. Only a minor fortification was attempted at the latter, and it does not survive today.

The walk was scintillating. We asked a man where the walk started. 'Over there,' he said, 'and up.' Up it certainly was. Up and up and up winding flights of steps which seemed that they would never get us to the top of the rough, narrow track. This was a walk to test our aerobic fitness! No gentle *Via dell' Amore*, this. Serious walking had begun, and very serious climbing. At last, we reached the summit, after more than a few false summits.

At 750 metres, the sea stretched out away from us and so far below that it seemed a world away. In the distance, we saw Corniglia which, despite its height above the sea, was far below us. And it looked so beautiful we had to persuade ourselves that it was real. No picture postcard could possibly convey the view which opened out before us, with 'our' gem of a village beckoning us. When eventually we completed the steep descent into Corniglia, we knew we had been walking.

How can the walk over the high track be described? Not adequately unless the picture painted includes the spiritual nature of it. The restless seascapes far below, the olives extending over huge areas—the former are of life of the moment, ever-changing into new life of new moments; the latter are life unchanging, in unimaginable longevity. The sense of exhilaration filled my whole being as I looked out over it all. I had to conclude then as I conclude now that it was and is all beyond my powers of description save to say that it is a visible, feelable, intimation of something elusive, invisible, yet unquestionably real.

You can without doubt experience the Cinque Terre on many levels of experience, and I found myself imagining, during the walk, what life must have been like for the villagers before the coming of the railway. All it takes now to travel between any two of the villages is a few minutes on the train; then it was necessary either to communicate between them by boat (and that would depend upon the weather), or to walk these hills we were walking. For them, there would have been two important differences; they would have been carrying produce for trading in one direction and any items purchased on the return journey, which highlights the other difference—their walk would have been twice as far as ours as well as twice as demanding.

At the end of our walk, I enjoyed a quick shower and change before we made our way to a local restaurant to satisfy our well-cultivated appetites with seafood spaghetti, lasagne with pesto sauce, grilled aubergine, mineral water and local white wine. A fine way to end a walk!

Our next adventure was the walk from Monterosso al Mare to Vernazza. We'd intended to make an early start, but it was so pleasant to enjoy a lazy beginning to the day that it was mid-morning before we got under way, commencing of course with another *locale* journey. At Monterosso we did some wandering, enjoying the fabric shops, the multi-coloured canopies over open-air eating places, and the general hubbub of the most crowded of the five 'lands'.

Monterosso, meaning 'red mountain', and at least as old as the Roman settlement known as Rubra, recalls the lofty hill overlooking the town where one "Rufus" (the red-headed), a descendant of the German Otto dynasty, once inhabited the fortified castle. The first documented evidence of the village as Monterosso, rather than Rubra, is as early as 1056. So the older villages run from the north (Monterosso to Corniglia); the younger (twelfth century) are to the south, Manarola and Riomaggiore.

After our investigation of Monterosso, we decided it was time for lunch. We plumped for Ristorante Pizzeria Bagni Fegina, where some of the tables were under a large canopy on the edge of the beach. The prospect of eating so close to the water with the scent of salt adding some olfactory pleasure was irresistible! In the event, it could hardly have been bettered. A magnificent seafood *risotto* and deserts of *tiramisu* for Anita and chocolate truffle for me, accompanied by an *acqua minerale* and a *vino bianco locale*, set us up nicely for the walk. Well, the *vino bianco locale* might not have done, but it was sheer pleasure.

We had thought the previous day's walk southwards from Vernazza to be difficult enough. What we now faced was another step upwards in ruggedness. Not only is it the most demanding of the Cinque Terre walks, we chose to walk it in the more demanding direction. This of course was unknown to us, though we could have predicted it had we taken the trouble to look at the contours on the map prior to the exercise rather than after it. There was some encouragement in the fact that the small number of people we passed on the way found it as challenging as we did.

On this section, we reached a height of 800 metres. The most breath-taking part is just before commencing the descent; the view down on the beautiful harbour of Vernazza is unforgettable. This time it was blue, oh so blue, for this was a calm day of glorious sunshine. No craft could move the day before without inviting disaster in that rogue sea, but today there were what appeared from our lofty vantage point tiny toy boats sailing through the gap between the breakwater and the cliffs. The reflection of the sun on the hemispherical cap of the church tower was simply beautiful.

We arrived late in the afternoon in Vernazza, ready more than anything else for a drink. Finding a canopied table in the harbour *piazza* we made short work of an astoundingly good *cappuccino* each before making our way uphill to the station. The short *locale* journey to Corniglia in the upper deck was quickly accomplished, and since we felt we had more than met our commitment to walking for the day we took advantage of a small bus conveniently waiting at the station. I had a vague sense of guilt that we were not climbing up the 365 steps, but the comfort of the bus soon calmed my conscience.

It was my last night in Corniglia. It had been a delightful time in the friendship of my walking companion with good conversation and the *camaraderie* of adventuring together. The next day I boarded an Inter-City for Florence, sad that my idyll in the Cinque Terre was over, but knowing that I had a wonderful mental picture gallery to draw on—pictures of one of the most beautiful small regions of Europe.

Chapter 7
Miracle on the Arno

Florence introduces itself in a surprising way. It is small.

To many people that may not be surprising at all. If Florence is simply a name associated with Italy, there is no reason for the visitor being startled by the city's diminutive size. However, even a nodding acquaintance with the Florence's enormous influence upon western civilisation would probably lead to an expectation of a large municipality. It is, after all, the city of Michelangelo, of Donatello, of Brunelleschi, of Dante, of Savanarolla, of the Medici and of a seemingly endless list of those who have left their indelible imprint upon European culture.

Yes, Florence is small. I walk across its cultural centre, from Santa Maria Novella station to the back streets of Santa Croce in about half an hour or so. Admitting that my walking pace is fast, nevertheless it serves to illustrate that this is no London, Sydney or New York. There are suburbs extending beyond the Santa Maria Novella—Santa Croce axis, but as major cities go, Florence, even including its wider residential area, is diminutive, perhaps even petite.

This settlement in the Arno valley has a clearly feminine aura. For example, with the exception of the grotesque Ponte Vecchio, the bridges which span the river exhibit the gentlest of curves culminating in dainty columns which seem to kiss rather than touch the flowing water. Even the Ponte Vecchio, ugly as it is, has its feminine touch, being the most famous location in Florence for buying cameos and fine jewellery. The horse-drawn carriages, in which those who like to travel in style can be transported from Piazza Signoria, show off the same delicate curvaceousness, the horses trained to place their hooves upon the cobbles with the light touch associated with high heels. While the clothes shops might not match in prices charged those of Milan's fashion centre or Rome's Via Condotti, their offerings certainly rival those of the larger cities in elegance and style.

Yes, Florence is small and feminine. In the days of Rome, it was considerably smaller. The churches of Santa Maria Novella on the western side of town and

Santa Croce on the east are both located outside the limits of Florentia. Everything to the south of the Arno is beyond the limits of the Roman city. In fact, Florentia, the settlement the Romans named, is easily outlined by looking at the map of modern Florence.

Let your eye follow the road from Ponte Vecchio into the centre of the city and you quickly see that in the midst of a disorderly web of streets lies a neater grid pattern, the trade mark of Rome. Florentia is bordered by Via Porta Rossa and Via della Condotta on the south, by Via de' Tornabuoni on the west, Via de' Cerretani and the Piazza del Duomo on the north, and by Via del Proconsolo on the 'Dante' side of town.

Little of Rome beyond the grid layout of the city centre exists today, but despite that lack Florence was the city which rediscovered Rome, as it rediscovered Greece, in a richer way than any other place. It provided the cradle for the Renaissance, a humanist child who quickly found that the Florentine nursery was not large enough. Renaissance art and science, letters and oratory, architecture and technology spread from their beginnings on the Arno to every corner of Europe. But Rome was not all that Florence rediscovered; she revived the ancient world.

When I am in Florence, I am reminded that while I had my physical birth in London, my spiritual self has roots in Florence, Rome, Athens and Jerusalem. And what rich roots they are! Small though she may be, Florence is for these and other reasons the adrenaline which makes my blood race.

To place your feet upon a Florentine street is to walk where Etruscans ventured, where Romans planted their orderly civilisation of law, *gravitas* and *veritas*, where Lombards made their Germanic presence felt, where Guelph and Ghibelline contested for Pope or Emperor, where Dante mused and longed for Beatrice, it is to browse where Michelangelo dreamed and Savanarolla thundered, it is to explore where Brunelleschi, Masaccio, Ghiberti, Leonardo, Vasari, Donatello, and how many more, lived an extraordinarily creative existence, it is to walk where the Wehmacht and Allied armies fought for supremacy in the leg of Italy. No matter how many times I return, I cannot contain the excitement of the experience.

But there is one name above all names in Florence—De' Medici. You simply can't get away from it. We shall return to that illustrious family, but before we do there is some climbing to be done. To ascend either Giotto's campanile (a somewhat claustrophobic experience), or Brunelleschi's great dome, both of which are part of the cathedral complex within the bounds of ancient Florentia, is to have all of Renaissance Florence open out before you.

To the east the view is dominated by the great church of Santa Croce, a truly massive structure which always seems to me to have departed from the concepts of poverty and humility espoused by the founder of the Franciscans, the order to which it belongs. It stands proud.

Santa Croce has a commanding presence. It is difficult, therefore, to associate it with *il poverello*, the self-effacing Francis. You could never say of him that he demanded attention. Yet that is precisely what Santa Croce does. It isn't only that it is huge—and it's certainly that. Its design is such that it has been constructed deliberately to dominate (lord it over?) the eastern side of the city. The effect is accentuated by the fact that its western portal opens out onto a very large piazza which draws every eye to the ecclesiastical masterpiece which has become the final resting place of the remains of so many immortals of Florence.

One whose remains are not in Santa Croce but who is remembered within its walls by an imposing monument is Dante Alighieri, a man who has no equal in Italy's hall of literary fame. His remains rest in Ravenna, but the spirit of the man is surely in Florence. One of the most delightful small family hotels I have enjoyed in Florence is the 'Beatrice' in Via Fiume. Named after the love of Dante's life, it is not difficult to lie in bed at the end of the day and muse upon the young poet crossing the Trinità bridge and seeing the girl who stole his heart walking primly by the river. It seems his love was not returned.

Perhaps Dante is not thought to be an especially romantic man, despite his love for Beatrice. It seems beyond dispute that one whose mind could later conjure up the horrors of the Inferno would hardly be likely to cause flutters in the heart of an impressionable young maiden, though we can conjecture that his skills with words might have had some appeal. But can we be sure that such a writer lacked a romantic heart?

A visit to the Dante museum provides some fine evidence of his physical appearance. As a younger man, he seems to have been strikingly good-looking, with piercing eyes, fine cheekbones and a sensuous mouth. Yet as he grew older, he became almost grotesque, mainly because his firm, jutting jaw began to dominate his face. Maybe Beatrice, had she lived long enough and if she'd observed his ageing face, would have been glad she had kept him at a distance.

His love for the girl he called Beatrice (she was almost certainly Bice Portinari, who married one Simone de' Bardi) started early. There is no need for speculation about it, because he tells us in one of his works, 'Vita Nuova', that he met her in 1274. She had just turned 8; he was not quite 9. There are those who argue that it was quite impossible for Dante to be in love at so early an age.

As one who was hopelessly in love at ten, I take issue with them. Could Dante have been in love just before his 9th birthday? Of course, he could! It isn't difficult at all to think of the boy whose heart was breaking as he thought of the pretty young Bice (so easily renamed Beatrice) whose eyes had so beguiled him. Alas, it was not to become the love story of the century, and Dante, in his twenties, married one Gemma Donati, by whom he had two sons and at least one daughter. Though it was a love to which Bice never responded, even so, and perhaps to the discomfort of Gemma, 'Beatrice' remained, it seems, the dream and energising force of his life.

Dante's own words in 'La Vita Nuova' (New Life), written in 1293, describe his feelings when first he saw her: 'Love dominated my spirit'. In the same paragraph, he describes her as 'this young angel'. These are the words of a man as love-sick as any before or after him have been. Boccaccio, his younger contemporary, in his 'Life of Dante', points out that there were a good number of people who saw Beatrice as an angel, so we might as well accept that, though only eight, she was well able to make young male hearts flutter.

In the same work, which he produced in 1321, the year of Dante's death, Boccaccio firmly states that the angelic picture of Beatrice stayed deep in the heart of her would-be lover until he breathed his last. Alas, Beatrice had long predeceased him. She did not live beyond her mid-twenties.

Yes, it seems Dante *was* a romantic, and I warm to him for that. But he was also a man well able to engage in the tougher areas of politics. He allied himself with the Guelph party, a not-so-surprising development given that Florence was overwhelmingly allied with that party. The Guelphs were the party of the Pope and therefore implacably opposed to the Emperor (emperor of the West, that is, since Charlemagne, long before, had been appointed with that title, a counterpoise to the Emperor in Constantinople). Those who supported the Emperor were associated with the Ghibellines and there were precious few of those in Florence.

The matter was not quite as simple as that, however. While the Guelph—Ghibelline conflict, which was often bloody, extended well beyond Tuscany, in Florence especially the Guelph cause suffered a major division, a split caused mainly by the wealthy bankers involved. The most uncompromising anti-

Emperor participants, including the banking families of Donati (the clan to which Dante's wife Gemma belonged), Pazzi (forever associated with the most scandalous conspiracy in Florentine history) and Bardi, formed the Black Guelphs. All three of those banks held papal accounts.

Those who wanted to take a more conciliatory line with the Emperor were known as the White Guelphs, and also included an impressive membership of banking families, the Cerchi, the Davanzati, the Frescobaldi and the Mozzi among them. The White Guelph bankers all held accounts associated with the Emperor and his supporters.

Dante was very public in his sympathies with the Whites and made no attempt to hide his view that Tuscany should be defended against the designs of the current Pope Boniface VIII, one of the most vicious and least moral of the line of St Peter, a line not short of incumbents able to make a moral man's hair curl. In 1300, he journeyed to San Gimignano in an attempt to persuade the leaders of that town to join an alliance against the 'Holy Father'.

His anti-papal (that is, anti-pope of the day) stance led to his banishment from Florence. Charges of corruption were trumped up against him, and a sentence of two years exile awarded against him. When other exiles were able legally to make their way back to the city on the Arno, Dante decided that voluntary exile was better than returning to a city too many of whose prominent citizens he viewed as being deeply corrupt. After some years of searching for a permanent place of abode he settled in Ravenna, where he completed the *Divine Comedy*. Not long after the completion of his most famous work, he died at Ravenna on 14 September 1321. His bones lie in a modest mausoleum in that city.

'La Vita Nuova', then, was his first work; 'La Divina Commedia' the last (the adjective 'divine' was added in the 16th century).

Much could be written about the museums and churches of Florence, but the details can be found in the guide books which are available in great numbers. This book is about what, rather presumptuously, I call my Italy. I shall therefore mention only the works, buildings and churches which more than any others draw me to the city.

When the de' Medici gained the Pitti Palace by purchase from the Pitti banking family, they decided to connect it with the Palazzo Vecchio, over the river Arno, so that they would have a private walkway between the two. They commissioned the great man Vasari to design the corridor. You can see it today.

Starting on the Palazzo Vecchio side of the river, the first thing to notice is that a first floor covered corridor runs from the Uffizi Gallery and continues by the side of the Arno to the Ponte Vecchio. Therein lies a tale. At the time of the De' Medici gaining the Pitti Palace the Ponte Vecchio was a single-deck bridge, as the others over the Arno in Florence are.

Moreover, it was lined with butchers' shops. Vasari built his corridor over the top, so the bridge became two storeys. A family such as the De' Medici was not keen on the smell from butchers' wares floating up into their private walkway between their palaces. Not surprisingly the butchers' shops soon left the bridge. Today it is a home for jewellers. Who was going to argue with a family such as the De' Medici? Incidentally, the name De' Medici indicates that they were not always bankers. Before their banking days, they were a medical family. Their destiny was to be the dominant force of Florence.

Cross the Ponte Vecchio and you will see that the corridor continues on its first floor level into the nearest building. Follow the road upwards to the Pitti Palace and you will see, if you look to your left, the corridor running from one building to another, entering the palace to complete the De' Medici private walkway. If that's not an indication of status, what is?

Every church in Florence is fascinating, but two in particular have special reasons for me to find them appealing. First, the church of Santa Maria Novella, close to the main rail terminus, has a special attraction. The church is beautiful in itself, but it contains one important work of art which stands out above all others for me. It is Masaccio's 'Trinità'. It represents a teaching of the Trinity of the Renaissance period, and it can probably be said that the teaching has not changed significantly, if at all, in the official corridors of the mainstream churches.

Not all will identify with that teaching of God as Three in One in a kind of mechanic-spiritual sense, with God the Father, Son and Holy Spirit co-equal. Yet Massacio's work is a magnificent exposition of it. The crucified Son faces us, God the Father is behind the cross and Mary in the foreground points to her stricken son, so that we, the viewers, will not miss the point. But where is the Holy Spirit? Some will say that it is clearly impossible to paint the Holy Spirit for the precise reason that spirit is not paintable.

But when you are in the church of Santa Maria Novella and standing before the painting, look at the Father's collar. Careful scrutiny will reveal that the collar is in the shape of a dove. It *is* a dove. Brilliant. The Spirit comes to the viewer from the Father through the Son. There is no mistaking the route of the Spirit in Masaccio's work. Nor is there any mistaking his artistic genius.

As you look at the façade of the church, in green and white marble, you can be impressed by, first, the successful attempt of its architect, Leon Battista Alberti, to bring his design into harmony with the structures of the area already erected and, second, the hard-to-miss fact that the whole façade fits neatly into a square. The width is equal to the height to the apex of the pediment, which bears the solar emblem of the Dominican order.

The plan of the church is a nave (the word represents 'ship', a symbol of the early Church) and two aisles. The transepts are short, so that the cross is most obviously formed by the nave and transept, excluding the aisles. The overwhelming initial impression is of the massive size of the church. The nave is 100 metres in length. Corinthian columns take the eye to Gothic arches. The vaulting is quadripartite, a form of ribbing which produces continuing groups of four spaces or partitions per apex. Quadripartite developed from the more complex sexpartite ribbing and being stronger, allowed higher cathedrals to be built.

Santa Maria Novella is a feast of architecture, but also of art. It is 'one stop' for works by Massacio, Botticelli, Vasari, Brunelleschi, Ghiberti, Ghirlandaio and many more men of art.

As you leave the church, you will notice that the *piazza* is rather unusually shaped, and there are obelisks there. The reason is that it is on the site of a Roman circus. I love to imagine the chariots almost flying past as I stand on the edge of the *piazza*, and hear the noise of the horses, the screaming of the charioteers, the roar from the crowds whose eyes are riveted to the action on the track. For the same reason, I am excited in Piazza Navona in Rome. I can see in my mind the drama of the race.

The other church which compels me to enter the doors is the Carmelite church in the Oltrano district on the Pitti Palace side of the river, Santa Maria del Carmine. The church appears rather plain in exterior, over-elaborate internally. It is in the rococo style, to my taste over fussy. To others, who enjoy the French influence, it might come as a delight.

As with *Santa Maria Novella*, the Carmelite church has precious work of Masaccio.

It is found, with the work of Masolino, his master, in the Brancacci chapel. The frescoes by master and pupil are considered by many to be the first truly masterful works of the Florentine Renaissance, and so, my perception tells me, they are. The pupil exceeded the skills and artistic sensitivity of the master, but that does not downgrade the collection of works. Together, they gave us a Renaissance experience to be taken in, absorbed and reflected upon. Unfortunately, time allowed in the chapel is limited, so reflection time is too short, but we make the most of the opportunity afforded.

For me, the finest work there is Masaccio's depiction of expulsion from Paradise. Adam and Eve are so painted that you can *see* their conscience-stricken grief. Rarely have I seen as striking a portrait of persons so life-like that they could step out of the painting and speak. There is perhaps a paradox that such life-like figures appear in a painting of a tale whose power lies in its being an aetiological myth, a study of what it means to leave innocence behind, even with the colourings of guilt, and begin the process of growing up in a hard world. They leave Paradise together, Eve using her hands to cover the private parts of her body, Adam covering his face.

Does this mean that Masaccio sees the expulsion being punishment for a sexual misdemeanour? It is a popular idea, but not one with substance. Not only is there no indication in the myth that the punishment was for sexual activity, such an interpretation runs counter to the obvious reason for humanity being in male and female sexes. Eve's covering of the sexual parts of her body suggests that Masaccio sees sexual activity is the cause for the expulsion. No matter. The painting is powerful and can be viewed in the spirit of its execution.

I have my own way of viewing it. The garden of Eden is innocence. We all have to leave it behind and face the more difficult world of growing up. We cannot return to innocence. A flaming sword guards the way back. The world of good and evil has to be faced and lived. Adam and Eve, as I see them in the painting, grieve the loss of innocence.

One other glimpse of Florence through my eyes will suffice. One of the great pleasures of Florence for me is to take a bus from the bus station by the railway terminus up to Fiesole, a delightful village which overlooks Florence and the Arno valley. Two elements of my ritual at Fiesole are, first, to look down at Florence and watch the lights of the city coming on. It provides magical moments, the more so if you are there with someone you love. It is infused with romance. And yes, my wife Ruth has stood there with me. The second element is dinner at a restaurant directly overlooking the valley. I know of no more romantic way to dine.

On the subject of romance, the Ponte Vecchio also provides a fine place of viewing. Stand on the side of the bridge looking downstream. Get there a little while before sunset. When the sun goes down, there is a wonderful picture of golden light shining over and through the Trinità bridge to the west. There are evenings, of course, when the weather denies you that experience, but not many.

Florence is well-known for many commodities. Two of them are decorated writing paper and leatherwork. As one who loves fine paper and a good fountain pen for writing on it, I am very fond of the paper products of Florence. There are good stationers' shops you ought to visit if only to see how exquisite is the work of the artisans. My own view is that, given the quality, it is foolish to leave Florence without a purchase or two.

Undoubtedly Florence has earned its reputation as a city of fine leather. In the market that winds its way around the Medici chapel of the church of San Lorenzo, leather belts and other products of the same material can be bought, sometimes by bargaining, at good prices. However, the best assurance of quality is found in the specialist shops, as you would expect. Ruth, for example, bought a magnificent leather jacket from a shop close to the Bargello gallery.

A garment of elegant appearance and superb quality, she bought it with the bonus of service from a salesman well-practised in the art of charming female customers. I don't think she would have missed it for the world. Whenever she wears the jacket, she is reminded of the fine quality of leather products sold in Florence, and of the salesman who fitted her out! She looks the height of fashion in it.

Let me take you now to one of the finest buildings in Florence, the Great Synagogue, Il Tempio Maggiore Israelitico di Firenze.

The Jewish population of Florence is in the region of 1,500 and has its origins at least as early as Europe's medieval period. The first synagogue in the city is believed to have been built in the 13th century. The present Great Synagogue was completed in 1882, a dozen years after the completion of the unification of Italy.

It is a lovely building, surmounted by a fine blue-green cupola in Moorish-revival style. The façade is porticoed at the entrance, above which is a beautiful semi-circular curve with a short tower at each end, each topped with a small cupola in the same colour to complete a glorious frontage.

When David Levi, a president of the Florentine Jewish community, died in 1870, money became available for building a new synagogue. He left his whole estate for that purpose, and a start was made in 1874. The building produced is a mixture of obviously Italian elements, and equally obvious Moorish influences. The synagogue was intended to note the Moorish -Spanish origins of the Sephardic Jews of the city. The architects were Vincente Micheli, Marco Treves and Mariano Falcini. Not the least of its attractions is the striped use of red and beige travertine and granite.

The synagogue was desecrated during the Second World War when Nazi forces used it a storehouse, an act which could only have been carried out on the orders of someone who had no regard for the sacred. However, being a Jewish building, it would have been fair game for German forces at that time, so much so that in August 1944, when the German army was in retreat up the Italian peninsula, German troops and Italian Fascists worked together to lay explosives to blow the synagogue up. It was mostly saved by Italian resistance fighters (*I Partigiani)*, courageous men (and some women) who worked at night to sabotage the work of the Nazi occupiers. They managed to defuse most of the explosive devices, reducing the damage to the building to minor. Such damage as was done was restored after the War.

That was not the end of the woes of the synagogue. The great Arno flood of 1966 which brought devastation to every low-lying part of the city brought inundation to the Great Synagogue. More restoration was done.

I am thankful that neither floods nor Nazis were able to destroy the Great Synagogue. It is one of the glories of Florence.

Florence is far more than the glimpses found in these pages, and you have to find its magic for yourself. You can't do it just by reading this book, though I hope it introduces you to the special nature of the city on the river. Before you visit it, however, do some serious reading on the Renaissance. You will find if you do that you need many days in Florence to investigate the products of the great outpouring of an unstoppable spirit of rediscovery and of artistic, engineering and scientific endeavour.

There really was a miracle on the Arno.

Chapter 8

A Wider Look at Tuscany

Tuscany is more than Florence. That city may be the capital, but it is not all that the region is or is about.

Sometimes I think that more words have been written about Tuscany in the last few years than any other part of the Italian peninsula. It isn't difficult to see why. It has some of the most attractive countryside in Italy, and perhaps the most varied, rising from the seacoast of the west to the foothills of the Apennines in the east. It boasts one of the best-known wine-producing areas (the Chianti) in the country and is dotted with enchanting hill-top towns across its length and breadth. The region's capital is Florence, one of the culturally richest cities in the western world, but there are riches in the wider region too.

A walk through the travel section of any large bookstore will soon reveal that on the shelves dealing with Europe there seem to be more guides on Florence and Tuscany than any other part of that continent. The shelves in other parts of the store are also not short of books set in the region. The dream-like memories of so many visitors to Tuscany have flowed through their pens to produce for us compelling, atmospheric books such as *Under the Tuscan Sun* and *Bella Tuscany* among many which set our imaginations on fire. And who has not seen at least one film set in Tuscany? My own favourite is *Enchanted April*; that delightful story of a group of women who escape from the dreariness of London weather for a few weeks in a Tuscan paradise.

People want to hear about Tuscany. It was my privilege to conduct two or three courses a year on the history and culture of the region, and I found it gratifying that people came to them in large numbers to find out what they could about this magnet for visitors in north-central Italy.

As for me, I greedily consume all the books I can find on Tuscany, and never allow myself to resist a video on the region nor avoid a visit to the cinema when a film on this beautiful part of the globe is showing. And I can't turn my back on any opportunity to visit it. Just offer me the excuse, and very soon I shall be driving through its country lanes, stopping in the villages for lunch with local wine at what is usually the only *trattoria* in the place, and enjoying, of course, a conversation with the lady who makes the lunch, and often her husband who pours the wine. The chances are that the cold meat in my panino (roll) is home-cured and the wine made from grapes grown not too away.

I want to take your imagination on a tour through Tuscany. It will be a journey through the places which I see as very special, and I hope you do too. So, join me on my 'travels through Tuscany'.

The first stop is not very far from Florence. I mentioned it almost in passing in the previous chapter. It is the small town or village of Fiesole. The church of Santa Maria Novella is very close to the bus stop, a fact I point out because there is a literary link between this important sanctuary in Florence and the small town up the hill. That link is provided by Giovanni Boccaccio, best known to us for 'The Decameron', a collection of salacious stories written from 1349 to 1351. The time of writing was significant, because in 1348 Florence, along with many other cities, suffered a dreadful outbreak of plague.

At the beginning of this bawdy adventure of story-telling, Boccaccio describes seven of his fictional relaters of tales, beautiful young women all, huddled in conversation in the church of Santa Maria Novella, sharing terrifying impressions of rotting bodies in the streets of Florence with many of the barely-living collapsing by the roadsides. Their conversation takes place in the Strozzi chapel within the church, but soon moves out as they decide to move up to Fiesole where they hope to find safety until the plague has passed.

They are joined by three young men and occupy their time by taking turns to tell sensual stories whose explicitly sexual content shocked the Florentine world of Boccaccio's day. It was explicit for the time, though it might not be considered graphic at all by modern readers. There were those who were deeply offended that he should write of the carnal desires of nuns, for example, and that, among other sexual references, he could write of a woman describing herself as fair and lusty, gamesome and fit.

One who found virtually every word of *The Decameron* offensive was Girolamo Savonarola who was offended by virtually everything he saw in the life of Florence. *The Decameron*, together with other books, adornments and miscellaneous 'vanities', was burned on the huge bonfire Savonarola lit for the purpose in Piazza della Signoria. There is a neat, if brutal, irony in the fact that when he fell prey to his enemies in Florence, he also was burned in the same Piazza della Signoria.

Fiesole, then, is the place where Boccaccio's fictitious story-telling young people sharing their sensual fantasies are set.

The ideal time to take the 20-30 m minute journey to the hill-top town is mid-to-late afternoon, so that you can enjoy wandering some of the narrow streets, sit with some coffee on the edge of Piazza Mino or Piazza Garibaldi (they are adjacent) and visit the Roman theatre before thinking about dinner. But to make the most of the visit, take a copy of 'The Decameron' with you, find a comfortable seat, and let Giovanni Boccaccio take you into his not quite respectable world for ladies and gentlemen. But surely we can be excused for just a little holiday from respectability? A book bound for the bonfire of 'vanities' surely needs a reading.

It is befitting, most dear ladies...

There, you've made a start. There is no plague to ride out, so you might not read a hundred stories, but that just means there will be a number left for reading at another time and another mood!

In the northern area of the Chianti lies the little town of Greve. It lies on the Greve river, and perhaps if it had no more to offer than its own townscape it would not require mention. However, a tale attaches to Greve.

Here lived the Gherardini family, who, though branches became associated with Verona and Florence, will always be linked with the valley of the Greve. The family, which still thrives, built a castle for their residence at Montagliari in the mid-thirteenth century above the Greve river. Next to the castle, the Gherardini built the church of Santa Maria della Neve. They moved into the castle in 1300, with the intention of making it their permanent residence. However, occupancy was short-lived: the castle was destroyed by Florentine forces soon after the Gherardini moved in, obliging them to move across the valley of the Greve to Vignamaggio.

The family has some surprises in store for those who wish to trace its history.

In 1479, a child, Lisa Gherardini, was born in the small branch of the family who stayed on in Tuscany. She became a remarkably beautiful young woman who married one Francesco Bartolomeo Giocondo. It is widely accepted that it was Lisa, known as *La Gioconda*, whom Leonardo painted, a work which is found today in the Louvre with the title, *Mona Lisa*.

Earlier, some of the family, under the headship of one Gherardino, left Tuscany, initially attaching themselves to Louis VII of France, then to Henry II of England. They were involved with Henry in the conquest of Ireland where they effected a name change. Gherardini very easily translates into Fitzgerald (or FitzGerald), the Italian Gherardini and the Norman Fitzgerald both meaning son of Gerald. Such became the family name in Ireland.

The story moves to America, where as immigrants the Fitzgeralds thrived as one of the leading New World families, eventually marrying into a Kennedy family. Can it be that one member of that family might live long in western memories?

These thoughts come easily to mind when driving through Greve in the Chianti and looking out over the Greve valley which at one time the Gherardini made their own fiefdom.

Greve might also stimulate in your mind, should you find yourself in the region, with the thought that the Gherardini are an ancient clan. They are recorded in documents of the ninth century AD now kept in the church of San Miniato in Florence.

They seem to have been a family with an inbuilt compulsion to fight, taking part in the White Guelphs v Black Guelphs conflict, as well as being invested in the broader Guelph/Ghibelline struggles of the 12th and 13th centuries. In 1300, the family members resident in Florence were exiled from the city when it became a *Signoria*, a city with a government headed by a *signore* or lord who ruled despotically. Dante Allighieri was exiled from Florence with them, and such was his regard for the Gherardini that he placed them in *Sphere V of Paradise* in the *Divine Comedy*.

They have been influential in other parts of northern Italy at various times as well as exercising considerable influence in Tuscany from the 9th to the 14th centuries. The family exercised significant power in the Veneto and Emilia Romagna from the 16th to 18th centuries. It also took part in the *Risorgimento* struggle which resulted, in 1861, in the partial unification of Italy, a work completed in 1870. Thus, they can claim association with Mancini, Cavour, Garibaldi and Vittorio Emmanuele, the major figures in the *Risorgimento* movement. The family has also had representation on the Great Council of Venice, a position of considerable prestige.

Today the Gherardini have residences in the Tuscany and Lazio regions.

The Tuscan countryside is indescribably beautiful wherever you go, and in some places towns or cities of great significance exist. In the Chianti region the high town of Radda, the heartland town of Gaiole, the monastic winery of Badia

Coltibuono and many other small towns are enchanting in their individual cultures.

At this point, it is appropriate to include something of the history of the Chianti area.

How old is the Chianti? The wine known as Chianti is on record as having been produced in the area at least as early as the 13th century, though it might cause some surprise to know that the Chianti wine as known at that time was white, rather than the light red we drink today.

What are the boundaries of the Chianti? In the medieval period the towns of Radda, Gaiole and Castellina joined forces to form the *Lega del Chianti*. This formed the heartbeat of the Chianti area, and within the boundaries existing today wines (the only wines) bearing the designation DOCG (*Chianti Classico Denominazione di Origine Controllata e Garantita*) are produced. As one who knows the pleasure of the taste of Chianti Classico, I look carefully for the DOCG classification.

Since wine is a matter of individual taste, and wine writers seem to me well beyond my interests as a simple wine drinker who enjoys the stuff in moderation, I content myself in saying that my own favourite Chianti Classico is the product of the Coltibuono winery. But then, perhaps I'm influenced by the fact that *Bardia a Coltibuono* is so strongly associated with Lorenza dei Medici, wife of Piero Stucchi-Prinetti and author of fine Italian cookery books, one of which is my well-loved possession. She is, of course, a member of the great dei Medici family, one of whom, the famed Lorenzo, was patron of the property which developed under his influence into the fine complex it has become. *Bardia a Coltibuono* is 'Abbey of Good Harvest'. It was founded in 1051 and was the property of the Vallumbrosan monks, a sub-order of the Benedictines, until 1810.

To describe it as idyllic is seriously to understate the matter. In the region of Gaiole-in-Chianti, it is in a country setting of rolling hills. The stone abbey, with Tuscan roof-tiles is built around its central feature of a fine square, castellated tower with Romanesque round arched windows, indicating that the central sanctuary area of the abbey is truly old. A cedar standing close by stands 20 metres in height.

It was my pleasure to visit Bardia a Coltibuono with my late wife, Ann, some years ago. We enjoyed a thoroughly pleasant afternoon being shown the kitchen, relaxing rooms, the cellar and the grounds. It will live long in my memory.

We became interested in visiting the Bardia after having watched a series of cooking programmes hosted by Lorenza dei Medici, filmed in the Coltibuono kitchen. If you, the reader, are passionate about cooking, note that classes are regularly offered at Coltibuono. You could not have a lovelier setting for learning.

Coltibuono is redolent of the dei Medici, but just 'down the road' is a winery associated with another famous name. Gaiole-in-Chianti will always produce in the mind of a history-lover the name Baron Bettino Ricasoli and therefore the winery, more ancient than any other. The Ricasole family has been associated with wine since 1141. In Australia, the country of my residence, the link of wine-making with the 12th century would be difficult to conceive. Very few Europeans here have family roots more than 200 years old.

How important is the Ricasole company? It is the fourth oldest company in the world which operates in the very place of its beginnings. That would have made it a fascinating business in its own right, even if it had not developed fine wines, and it has. But it can add to that fourth place distinction the honour of being the second oldest wine producing company in the world operating still on the block of its founding.

But there is more. In 1872, Baron Bettino Ricasoli confirmed his invention of that special drink of Tuscany, Chianti. He described it as having its special aroma from the *sangiovese* (or *sangioveto*) grape. The *sangiovese* was and is the greatest grape percentage of Chianti. So, we owe that fine drink to Count Bettino Ricasoli. Most of us would consider that to be sufficient for lasting fame, but Bettino had more achievements to his name. He was the first Prime Minister of the partially unified Italy from 1861 to 1862 and 1866 to 1867 and member of the Italian Chamber of Deputies from 1861 to 1880. Before 1861, he had been Mayor of the City of Florence (from 1847 to 1848).

Such a man was Bettino Ricasole. When you have a glass of his fine Chianti, drink a toast to that remarkable contributor to the politics and to the pleasure of Tuscans. We enjoy the pleasure contribution when we drink Chianti from Gaiole.

I take you now away from the Chianti to the town of Lucca.

Lucca has a strong hold on my heart for a quite different reason. I love its rampart walk; I love its church of San Michele in Foro, built on the site of the Roman Forum, I am fascinated by the Piazza dell' Anfiteatro, the wonderful curving space that was once the Roman amphitheatre and is now a major Lucca meeting place, and a wonderful location for sitting at an outside table under a canopy and drinking coffee or wine.

The town is a treasure of interest. But my major reason for loving Lucca is what I may call the ghost of one of its most famous citizens, Giacomo Puccini, or to give him his full name, the length of which I am delighted I don't have, Giacomo Antonio Domenico Michele Secondo Maria Puccini. It seems his parents spread their bets on the blessing of the saints upon their son.

One or more must have blessed him, for he produced music that tugs at our emotions with almost every bar.

The statue of the seated Puccini outside his house depicts a prosperous, elegant man. The house itself, at number 9, Corte San Lorenzo, is today a wonderful museum of the life of the man. Much of the furniture used when the family lived there is still in place, and for me the most interesting piece is the piano upon which he wrote his uncompleted (by him) opera, Turandot.

Turandot was the last opera he composed, but two scenes remained for completion at the time of his death in 1924. They were completed from Puccini's notes by Franco Alfarno. Would the final scenes have been very different musically, had Puccini completed the whole work? Perhaps, but I shall continue to enjoy the sublime listening experience of Turandot at every opportunity, and for that matter my other favourites, Manon Lescaut, La Bohème, Madama Butterfly and La Fanciulla del West. It might be that those who are authorities on Puccini will criticise my choice. I care not. While I love all of Puccini's output, these are my favourite five.

Was Puccini easy to get on with? His relationships with his librettists suggests he was not. However, he had good reason to be particular about his *libretti* and have some head-to-heads with his wordsmiths. It seems that the failure of Edgar was able in no small measure to be sheeted home to the *libretto*.

Were his relationships with women an indication of a difficult personality? That's hard to say, but what can be said is that his sexual relationships were best described as irregular. In 1884, when not quite 26 years old, he commenced an affair with Elvira Gemignani who was married to one who would today be called a serial adulterer. Elvira Gemignani became pregnant and she, their son Antonio and Puccini moved in together. They were not free to marry until the death of Elvira's husband, Narciso in 1903, a death caused by Narciso's being shot by the husband of one of his lady friends.

There was to be no 'happy ever after'. The marriage of Elvira and Giacomo was quarrelsome and Puccini was himself a man of one adulterous affair after another.

I am, then, one who loves the music of a man I probably would not have liked, had I met him. But please play me his music.

1903 was significant not only for the death of Narciso Gemignani; it was also the year in which Puccini could have lost his life had he not received medical attention when he did. He was on his way by chauffeured car with Elvira and Antonio from Lucca to Torre del Lago, where he spent a good deal of time, when, in treacherous weather, the car left the road and rolled over. Elvira and Antonio received no serious injuries, but Puccini and the chauffer were not so fortunate. Puccini was the most seriously affected with a fractured right leg and chest injuries. He was under treatment for many months and could well not have survived the accident, given that a portion of the car was pressing heavily upon his chest as he lay trapped under it.

Torre del Lago is important for Puccini-lovers. After 1891, he spent most of his time there, built a villa in 1900, and lived by the lake until 1921, when he moved the short distance to Viareggio. The villa at Torre del Lago, which is open to the public, is a museum of his life. He is buried at Torre del Lago. Elvira and Antonio survived him.

Such a ghost wanders the streets with me when I am in Lucca.

I could take you to Pisa, to Siena, to San Gimignano and other places of great interest in Tuscany. They have become, however, mostly tourist honeypots. I enjoy them all, but the guidebooks will supply all that is needed to find your way around them. Don't be put off by their lack of treatment here; it's just that they are not part of the emphasis of this book.

Chapter 9

Byzantium on the Adriatic

Why go to Ravenna? Because it is a memorial to Byzantium in Italy, and a reminder of the Emperor Constantine's decision to remove his centre of empire from Rome to that city in AD 330, with implications not only for Italy but for Europe when eventually an Eastern Emperor and a kind of Emperor of the West held sway over their respective parts of Europe. Eastern Emperor? Yes, because Constantinople (the modern Istanbul) is on the border of Europe and Asia. To enter Asia from the modern city is no more than a matter of crossing a bridge.

The title of the chapter is 'Byzantium on the Adriatic', and while that is true for the reasons that Ravenna appeals today, it should not obscure the fact that the city has been under the control of conquerors of many kinds. The point of the title is that Byzantium is the mark most strongly left on this city on the delta of the River Po. I have also used the words, 'on the Adriatic'. That is not misleading but not entirely true. It is not far from the sea, and my justification lies in the Candiano Canal which links Ravenna with the Adriatic.

That explained, let's proceed.

Four stirring lines from Oscar Wilde's long poem, *Ravenna*, read:
O lone Ravenna! Many a tale is told of thy glories in the days of old.
Two thousand years have passed since thou didst see
Caesar ride forth to royal victory.

So we are introduced to the world of Ravenna's past glories, but we should not think that some do not exist now. They do, most especially in their Byzantine buildings and mosaics. And we are introduced also to the fact that it was from Ravenna that Caesar set out to cross the Rubicon and set in motion a movement of history that could not be stopped. I feel a sense of pleasure in relating that because it was from Ravenna that I also set out to cross the Rubicon some years ago. Alas, I was not on a warhorse leading an army, but driving a car I had hired in Ravenna for the journey.

129

My most vivid memory of the Rubicon (to continue with its ancient Latin name) is the surprise I received when discovering it to be a rather insignificant river to look at—not a great water highway by any means. But then, as reason returned, I realised that it did not have to be a river of great width and depth. Its importance does not lie in size, but in historical importance. I could claim no importance whatever to my crossing except that it was a personal ambition realised.

Caesar's crossing, in 49 BC made conflict with the Republic's rulers inevitable. Once he had crossed with the legion XIII, *Gemina* (*Legio tertia decima Gemina,* the 13th Twin Legion), he is said to have uttered, *Alea iacta est,* 'the die is cast'. It was indeed cast. That little river, Rubicō, from the adjective rubeus, 'red' because mud brought down from the hills coloured its waters, was from that moment destined for fame in western European history.

Yes, it was from Ravenna that Julius Caesar set out on his fateful journey. How could I not feel the heartbeat of history in Ravenna and on crossing the Rubicon? In my imagination, it was not difficult to see 'Caesar ride forth to royal victory'.

Caesar was not the only influence that brought me to Ravenna. The city lives with the name of another, very different person who has already been mentioned in this book, one Dante Alighieri (1265-1321). His exile took him to Ravenna, and it is there that his tomb can be found. Those with an appreciation of the great man's work will be surprised by the modest structure that commemorates his person and his work. It is simple, unexpectedly small, and of little architectural merit. But don't let that put you off. A remarkable tale is brought to mind as you stand before the tomb. It is a tale of a corpse which, while not as mobile as that of Santa Lucia and certainly not as well-travelled, is nevertheless one which has known more than the usual share of movement.

The story starts with Dante himself, whose body would almost certainly be buried today in Florence had he, in his native Florence, chosen the side other than the one he did in the intra-Guelph conflict following the Guelph's defeat of the Ghibellines. The Guelph-Ghibelline conflict was one between supporters of the Pope (the Guelphs) and supporters of the Holy Roman Emperor (Ghibellines). Florence was a supporter of the Pope and therefore a Guelph city. However, the Guelphs divided into two warring factions, the White Guelphs (*Guelfi Bianchi*) and the Black Guelphs (*Guelfi Neri*). The Black Guelphs remained supporters of the Pope, but the White Guelphs, while having no truck with the Emperor, wanted far less papal influence in Florence, and were especially opposed to Pope Boniface VIII.

Dante was born into this time of conflict. He gave his allegiance to the White Guelfs and to his cost, they lost the fight with the Black Guelphs in 1301 with the result that he was exiled from Florence, the Black Guelphs now being the unchallenged ruling party. Exile was perhaps the most painful punishment that could be imposed on Dante, whose love for his home city of Florence was intense.

He became something of a wanderer during his exile, spending time in Verona, Liguria and Lucca. In 1318, he was invited to make his home in Ravenna, an invitation he took up. Away from his roots and all that gave meaning to him, the pain of exile for him can hardly be imagined. He died in Ravenna in 1321.

His body was buried in the church of *San Pietro Maggiore*, now the church of *San Francesco*. That might be considered the end of the Dante story, excluding his enduring fame, but not so. The city of Florence was compelled to recognise the genius of Dante, who was rapidly becoming recognised as among the greatest—if not *the* greatest—of the poets of the Italian peninsula. A conviction grew that as a native of Florence, his body should be interred in that city. It took some time for action to be taken, but in 1519 Pope Leo X decreed that Dante's body should be transferred from Ravenna to Florence. Not surprisingly, Ravenna was not impressed. The story is that an empty coffin was sent to Florence, and the remains of Dante were reburied in or close to a Franciscan monastery in Ravenna.

Two centuries later, in 1830, the sculptor Stefano Ricci completed a 'tomb' for Dante in Florence's massive church of Santa Croce. It has become the city's memorial to its greatest literary figure. It stands in the church as a huge presence, a memorial to a man whose literary contribution deserves the same adjective. The memorial contains the inscription, *Onorate L'Altissimo Poeta*, 'Honour the Most Exalted Poet'. Dante is indeed the highest figure as he sits at the apex of the 'tomb'.

When I first stood before this monument, I was aware that the Florentines were telling me that the author of *The Divine Comedy*, which deserves perhaps the appellation of the greatest epic of the Christian west, and of much else besides, was a son of Florence. They can be justly proud of him, and in case you don't get the point, to the left of the western façade as you enter the church, you can see the commanding statue by Enrico Pazzi of the great man on a pedestal which ensures that you have to look up to him. The Ricci monument does that too, of course.

The body, though, remains in Ravenna, and as I looked at the mausoleum, almost certainly the final destination of his body, I found myself wondering if he was experiencing a stay in Purgatory, in the Inferno or in Paradise. I wished him well and hoped it was the last-named.

Incidentally, the title *Onorate L'Altissimo Poeta* was taken up by Isaac Asimov when he published his science fiction work of two professors and the calling up of spirits of the illustrious literary dead. The story, published in English in 1954 and Italian in 1957, can't fail to conjure up the Dante memorial in Santa Croce, if only because of the inscription. I wonder if Asimov was cocking a snook at Ricci's great monument?

This chapter can't end without mention of the mosaics of Ravenna. They are said to be the finest in Europe, and that alone should make Ravenna a place for the artistic to explore. Having visited Venice, Istanbul and Palermo, and many other European places of mosaic attraction, I have no argument with the claim. Those of Ravenna are magnificent. The *tesser*ae are skilfully laid in such an irregular way that the light glints in reflection from them, so that to gaze upon them is to look at what seem to be living displays.

They can be seen in many ecclesiastical buildings in the city, but to see the oldest, visit the Galla Placidia mausoleum (*Mausoleo Di Galla Placidia*) and to the Orthodox Baptistery (*Battistero Degli Ortodossi*). The tomb of Galla Placidia, a mid-5th century AD mausoleum, is one of the more colourful expositions of mosaics, presenting predominantly blue themes. Not only are the mosaics old, the building itself is the oldest in Ravenna. Themes include The Good Shepherd, *San Lorenzo,* walking towards the grill upon which he suffered his final torture of being roasted alive, and symbolic features of stags believed to represent souls.

The sarcophagus is said to contain the remains of Galla Palicidia, daughter of the Emperor Theodosius I. She died in AD 450. Does the mausoleum contain her remains? They are said to have been interred there, but there is no absolute certainty. A fire in 1577 burnt the contents of the sarcophagus, adding difficulty to the quest for certainty.

The Orthodox Baptistery also has magnificent mosaic work, in this case featuring strongly contrasting colours which produce a brilliant effect. For me, the finest effect is that of the scene at the apex of the dome, depicting the Baptism of Christ and the Twelve Apostles. It is a worthwhile investment of time to visit the Baptistery if only to see the dome scene.

The next oldest mosaics are to be seen in the Arian Baptistery, where the chief scene, not surprisingly, is another of the Baptism of Christ and the Twelve Apostles, beautifully portrayed.

The Baptistery takes our thoughts to a very important schism of Church history, a confrontation to which I shall return shortly. Before doing so, note that the churches of St Vitalis and St Apollinaris The two should be included in the mosaics tour.

So we turn our attention, in drawing the chapter to a close, to the Arian Baptistery. Why? Because Arianism was a thorn in the flesh of the Catholic Church for a very long time, and it is useful to know something about it before visiting the Baptistery. The Arian story is one of the most compelling in all of European history, not only Church history.

The story began in Alexandria early in the 4th century AD when Arius, a presbyter of the Church, proclaimed that Jesus Christ was created by God, and was therefore not equal with God. This is a simplified beginning of the ensuing controversy because this is not a book on Christian theology. Suffice it to say that such a position was contrary to the official Church view and was rejected and declared a heresy. Arius, of Libyan lineage, was raised in Antioch but is always remembered for his statement in Alexandria that started a movement that divided Europe.

While the Church denounced his views, the Emperor Constantine sent a letter to Alexandria in which he treated the controversy as an insignificant disagreement about words, a kind of storm in a teacup as we would say today. How wrong an Emperor can be. Arianism grew in its influence, and no matter how strongly Church councils condemned it the movement continued to attract followers so that it became one of the strongest schisms in the history of the Church. The controversy was so long-lasting and so difficult for the Church that in the year AD 800 in Aachen, the Pope of the day anointed Charlemagne of the Franks *Emperor in the West.* How so?

There was already an Emperor in the East, in Constantinople (once Byzantium), and the Frankish people had one great attraction for the Papacy. In a continent where so many groupings were Arian, the Franks were Catholic. So a Catholic alliance of Pope and Emperor was established, an arrangement which would probably not have happened had not Arius, over four centuries earlier, not proclaimed his belief about the relationship of Jesus Christ to God the Father.

When I stood at the Arian place of baptism in Ravenna, all of this was in my excited mind and I saw Europe breaking religiously into two with a fracture that would take centuries to mend. Think of these things when you visit the Arian Baptistery in Ravenna.

Leaving Ravenna, you will take with you rich thoughts of Dante, of mosaic art, of Byzantine architecture, of Church history and a great schism in Europe, among other rich memories. That makes Ravenna a place not to be missed.

Chapter 10
Unforgettable Umbria

It's Saturday night, and I'm sitting on the cathedral steps overlooking *Piazza Quattro Novembre* in Perugia and I'm feeling the throbbing excitement of the medieval city at night. The piazza is one of those places which remains as alive at the weekend as a Paris boulevard until at least two in the morning, chiefly because there are so many young people in the city. This is the meeting place above all others on a Saturday night. The young person who does not come to *Piazza Quattro Novembre* on the last evening of the week is a rare bird. The television cameras are here, filming a variety show, and the atmosphere is buzzing.

I've found a group of friends who are also students at the *Università Per Stranieri di Perugia* (the University for Foreigners), and they are talking about star signs and drawing conclusions about the respective characters and personalities.

'What is your star sign, Tony?'

They are amazed that I don't know. Rana is especially taken aback and declares that she has never met anyone who does not know his star sign. Rana is Iranian, and totally illogically I think of the 'wise men from the east' in Matthew's Gospel, almost certainly Persian astrologers, and I conclude that Rana's reaction is hardly surprising.

'When were you born?'

'April 8.'

'That makes you Aries.'

'What does that mean? What does it say about me?'

I am sure that I am not energetic—well, I might be energetic—but I don't believe I am assertive—or am I? Now she has me thinking.

There follows a discussion of the characteristics of various personalities, based upon the constellations at the time of their birth. I find myself thinking that astrology was once a very powerful influence in these parts. In north central Italy, there were chairs in astrology during the 14th century at Perugia and Bologna, as well as at more distant centres such as Padua and Paris. I find myself thinking, too, how strange it was the Church itself became influenced by the astrological world-view, and I share this thought with my fellow- students.

'I don't think it's that surprising,' says Rudolfo, a Swiss, 'because, after all, the Greek and Roman worlds accepted it totally. Christianity was born in a Greco-Roman world.'

'But Rudolfo, to accept the tenets of astrology is to accept the omnipotence of the stars in the life of a person, whereas Christianity teaches the omnipotence of their Creator.'

Inevitably, the discussion is inconclusive, but lively. All over the piazza, there are small groups in animated discussion. Every Saturday night, it is the same here. You get into a lively discussion about something, and it doesn't really matter what it is. It's part of the life of Perugia, a place where anything and everything is discussed, usually with passion.

My fellow-students disperse, to wander along Corso Vannucci, which takes its name from Pietro Vannucci, an artist celebrated in these parts as *Il Perugino*, one of the men who give Perugia pride in its past, and I move a little higher up the terrace of steps, and sit for a little longer, watching the stage and the camera crews. There is the usual buzz in the air. The *Passagiata*, the evening stroll-cum-parade when locals dress well to catch up with others for a chat, has passed.

The space now belongs to young people and when young people are gathered, there is excitement, a kind of invisible electricity in the air. I listen to their animated discussion and laughter, I look at happy faces, I see intelligence in their eyes, for many of those present are young people studying at the University for Foreigners or the University of Perugia. Even though similar gatherings occur in Piazza del Popolo in Rome, in Piazza Umberto in Capri, and for that matter in any other Italian city, I know I don't want to be anywhere else. This, at this moment, is my world. This is medieval Perugia with very modern young people celebrating. Yes, I am loving being in Piazza Quattro Novembre.

It's now midnight and people are still pouring into and out of the piazza. Being somewhat older than the youth I am watching, I decide that in just a little while I must return to my studio flat and give some priority to sleep.

Living in Perugia while studying was one of the fine experiences of my life. The only disadvantage at the time was that I was away from my wife and family, but that significant lack aside, I enjoyed the experience immensely.

The University for Foreigners is in the elegant Palazzo Gallenga, a fact which makes study a very fine undertaking. Palazzo Gallenga is in delightful Piazza Fortebraccio, immediately outside the huge Etruscan arch in the equally massive Etruscan walls of the city. The arch is truly impressive, reaching to a considerable height, topped with a Roman structure which itself has higher medieval additions. The arch passageway is over 30 feet high, or 9 metres. This makes it twice the height of a London double-decker bus. Two rows of voussoirs (wedge-shaped stones) form the graceful arch, held in place by a keystone at the top. Above the major arch is another formed by voussoirs, making a total height of 60 feet (18 metres).

The arch was built in the second half of the 3rd century BC and restored by Augustus in 40 BC following his victory in the Perusine War. The city became known then as Augustus Perusia. The inscription of that name is on the inside of the arch.

The origins of the university are interesting. It is the oldest university in Italy offering courses in Italian language and culture exclusively to foreign students. It was the dream-child of a lawyer named Astorre Lupattelli, whose ambition for many years was to establish such an institution in Perugia. His dream was realised when, in 1921, the university was opened with high aims.

Its early courses were held in two major centres, the halls of the University of Perugia and in the smaller, but brilliantly appointed Sala dei Notari in the Palazzo dei Priori in the city centre. From 1927, the university had its own premises in Palazzo Gallenga. As a student, it is easy to love Gallenga in its warmth of welcome and its elegance.

There was a period when the official aim of the university diverted from Lupattelli's commendable ambitions for the institution. The foundation date of 1921 is the clue. Fascist influences became dominant and the University for Foreigners was drawn into the Italian state's official requirement that teaching institutions were to 'spread the superior Italian culture around the world'. Today that purpose is long gone. High quality courses in language and culture are the major curriculum ingredients.

The location of Palazzo Gallenga introduces one of the major reasons for the charm of Perugia. Having Etruscan roots, it sits on the top of a considerable hill. It was the Etruscan custom to build on defendable eminences. The journey on the bus from the mainline railway station, stazione Perugia di Fontivegge, on the flatter country below consists of loops and sharp bends that emphasise all the way up to Piazza Italia at the top how steep the slope is.

During my time living in Perugia and subsequent visits, the charm of the city never paled. I am as much in love with Perugia as when I first set foot in it. I have not been able to resist returning a number of times. The cafés and restaurants tucked away in the narrow streets, the Roman viaduct running into the city and now one of the charming walkways of Perugia, the huge Etruscan well with its massive masonry, the Pallazzo Priori housing the Umbrian Museum, two sumptuous guild meeting rooms and other public offices, have their own attraction as they dominate the city centre.

Piazza Italia at the highest point of the city is compelling in its graciousness and is the place where many visitors first step onto the pavements of Perugia, it being the terminal stop for the urban buses. The churches and other ecclesiastical buildings are structures of endless fascination. The story of Perugia could go on with mention of so many elements of the city's make-up.

Yet sometimes, the simple, everyday things bring pleasure out of all proportion to their evident importance. A small *allimentari* and market at Porta Pia, where my studio flat is located, brought me endless pleasure as I shopped there most days for the everyday necessities including, of course, food. You quickly discover in Italy that only fresh food is sold. That's one of the great delights of eating in the country. I also quickly discovered the delights of the *mercato coperto*, the covered market where you can buy just about anything and know that it is as fresh as any food you could buy anywhere.

Perugian chocolate became part of my fascination with the city when, on a visit after my time at the University for Foreigners, I found I was there during the Eurochocolate Festival.

What a time that was, with chocolate stalls everywhere from Piazza Italia to the cathedral. I have never seen such a chocolate celebration.

The fact is, Perugia is a magnificent city. On one visit, my wife, Ruth, and I stayed in part of a palazzo opposite the Palazzo Priori. We could hardly have been more at the centre of things and loved every minute. I look forward to staying in Perugia again someday before too long.

North of Perugia lies the town of Sansepolcro. Getting there provides the opportunity to travel on the privately-owned Umbrian Central Railway (Ferrovia Centrale Umbria), an unusual company to say the least. It contracts services for the national passenger operator Trenitalia. The trains leave from Sant' Anna station high on the side of the hill, a little below Piazza Italia. They might well be the most graffitied trains in Europe, a feature that makes them colourful at least. The line runs from southern Umbria, north to Sansepolcro just over the border into Tuscany.

The journey's most remarkable section is the leaving of Sant' Anna on departing Perugia and returning up the hill to Sant' Anna at the end of the day. The gradient is extraordinary, seeming to defy all the rules for steel wheels on steel rails that civil and mechanical engineers ever devised. When I first made the journey, I could not understand how a train could manage to get to the top. As the train ascends to Perugia the sound of grinding and groaning of a locomotive working very hard is unmistakeable. But it does it and moreover it does it every time. On the descent, you can almost feel the train's sense of relief when Ponte San Giovanni is reached and the more level journey begins.

Why go to Sansepolcro? Principally because in the Museo Civico hangs the magnificent Piero Della Francesca painting 'Resurrection'. More of that in the next chapter. For the present, muse on one of the most interesting railways in Italy. One of the bonuses of making the whole journey from Terni in the south to Sansepolcro via the wonderful climb up to Perugia is that it takes you the length of Umbria through some fascinating countryside on a train which, no matter the graffiti on the outside is comfortable enough and clean enough on the inside for you to enjoy a pleasant journey.

When thinking about country journeyings in Umbria, a useful piece of knowledge is that the Tiber, which runs through the heart of the region, is in broad terms a dividing line between areas which were principally Etruscan west of the river and those which were mainly Umbrian to its east. The river passes within five kilometres to the east of Perugia, an Etruscan city.

Crossing the river, you head for the city of Gubbio, once under the control of the Duke of Urbino and the Montefeltro family (from 1384 to 1508). The palace of the Dukes of Urbino still stands at the end of a narrow road that has become at the height of summer essentially a tourist road. It is a road where it might be advisable to ignore the hordes of tourists and walk the street, if only because the ceramics for sale are worth an appreciative look. You might choose to buy, but even if you don't, you'll get a good idea of the typical Umbrian ceramic patterns.

You should also take the cage-lift, which is a kind of chairlift but with stand-up cages for two, up the hill to the church of Sant' Ubaldo, a simple and pretty church in a magnificent location. As you climb in the chairlift you get the finest view of the Roman theatre below that is available anywhere in Gubbio.

You notice that in the church there are some interesting large wooden arrangements that look like giant egg timers or hour glasses. They are the *ceri* used in Gubbio's annual *Ceri* Race, not really a race at all. It takes place on the 15th May and features three guilds of the town. Each wooden structure, weighing 400 kg, is known as a 'candle' and is surmounted by a statue of a saint. The three are Sant' Ubaldo (patron saint of Gubbio and protector of bricklayers), San Georgio (protector of milliners) and Sant' Antonio (protector of farmers).

The 'race' is gruelling, an uphill run of the three teams, each carrying a 'candle', for 4 kilometres. It is no race for weaklings, and custom decrees that Saint Ubaldo must win. Even so, the race is run at a furious pace. It usually lasts for less than 15 minutes, which says a great deal for the fitness and strength of the participants, given that the race is a constant ascent of serious gradients. It brings a great deal of excitement from the spectators. As is usual in Italy for a race, it is preceded by a colourful procession.

Why is it run? It celebrates the help believed to have been given to Gubbio by Sant' Ubaldo in its 1151 victory over an alliance of eleven other towns. Gubbio was Ghibelline in the 11th and 12th centuries' Guelph—Ghibelline conflicts. The alliance was Guelph. Certainly, the victory was remarkable. You make your own mind up whether Sant' Ubaldo had a hand or not, but the background adds an important dimension to the race for the watchers.

Sant' Ubaldo died on 16 May 1160. The race is held on the eve of his death.

Gubbio is home to an interesting legend that led to a strange burial, the only burial of its kind I am aware of. The legend has it that in the 13th century an enormous wolf brought terror to the countryside around Gubbio. The predations of the creature came to the attention of Saint Francis, so he decided when passing through the area to apprehend the wolf and discipline it for its unacceptable behaviour. The wolf was reduced to tears (Do wolves have tear ducts?) and became thoroughly repentant for its 'sins'.

He promised never to behave in such a way again and as a pledge of good faith held its paw out to Francis. Il Poverello accepted the remorse and the promise. The wolf became a local pet and when, full of years, he passed into wolverine after-life he was buried in consecrated ground. Hence, 'The Wolf of Gubbio' has become central in the folklore of the city.

A celebrated figure in Gubbio's history was a man who made a major contribution to its prosperity, one Maestro Giorgio, remembered affectionately by those in the ceramics industry in the area. The origins of Gubbio's ceramics specialisation lie in the medieval life of the city. Giorgio di Pietro was born at Intra on Lago Maggiore sometime between 1465 and 1470. Thus, we don't know how old he was when, probably in 1489 he moved to Gubbio with his brother Salimbene. We can only surmise that he was between 19 and 24.

In Gubbio, they formed a business partnership with a potter of the city, Giacomo Paolucci, the purpose of which was to produce pottery of *maiolica*, a technique of tin-glazing. Giorgio added red and gold lustre in a third firing which provided a glowing finish that other pottery-producing towns were unable to emulate. Gubbio gained an important commercial advantage that put it in Giorgio's debt. It became the basis of the Gubbio style of pottery, making the city a good place for pottery-browsing still.

In 1498, Maestro Giorgio was granted citizenship of Gubbio by Guidobaldo da Montefeltro, Duke of Urbino, a citizenship with its privileges confirmed in 1519 by Pope Leo X, who described him as 'an excellent master in the art of *maiolica*', and one who 'brings honour to the city, Lord and people of Gubbio'. He became known as 'Maestro Giorgio delle maioliche'. The business passed on to his sons. He died in Gubbio, but there is no known marked grave.

The city is important to see even if you have no interest in pottery. It lies in a gorge formed by what in Italy is known as a *torrente*, or torrent. The difference in Italy is that even without water or with very little of it, it is a torrent. The ramparts are impressive and the yellow ochre of the buildings remarkable attractive. Yes, Gubbio is very much for visiting.

One of the best-known places of Umbria, and one of the most over-run with tourists is Assisi, the city of Saint Francis. It's a city of pink buildings, long and narrow, on the slopes of Monte Subiaso. Its major focus is the basilica of Saint Francis, consisting of an upper church and a lower church, both galleries of devotional art.

The two Assisi earthquakes of 27 September 1997 were devastating for the art world and tragic in the loss of life associated with them, the first at 2.33 am measuring 5.5 on the Richter scale, the second at 11.42 am reaching 5.7. Damage included the vaulted ceiling, many Cimabue frescoed works and some of Giotto's frescoes. The Upper Church received significant damage, but the Lower

Church was virtually unscathed. That meant that my favourite artwork of all those in the basilica, Cimabue's Saint Francis, was preserved undamaged.

Not long after the earthquake, I visited the basilica and was thrilled by the beauty and serenity Cimabue has managed to depict in Francis. I visited the basilica again some years afterwards and was no less excited than I had been at seeing the work intact after the earthquakes.

Sadly, the second earthquake took the lives of four people, two surveyors and two Franciscan friars who were in the basilica assessing the damage from the 2.33 am *terramoto*. About 20 escaped.

The 13th century church of Santa Chiara also received some damage, as did other structures.

I learnt something else after the earthquakes, and that is that Italians don't just put up scaffolding for functional purposes. They make sure that it is as inoffensive to the eye as possible. I do believe that the scaffolding I saw holding parts of building up was brass, or made to look like brass. Extraordinary, yes. True, yes.

The station is some distance below the town, so a taxi connection is necessary. However, there are scheduled buses from the Piazza Partigiani bus terminus in Perugia. They stop at Porta San Pietro in Assisi leaving a walk uphill to the basilica. It is a short walk—a few hundred metres—so it isn't all bad news.

The other Umbrian city that I think of very warmly is Orvieto, sitting high on its hill of tufa rock. Its massive tuffet is a pedestal with sheer rock sides all the way round. The road entrances to the city (there are two) have considerable climbs for the visitor to make. However, no vehicle is required for making a visit because on leaving the railway station on the western side, you can take a funicular to the top of the cliff-face at Piazza Cahen.

The major reason for visiting Orvieto lies a bus ride to the south-west in Piazza del Duomo. However, before leaving Piazza Cahen, you should spend an hour at the Pozzo di San Patrizio (Saint Patrick's Well). I suggest an hour if you are fit because the well, which has a downward spiral staircase and a separate upward one (descenders and ascenders never meet), is 62 metres (200 feet) deep with 248 steps to be negotiated. 496 steps need a bit of time, especially the half of them which must be climbed. Why go down? Because to do so is to experience the finest 16th century civil engineering.

Originally, the well had a survival purpose. Its digging and construction was authorised by Clement VII, a de Medici pope, as a water supply for the city should it come under siege. He had good reason to commission the work. He had fled Rome in 1527 after its sacking by the Holy Roman Emperor Charles V and taken refuge in Orvieto. Should you be tempted to make the descent (and you should allow yourself to be so tempted if you are fit enough to make the journey), then let your imagination run as you take to the steps. The well was built not with human water carriers, but oxen.

The double helix arrangement certainly avoids upwards and downwards crushes of people to become entangled, but its purpose was to allow oxen bearing water carriers to descend, be loaded with their water cargo and ascend without turning and not meet other oxen on their way down. When you make the journey, you will realise that the steps you are using are far from wide enough for water-bearing oxen to pass.

The man responsible for the construction of this extraordinary feat of engineering was one Antonio Cordiani (1484-1546), popularly known as Sangallo the Younger. He was a Florentine, so there was a neatness to his being commissioned by a de Medici pope whose own associations were principally with Rome and Florence.

Sangallo has a good many commissions to his name in Rome. My own favourite is the church of Santa Maria di Loreto, a beautifully balanced edifice, elegantly domed above a rectangular form which descends to a larger one, pilastered in attractive patterns which do not seem to coincide with any of the three principal classical orders. A beautiful building.

To return to Saint Patrick's Well, the work was completed in 1537 and from that year Orvieto had available cold water of great purity. (Did the oxen supply impurities? I don't know.)

Why was it called 'Saint Patrick's' Well? It seems to have been given the name in the light of the Irish legend that Saint Patrick could give access to Purgatory, that is, to the very depths. Hence the access he gave was 'bottomless'. The Pozzo di San Patrizio might not be bottomless, but it is certainly deep. It seems to be responsible for the saying, or reflects the saying, that a man careful with his money has pockets like Saint Patrick's Well, that is, they are bottomless.

The Piazza del Duomo is the centre of what is rather a quiet city. The piazza is spacious and grand.

On one of its sides stands the Palazzo dei Papi, the Palace of the Popes. It is a massive building, built of the volcanic rock the city sits on. Its major interest is the fourth floor, which houses the Cathedral Museum. Besides housing ecclesiastical artifacts, it has a Madonna by Simone Martini and sculptural works by Maitani, the Pisanos and Arnolfo di Cambio.

The other major building on the piazza is the Duomo, or cathedral. It is one of the most exciting cathedrals in Italy for me, with its harmonious western façade, completed in 1600. It is surely one of the most striking and colourful cathedral façades in Italy. While the cathedral architecture is principally located in the transition from Romanesque to Gothic, begun in 1290, the façade is a Gothic masterpiece. It takes the eye upwards via soaring vertical lines and gables as slim as they can be while still being gables. The buttresses, also as slim as they are able to be, clothed in small slabs of coloured marble, compel the eye to look upwards. The effect is sumptuous and the architectural intention is surely that the viewer should look upwards to heaven. The final impetus for the heavenly journey is supplied by the pinnacles which seem to say, 'We've shown you the way, keep looking upwards.'

What was the cathedral's purpose, apart from the obvious one of becoming a place of worship and the seat of a bishop? Its very specific purpose was to be a place of housing the relics of what became known as 'the miracle of Bolsena'. The story has some charm or a touch of the grotesque, depending upon how you relate to it.

The tale is set in 1263 when a German priest stopped at Orvieto's neighbouring town of Bolsena on his way to Rome on a pilgrimage. He was by all accounts a priest of faith and piety, but one who found difficulty in the doctrine of transubstantiation, that is, the teaching that Christ is really present in the Host at Mass. While functioning as the celebrant at Mass in the church of Saint Christina, he had just finished the words of consecration when blood began seeping from the consecrated Host. It began to drip to his hands.

He interrupted the Mass and made his way to Orvieto where he related what had happened to the Pope, at that time Urban IV, who then sent messengers to Bolsena to investigate the matter. Their report substantiated (pun intended!) the story and Urban commanded the Host to be brought to Orvieto together with the linen cloth that bore the bloodstains. That was duly done and the relics found their eventual home in the cathedral.

The story of the miracle finds its conclusion in Orvieto, the city that at one time was the home of the popes.

The interior consists of a nave and two aisles in alternating black and white stone. It houses fine fresco work and is in my view as elegant within as the façade is without. It is one of the most pleasing cathedrals to spend time in.

Orvieto was an Etruscan city and it is no surprise then to discover that it has an Etruscan 'city of the dead'. It consists essentially of 'rooms' cut into the tufa rock to house the bodies of the dead. My strong impression as I walked through the necropolis was that I might go into one of them and have afternoon tea with dead Aunty Etrusca. Bizarre I know, but that was my odd thought. Don't be put off by the slight flippancy in that remark. The necropolis is a very important visitable example of Etruscan burial practices. I found myself greatly excited by the experience of walking through it and letting my imagination run. Perhaps you, too, will find it exciting.

So, dead Etruscans provide the farewell to *Bella Umbria* in this book. But it is very much a region for the living to enjoy.

Chapter 11

An Apennine Interlude

My fascination with Piero della Francesca started when Annie, my first wife, and I stumbled into the uninviting church of San Francesco in Arezzo many years ago, there to find the wonderful frescoes devised by his vivid imagination and executed by his gentle hand. I say 'stumbled into' because seen from the outside the church has a forbidding look to its plain façade and it was my intention to walk straight past it.

Annie though, could be quite persistent when her curiosity was aroused. It was she who insisted that we go in. One look was enough to fire my imagination. How could I find out more about this extraordinary artist? Where could I see more of his work? The quest had begun. I searched out his work in Urbino, in Sansepolcro, in Florence, in London, in Perugia, in Monterchi. And what an exciting experience it has been!

Piero is the gentle painter whose work I will travel anywhere to see. There is a lightness of touch in his execution which tells me that composing a picture and putting it on canvas was never a labour to him, but always an act of love. I see him with a tear in his eye as he carefully composes that face of infinite compassion on the 'Pregnant Madonna' now to be seen in its own gallery in Monterchi; I see him standing back from the canvas in amazement at his own work, gazing at the triumphant look on the face of the risen Christ in the painting Aldous Huxley once described as 'the greatest small painting in the world', the *Resurrection* at Sansepolcro. I was surprised to discover, by the way, that the painting is not so small. It occupies a goodly portion of one wall in the gallery. And the robe of Christ! It is the most delicate of pinks, a colour which I have seen in so much of Piero della Francesca's work, and is for me almost his signature.

The point was, how could I see the 'Apennine' works of Piero?

It happened quite by chance. I was on my way to somewhere else when I found a very, very special place. Serendipity is surely the gateway to life's most magical experiences, those moments of discovery which no careful planning can possibly supply. It was the gentle Piero who first took me into the Apennines.

I had a long weekend free from study in Perugia. My last lecture for the week was on Thursday, then no more until Tuesday of the following week. Four whole free days to do something with, and I determined not to waste a moment of it. As I thought about what to do with those four days, my only such lengthy break during the course, the idea of seeing some of Piero della Francesca's most intriguing work began to take shape.

Now the break in studies gave me the opportunity to see three of his very special paintings I had not seen before but had longed to view for many years. One was in the small Tuscan village of Monterchi, the other two resided in the Le Marche city of Urbino. Monterchi is the home of the *Madonna del Parto*, or 'The Pregnant Madonna'. The National Gallery of Le Marche possesses the *Madonna Senigallia* and the 'Flagellation'.

When Friday came, I took the bus through the narrow streets down to Fontevegge, Perugia's FS railway station, and there hired a car for the long weekend. My odyssey had commenced! In true Tony Gates style, I set my face towards the first stop on the journey, Monterchi, intending to get there by the shortest possible route. However, I still hadn't managed to get the amazing network of roads around Perugia under my belt, and while I can't remember any details at all of my journey out of the city, it was an experience of total lostness!

The major roads around Perugia are fast and furious, with tunnels here and there, and very little opportunity to turn around once you find you are going in the wrong direction. It must have taken me half an hour of 'wrong directioning' before I managed to point the car in towards Umbertide and Citta di Castello, from whence I would have to turn off the main road for Monterchi. Ah, well, I saw more of the countryside than I'd intended, and that was far from being loss.

The minor road from Citta di Castello is a delight, following the Tiber Valley with the Apennines to the east, the hills of Tuscany to the west, and the sparkling waters of *Lago Trasimeno* (Lake Trasimeno). It was a tranquil day, the sort which guarantees peace and pleasure whatever you are doing. The green hills all around me and the cloudless, blue sky above seemed to make every colour intense.

The terrain began to rise a little, and then Monterchi appeared, high on its hill. I drove the winding road up to the village, parking just outside the old walls.

Before visiting the *Madonna del Parto*, I decided to walk through the streets to absorb the atmosphere. I was quickly rewarded. Every street is lined with picturesque houses which wear their age well and exude charm. I found the main piazza populated with a large number of artists; everywhere I looked people were seated at easels, concentrating intensely on the task of interpreting on canvas the beautiful village around them.

Open-necked shirts and jeans seemed to be the painters' uniform, and one or two even contrived to look more French than Italian by wearing berets at rakish angles. I couldn't see one painter below middle age, which means, perhaps, that the reflective experience of painting has a special appeal when the hectic years have passed. I have to admit that as one who enjoys using watercolour, the appeal is irresistible. If I were to return to Monterchi in the near future, I would certainly take my paints and brushes with me.

I walked out onto the wall which looks westwards over the Tiber Valley, crossing an arch which traverses the road to the school now converted into a gallery to house Piero's wonderful work. The view which confronted me is quite beyond the power of words to describe. Falling away before me was the most massive vista across the valley so that my eye was able to take in detail for many, many miles, all so clearly defined by the glorious sunshine. Is the light always so bright here?

Besides the charm of the village and the wonderful views towards the Tiber, is the light itself a reason for so many artists finding their way to Monterchi? Or does Piero attract them, and while here they put their own skills to work? As a very amateur painter I have a strong desire to return to Monterchi with my own painting gear. The peace of this hilltop village is reason enough to return.

But it was time to see the *Madonna del Parto*.

It is for me one of the truly sublime works of Piero. It is a detached fresco which shows the 'with child' Virgin Mary looking regal as well as serene. She stands under a canopy, obviously pregnant, wearing a full blue gown from neck to feet. Two angelic figures, one on each side of her, hold back the curtains as though to present her to her audience. This is a glorious pregnant Madonna.

I stood looking at her for a long time, trying to get myself into the mind of an artist who could produce so moving a picture of a woman awaiting confinement. Then I remembered that Monterchi was the village of Piero's mother. Monterchi and pregnancy went together for Piero. Could it be that while the picture is clearly one of devotion to the Virgin, something of adoration for his own mother is in the fresco? The first thing that draws the eye is the gentle oval face of Mary. Do we have a glimpse in that face of how Piero saw his mother? It is not something he could admit, of course, but I cannot help wondering. We know that in 1459 Piero visited the village to pay homage to his mother.

The fresco is not now where it was painted. It was probably executed sometime between 1459 and 1465, though it could have been commissioned a few years earlier. It is not known who the commissioner was. It was painted in the chapel of *Santa Maria di Momentana*, situated on the slopes of Montione, a word from the Latin *Mons Iunonis*, Hill of Juno.

Due to an earthquake, the picture was moved in the late 18th century to the newly built cemetery chapel. In 1919, it was moved as a temporary measure to a gallery in Sansepolcro but returned to the cemetery chapel in 1922.

The detached fresco became the focus of an extraordinary incident 22 years later. In 1944, there was concern throughout Italy that great works of art were in danger from bombing and shelling and a great deal of thought was given to how they might be protected. The *Madonna del Parto* was considered to be at risk, so a plan was made to protect it in an alcove enclosed by a brick wall, to make it as safe from explosives as possible. The Italian Government sent two scholars from Florence to Monterchi to supervise the placing of the fresco in its place of safety and to ensure that its refuge was suitable for the painting's storage.

What followed was more like a scene from *Monty Python* or *Fawlty Towers* than a real event. When the two Florentine scholars arrived at Monterchi, they must have looked authentically Italian, as of course they were, because some of the locals were convinced they were Germans disguised as Italian academics who had anything but the security of Piero's work in mind.

Accordingly, some Monterchi women rang the church bells to alarm the population. A crowd with hoes and clubs arrived at the scene, apparently looking very menacing, determined to protect the Madonna. Once the comical misunderstanding was sorted out, the professors from Florence, no doubt a little shaken, were able to do their work.

'The Pregnant Madonna' is not a work to spend five minutes before. It needs time for reflection and for its sheer wonder to percolate through the viewer's soul. I left the little elementary school and Piero della Francesca's *Madonna del Parto* with very great reluctance but encouraged by the thought that another of Piero's great works awaited me at Urbino. The barely more than a girl Mary of the gentle face touched by anxiety went with me, reminding me that I had engaged with one of the art world's most beautiful and moving paintings. She had entered into my deepest emotional self at Monterchi.

From the village of Monterchi, I made my way up the wonderful hairpins of the Apennines, surely one of the most satisfying driving experiences of Italy. They seem endless and require real driving, with plenty of gear-changing and coaxing on the bends which in places come close to doubling back on themselves. It means that the climb takes a long while to get to the top. The constant 'tacking', as it were, uses many more kilometres than an impossible straight line up the mountain would do. But that suited me well. I didn't want it to be over. It was a wonderful driving experience that I could have indulged in all day. I couldn't enjoy the views, of course, but I knew I had that pleasure on the descent of the return journey. Bring on the return journey!

My destination was Urbino, a city I had one strong reason for visiting. Again, Piero was the attraction. His 'Flagellation' picture is located in Urbino and I was determined to stand before it and take in as much of the artist's meaning as I could comprehend. Many have said that the artist's intent is too much of a mystery for them to be able to interpret the work with any confidence. Well, that just made it all the more important to try my hand. I, who am a cryptic crossword and word-games enthusiast, was as prepared to be wrong as any other attempted interpreter. Add to that my love of fine art, and especially of the work of Piero della Francesca, and you have all the reasons necessary for my decision to drive to Urbino.

It was not to be a straightforward journey, however. Once over the top of the watershed, and I knew when it was because I felt the change of angle of the car, and after stopping for a lunch break, I made a distracting discovery. However, before moving on to that I must comment on my lunchbreak stop. I walked into a café just past the top of the hairpins and immediately felt that I had walked into a closed establishment where the door had inadvertently been left unlocked. Not a soul was in sight, not at the tables, not behind the counter.

It was a Sunday, but even in Italy, not everyone was at Mass, surely. I called out. No response. I walked to the far end of the room where there was a door that I might call through to see if anyone was available to serve me. Then I heard a sound, a kind of conversational buzz that rose to excited exclamations. I called again, but there was no way I would be heard above the noise that was now growing in strength.

There was only one thing for it. I would go through the door and make it obvious I was a customer to be served. It felt like an intrusion, but I was hungry and didn't know when I would find another eating place. What I found on going through the door was a large lounge room filled with men, many of them young, and a television receiver. The television provided the reason for the empty café. Yes, it was Sunday, but it was not the Church which was holding sway. The Italian Formula One Grand Prix was on and the room was filled with Ferrari supporters, some of them wearing the red of the cars, and one wearing a scarf with the prancing horse emblem.

Nothing was going to interrupt the excitement. *'Avanti! Avanti!'* 'Come in, come in!' I, who was a total stranger, was being invited to be part of it as though I were a member of the village family. Hungry though I was, nothing could have persuaded me to say, 'No'. This was something to be enjoyed, to be part of. Satisfying the hunger could wait.

I stayed and enjoyed not only the race, but the atmosphere of the room and the obvious inviolable priority of the afternoon. While I was there, a couple of locals also came into the room to warm welcomes. At the end of the race, Ferrari claimed the chequered flag and the room was in uproar. My back was slapped, and I was treated as one of them.

It was a never-to-be-forgotten experience. I shall always be glad that I accepted the call to stay. The proprietor sold me a *prosciutto* and *formaggio* panino and wished me well for the remainder of the drive, though he could not understand why anyone would want to go to Urbino.

I took the food to the car and sat for a while consuming one of the best ham and cheese rolls I had ever had. And as I ate, I congratulated myself on my luck at having had so rich an experience in the Apennine heights.

My intention had been to find a bed in Urbino for the night and enjoy Piero's work the next day. However, the Italian Grand Prix had put me well behind that schedule, and I had not the slightest regret. I decided that it would now make more sense to look for a B&B or hotel somewhere along the way and continue to Urbino the next day.

So off I went. Before long I saw a sign pointing to the left, indicating that the road leaving the main one went to a place called Borgo Pace. That was intriguing, suggesting to me that it must be a place of peace. It might not be of course, but never mind. It was the name which resonated, and no facts were going to dampen it. As I continued to drive eastwards along the gently descending fell, I couldn't get the name out of my mind. Borgo Pace—what thought it produced! I went on driving towards Urbino, still with the intention of finding a bed along the way. Eventually, it became too much for me and, resistance defeated, I made a U-turn and headed back towards the signpost that had captured my imagination.

When I came to it, I made the right turn and found myself driving over a charming small stone bridge and quickly after that into a sloping piazza. To my right was a hotel. I parked the car outside and prayed that there was a vacancy. This is where I wanted to stay the night. I wanted nothing less. I was not willing to settle for anything less. I walked in through the main door and asked the lady behind the counter if she had a room vacant for the night. My heart leapt when she replied, in English, 'Yes sir. We have a room.' I asked the price but would have paid anything for it. In fact, it was a very reasonable figure.

I took my overnight bag up to my room, then went out to explore.

I started with the stone bridge I had driven over. It turned out to be more than just a fine structure. A plaque told me that it had been blown up by the retreating German army during the Second World War and had been rebuilt by local men. How grateful I was for those local men I would never meet. They had restored a lovely part of a lovely village.

From there, I wandered across the piazza to discover on my left a telephone booth that looked very familiar. I, a Londoner, was quickly reminded of the telephone booths of my youth, red, full length doors, totally enclosed for privacy, and because of that they always had a certain odour of human use resting in the telephone hand pieces. As I recall them now, I am certain they could hardly have been healthy instruments to use. 'But,' I thought, 'I didn't know Italians had similar phone booths.'

They didn't. I discovered when I approached it and examined it more closely that it was an English King George VI post office telephone booth. What was an English King George VI phone booth doing high up in the Apennines of Italy? I have always thought of myself as a person difficult to surprise. But on that day, I certainly was surprised. I never did find out how it got there in the tranquil village of Borgo Pace.

Wandering through the village I came to a high, magnificent bridge over the River Metauro set in a very deep ravine.

The Metauro is formed by the Meta and the Auro, two torrents which meet to form a river which, in times of strong flow, can be a rushing conduit.

While it is not known precisely where on the river the encounter took place, in 207 BC Hasdrubai Barca, whose support was important to Hannibal for the success of his Italy campaign, was defeated by Roman forces under the commands of consuls Gaius Claudius Nero and Marcus Livius Salinator. To look over the high bridge down into the valley of the Metauro is an opportunity to think on a battle which had a great deal to do with Hannibal's designs on Rome.

I slept that night after thinking of great things on the Metauro, though of course without locating the battle necessarily at Borgo Pace. In any case, the name made me think more of peace than of war, a strange sort of paradox.

My decision to make the very short diversion into Borgo Pace had proved to be a good one. It is an absolutely delightful village, tucked away in rugged, but well-treed, country, as pleasing a place as I have ever stayed in. I resolved that one day I would take my wife Ann, who has since died, to see it. I made her that promise when I returned to our home in the Adelaide Hills. Before I was able to fulfil that promise, cancer struck her. When I returned to Borgo Pace, I took her with me in my heart. It was an experience of emotional catharsis focussed in the little church of Santa Maria Nuova in the village.

To return to my first visit to Borgo Pace, the next day I continued my journey to Urbino. I walked to the Galleria Nazionale delle Marche where 'Flagellation' was to be found. I stood before it for over an hour, longer than I had expected to study it.

As I stood before the picture, absorbed in it, scarcely able to believe that at last I was seeing the real depiction, a female voice to my left, and slightly behind me, said, 'What do you make of it?' It was a cultured voice. I turned to see my questioner. She was pleasantly dressed, possibly a little younger than I but not much, and attractive. What *did* I think of it, I who had no art training and was standing before a work which has baffled experts the world over?

The painting is an unusual composition, having two centres of interest, one to the right where three men, in the close foreground, are in conversation, and one to the left where, in the middle distance Christ is suffering flagellation prior to his crucifixion. In the left hand scene, the flagellation takes place in a spacious gallery of Corinthian columns and a decorative, coffered ceiling. Five figures are involved, including Christ. One of them is seated, having his upper body clad in a garment of delicate pink, a colour that seems always to characterise, for me, Piero's work.

The figures in the right-hand scene have no interest at all in the flagellation going on quite close by. They are part of the total scene, and the superb perspective work shows them to be standing well forward of the flagellation, as well as to the right of it. One of the clearly enigmatic features of the picture is that the flagellation scene is illuminated from the right whereas the scene of the foreground three men appears to be illuminated from the left, so that the illumination is proceeding out of the picture on both sides.

In the various expert interpretations, most of which conflict, the seated figure is seen variously as Pontius Pilatus, the Byzantine emperor John VIII Palaiologos and Sultan Murad II. Perhaps that alone indicates that answers are still wanting for interpreting 'Flagellation'.

Working on the basis that in art every person has the right to personal expertise, I set my mind to articulating what it meant for me, and I might add continues to mean for me. It is far simpler than any of the professional interpretations, none of which I dismiss. I am not qualified to do so. They are all interesting, but I have to make sense of the picture for myself. And for me, the reaction is essentially spiritual. I know that this flies in the face of many expert interpretations which see the picture as political.

But remember, everyone in matters of art is his or her own interpreter because art has to mean something not for the whole world, but for him or for her. I might add that I see the spiritual as to do with reality, not in the Platonic sense, but in a Greek sense, nevertheless. I see it in the dual senses of the word *alētheia*, the close alliance of Truth and Reality. In the 'John' corpus of writings of the New Testament, for 'Reality', read 'Divinity', the Reality that (or Who) is communicated through the *Logos*, the communication of the heart of things.

The focus is upon the three foreground figures, as Piero obviously intended it to be in placing the flagellation scene a step back in the composition, though it remains important, viz. the title of the picture. The world goes about its business oblivious to the realities that can transform its thinking. It matters little what the foreground figures are discussing. The important thing is that they have no interest in the punishment of goodness that goes on behind them. They are not looking at it. They have no concern with it.

Yet goodness has to be punished and rejected. It is always a threat to vested interests. And I see the seated figure as vested interest. What am I, the viewer, to do about it? Is Piero asking us to bring, in our minds, the background scene forwards and make our personal reactions to it, to embrace goodness whatever the cost might be to our own vested interests? To make, at least for ourselves and in ourselves, the punishment of supreme goodness at a point in time, not to have been in vain, and to let it work transformatively within us?

It is not the view of art experts, and it might not be Piero's intention. No matter, it is the impact of the picture upon me, and I shared it with my questioner. It led to a deep discussion, which we continued over coffee at a bar outside the gallery. She too was not an art expert but loved great paintings. I have forgotten her name, but not the richness of the conversation.

The art historian Kenneth Clark is said to have called 'Flagellation' the greatest small painting in the world. Since Aldous Huxley gave the same appellation to Piero's 'Resurrection', I feel privileged to have stood before both pictures.

Reluctantly, I had to end my time with my intelligent and charming coffee companion and return to my car. I had to return to Perugia and my studies.

The return journey involved the wonderful hairpins on the escarpment, this time descending. The views over the Tiber valley were not to be forgotten. A few years later, I was to drive down those hairpins again to re-experience the vista opening out before me. Stunning.

I mention two other places in the Apennines among many that are special to me.

The first is the delightful village of Fiumalbo, where I spent a week while engaging in the pleasures of watercolour. The hotel I stayed in with Ruth is on the Piazza Iolanda in the centre of the village. The hotel is truly charming, with lovely views of the piazza. One window of our room looked out over the heart of the village, including the little oratory and roofs of rounded tiles. Another looked towards the hills. I have very fond memories of Fiumalbo.

It is high in the Apennines about 70 km south-west of Bologna and approximately 50 km from Modena. The location is tucked away from noise and bustle, a peaceful place, in the vicinity of to the border with Tuscany, not far from the confluence of two rivers, the Rio Aquicciola and the Rio di Pozze. Their waters mix to form the Rio Scoltenna. It is situated in the Frignano Park (*Parco del Frignano*), an area of 15,000 hectares that Fiumalbo shares with other small villages but is surely the loveliest. The park begins at an altitude of 500 metres and reaches 2,000 at the summit of Monte Cimone.

There are spectacular views, as I discovered on drives to some of the villages. The statistics locate the village, but for me, the charm of Fiumalbo lies in the experience of 'difference' I find there. The people live close to the land. The major shop is the size of a very mini-supermarket, and well it might be because the villagers do much of their own vegetable growing, some of their own pasta making, and have little time for prepared foods from the shelves. In Fiumalbo, village life, so quickly disappearing in much of the West, is alive and well, still giving inhabitants their purpose and community bonds. Yes, that's where the enchantment is for me.

In the small village of Fiumalbo, community bonds are alive. Even visitors such as I are greeted in the piazza and the lanes with *Salve!* The centre of the life of families is still the Church, so that for me the oratory in the little piazza symbolises the unifying spirit of Fiumalbo. My fervent hope is that this little community of sanity and human interaction never becomes a tourist 'destination'. In Fiumalbo, I feel a kind of spiritual rightness, as though this is how once we were and were meant to be.

For those readers of this book, who surely are travellers or travel readers who want more than the well-known sights, and find their way to this special place, Fiumalbo will be a compelling place to stay, to soak in its own village culture and from which to venture out to discover the mountain life of the Modena province. Leaving it will be painful.

Those who are familiar with Venice and have an ear for language will at times feel as though, if they close their eyes, they are in the city of the lagoon. Why is that? Fiumalbo has its own dialect which differs even from close-by villages. It belongs to the northern Italian linguistic cluster but is a kind of bridge between that group and the central Italian clutch which is largely Tuscan influenced. The result is that the Fiumalbo dialect has similarities with *Veneziano.* That's one of the fascinations of Italy. While Italian is an important unifier, many local languages or dialects are spoken when locals speak with locals.

The village, of many stone houses, is of uncertain age. The name derives from *Fiumen Album* and is appropriate given that rivers run on both sides of the settlement.

Saint Catherine's church is a special place. It houses a collection of sacred art which provides a pleasant hour or two's diversion.

The Oratorio of the Immaculate Conception is on the side of the piazza opposite our hotel (*albergo*) *Appennino,* and a delight to see from a window after dark when it's illuminated by the lemon glow of street—lights. Somehow, it's picturesque even though it should not be, given that its shape is approximately in the form of a small Nissen hut. To enter it is to sense an atmosphere which seems only to be generated in a building where there have been centuries of worship. Somehow you know that this building has been precious to many who have gone before.

On a lighter note, those who love sweet things for the palate might be attracted by the crunchy 'Brittle of Fiumalbo', a treat still produced in the Modena—Fiumalbo area of the Apennines from a recipe which is still protected. It is often made by twisting the brittle mix around a thin rolling pin to produce a tubular shaped confection which is nutty and sweet; some might say it's addictive.

Those who find the history of human migration fascinating will want to see the Celtic huts at the village of Valdara, 6 km away. To see evidence of the passing through of the Celts, including the foot of dominant Monte Cimone, is to live history. The huts might or might not be unique, but they are certainly interesting. They are stone, as might be expected. The gables look very strange, with steps of stone, protruding to look like distorted sideways teeth, following the pitched line of the roof, which provides the major structure of the hut, which is severely lacking in window light. Does that say something about the harshness of winter? The steps are said to be there for thatch maintenance.

You will leave Fiumalbo with an ache in your heart, as I did. My heart warms whenever I think of that delightful village.

The other place in the high country to mention could not be more different from tiny Fiumalbo. It is Maranello, the home of Ferrari.

I went there with my wife Ruth and Silvio, an Italian friend who drove us there from Palagano. It was not long after Michael Schumacher's terrible skiing accident. To see, in the Ferrari enclosure and museum, signs proclaiming, 'Forza Michael' was very moving. Yes, we wanted him to be strong, but more than that we wanted a miracle. We wanted to see the pre-accident Michael, who had brought us so much excitement on the track, enjoying life again. We were not unaware of the seriousness of the damage that had been done to him, and grieved for him.

Even so, the Ferrari museum, red everywhere and the prancing horse everywhere, is a place of absorbing interest for Formula One racing followers, of whom I am one. I have been so since the days of Stirling Moss and Mike Hawthorn, Maserati and Vanwall, and cars very different from those of today. I and others have seen the days of dominance of Vanwall, of Williams, of McLaren, of Mercedes, but always in the leading group there has been Ferrari. And here I was in Ferrari heartland. It was thrilling! Nothing was more thrilling than the exhibits, in a circle, of successful Formula One Ferrari cars year after year, each car facing into the centre of the circle.

I felt extremely fortunate that day. I was where almost any Formula One follower would love to be—at Maranello.

One of my most valued possessions as a lover of fountain pens, and hater of ballpoint pens and their like, is a Ferrari fountain pen in Ferrari red with the prancing horse on the clip. Oddly, perhaps, I did not buy it at Maranello, mostly because I did not see one there. However, during the week following I was staying in Venice and on a visit to the university bookshop saw in the window the Ferrari pen that is now in my possession. It is a fine instrument that I love to have in my hand. I recall that some years before Michael's accident, the Ferrari which he had driven in the season just closed was on display in a showroom in Venice's *Mercerie*. I wandered around it with great appreciation of the fine machine I was inspecting so carefully, blissfully unaware the so devastating accident to come for Michael.

There are so many places in the Apennines I have enjoyed, but the chapter has to find an ending. I hope it has supplied something of the variety and feel of at least a small part of the multi-faceted mountain range.

Having written of Piero della Francesca's works in Monterchi and Urbino, it is important not to leave the chapter without a further comment on his greatest work, *Resurrection*. It is not only his greatest work, it is one of the truly superb paintings of the world, described by Aldous Huxley as 'the greatest painting in the world'.

It is to be seen in the Museo Civico in Sansepolcro, just over the northern border of Umbria in Tuscany.

For someone on a tour of Piero's work, the journey, Sansepolcro (*Resurrection*), Monterchi (*The Pregnant Madonna)*), and Urbino (*Flagellation*) is a feast of art appreciation.

It has been my good fortune to visit Sansepolcro twice to gaze upon *Resurrection*. It is truly magnificent. Christ has his foot upon death. He is commanding, an unqualified victor. His eyes, extraordinarily powerful, compel the viewer to gaze at them and allow their declaration of victory to be *felt*. I have no argument with Huxley. This picture is without a superior. At 89 inches by 79 inches (225 cm x 200), it is commanding in the gallery. However, there is a story.

The painting might very easily not have been there today. It owes its survival to a British officer of the Royal Artillery, Anthony Clarke. Following the terrible battle of Monte Cassino, the allies were advancing up the leg of Italy with the Germans in retreat. Clarke, close by Sansepolcro with his unit, was ordered to shell the town to flush out German troops who might be there. However, he remembered Huxley's description of *Resurrection* and the fact that it was in the town he was about to shell. He disobeyed orders, refrained from shelling and preserved the painting. It was later revealed that there were no Germans in Sansepolcro, but Clarke did not know that at the time.

Today you will see on the street map of Sansepolcro, via Anthony Clarke, quite a long thoroughfare running off via Costituzione. So Sansepolcro houses Piero's greatest work and remembers its saviour. I am grateful to Anthony Clarke and glad that the Royal Artillery had an art-loving officer in the advance to Sansepolcro.

Chapter 12

Ecclesiastical Eminence to Imperial Retreat

On the way from Rome southwards into Campania, there is a towering mountain rich in the history of the human struggle. It bears the name Monte Cassino and lies in the southern part of Lazio.

Monte Cassino first came to my attention during boyhood. The Second World War was in the Allied ascendancy phase. One day, I was in our local cinema; I have no idea at this moment what the films were, but I do remember the newsreel. Those were the days when you got two films and Pathe News for your money. The newsreel that day featured fighting at Monte Cassino. My father was away in the Army, and only long afterwards did I discover that he was at Monte Cassino in the Royal Artillery.

Since then, I had a strong desire to visit it, a need strengthened by reading of Benedict, his sister Scholastica and the monastery's eminence overlooking the landscape far below including the town of Cassino.

The height of the mountain is such that you can't avoid seeing it as you pass southwards on the Autostrada del Sole on the way to Naples. To see it from a train you have to take the inland, secondary Naples route in a second class only stopping service via Caserta, rather than the crack express route via the coast.

It was from the railway, as my train waited at Cassino station, that I first gazed up at the remarkable Benedictine building at the summit of the mountain. It did not realise my dream of visiting it; in fact, it generated considerable frustration. So near, yet so far. To look up at it in its commanding position, but not be able to climb the hill and enter that striking building with all its history of spirituality but also of warfare, was scarcely bearable.

Since then, I have seen it a number of times, including visiting that wonderful place. Each time I do see it, my mind runs back to a small village in south Hertfordshire. It bears the name Ridge and is little more than a cluster of houses around a church. One day some years ago, as I walked through the churchyard, I stumbled across a grave I had not noticed as I ambled around reading headstones. The stumbling was literal because the grave was surrounded by

160

reasonably high grass; I came close to falling forwards as my foot caught in the stonework. I looked down and read an inscription which told me, to my considerable surprise, that beneath the stonework lay the remains of the Right Honourable, the Earl Alexander of Tunis.

So humble a grave for so eminent a soldier! Field Marshall Harold Rupert Leofric George Alexander, first Earl of Tunis, was one of Great Britain's most distinguished Second World War soldiers. However, his record of service goes back to the First World War in which he served as a commissioned officer in the Irish Guards. He served in India between the wars. He will always be remembered for his remarkable record in World War II in which he supervised the latter stages of the evacuation from Dunkirk, contributed strongly to stopping the Japanese advance in Burma, held the post of Commander-in-Chief, Middle East (where his strategy was a major factor in Bernard Montgomery's Eighth Army victory over Rommel), and was Commander of the 18th Army Group in Tunisia. At the time of the great battle of Monte Cassino, Alexander was in command of the Allied armies which overcame the German forces in the bloody push from the foot of Italy to Rome and beyond.

It was perhaps Alexander's misfortune that he was the man in charge during Monte Cassino's darkest hour, because he will surely be seen by historians as carrying a significant share of the blame for the great monastery's destruction, a sad addendum to a brilliant military career.

Monte Cassino's place in modern history is brought about by that bloody battle which lasted from October 1943 to May 1944 when the two sides fought for control of that amazing eminence. Hitler had made it the power centre of his defensive Gustav Line, by which he hoped to halt the Allied progress from the foot of Italy to Rome, 87 miles away to the north-west. Though he didn't succeed in his objective, he certainly caused the Allied forces some major casualties as the battle stretched out seemingly interminably.

You only have to see Monte Cassino to understand the difficulties of storming it. It towers above everything around it, having an escarpment so sheer that even the one face able to accommodate a road demands that the approach to the summit consist of tortuous hairpin after tortuous hairpin. At the foot of the mountain as it is approached from the south flow the rivers Rapido and Garigliano, adding further complications for attacking troops.

The German forces were well established in their defensive positions, well able to see troops approaching their fortress, rather as medieval defenders of high positions had the advantage over very visible attackers below. During the latter part of 1943 the Allied battalions had little success. The great Benedictine monastery at the summit was destroyed by bombing, led by units of the American Air Force, in the misguided notion that the Germans were occupying it. In fact, the Germans had already removed both the monks and the treasures from the building.

At the beginning of January 1944, the US 5th Army made some progress as they crossed the Garigliano River. As the battle wore on losses became very heavy on both sides during heroic fighting. The task of storming the German positions at the summit was given to the Polish Corps under the command of General Anders. The ground to be covered was appallingly difficult and complicated by a mass of land mines. More than one thousand Polish graves in the nearby military cemetery are testimony to the terrible problems the Corps faced. Their tenacity and bravery kept them at the task of inching closer and closer to the German positions.

A dominant white marble obelisk bears the inscription, 'We Polish soldiers have given our bodies to Italy, our hearts to Poland and our souls to God for our own and others' freedom.'

Courageous fighting by the French under General Juin, advancing over the Aurunici and Ausoni mountains to the Germans' right, tightened a pincer which caused the Führer's forces to abandon the mountain on May 18. The road to Rome was open. The advancing Allies were joined by forces from the Anzio beachhead and Rome fell. Today all is quiet, and a great sadness seems to me to hang over the German and Allied military cemeteries.

The town was destroyed, so that what we see today is almost entirely of post-war construction and therefore functional rather than beautiful. But it has a history far more interesting than its modern face. It began its life as Casinum, inhabited by the Volsci people of the ancient world, who spoke a language which has an envelope of mystery around it, but clearly has strong relationships with Latin. It was absorbed into the Roman sphere of control in 312 BC.

The most important year of its history was AD 529 when Benedict of Nursia (in modern Umbria) established a monastery on the summit of the mountain, on the site of the Roman fortification of Casinum. Worship had taken place on the site in the temple of Apollo, but Benedict very quickly Christianised the mountain. That monastery, eventually to become an abbey, was destroyed by the Lombards in 589, the Saracens in 884, the Normans in 1030, and the Allies in

1943. Each time it has been rebuilt lovingly and impressively. It remains the mother house of the Benedictines and the most important centre of Western monasticism. Benedict's Rule is taken by devoted followers throughout the Western world. It is an important centre of learning, and one Paul the Deacon (720-799) established at Monte Cassino a tradition which has resulted in a rich vein of historical scholarship.

The Benedictine Rule (*Regula monachorum*) seems radically out of step with the values holding the field today. Its emphasis upon intellectual study and manual labour, upon chastity, obedience and poverty, sits strangely alongside what seem to be their opposites in the wider community. I can't help noticing that the many Benedictines whom I have met seem to be very much more content than the wealthy and hedonistic.

It was my great joy to visit the monastery on a Pentecost Sunday some years ago. As I wandered into the sanctuary the Pentecost Mass was in progress. It was a compelling moment in which great solemnity and spontaneous celebration were mingled. I felt lifted into that unseen world which surrounds us with realities which touch us so powerfully at those times when we are spiritually prepared to perceive them. During that wonderful service, images of Benedict, of Scholastica, of the Abbot Desiderious who became Pope Victor III, of the Abbot Gregorio Diamare, the man responsible for dealing with the Germans concerning the removal of the abbey's artistic treasures to ensure their safety, of Captain Maximilian Becker of the Hermann Goering Division, the man whose commitment under-pinned the survival of those treasures which were all around me at the mass, and of countless faithful, disciplined monks, swam before my eyes of imagination. When I left the Abbey, I had to force myself back to earth.

As with so many of the great buildings of the world, Monte Cassino Abbey is beyond description. It has to be visited and its wonder breathed in with spiritual inhalation. To use the current term, the air at Monte Cassino is thin. The journey from the material to the spiritual is very short. The Renaissance glories of its major rooms (especially the sanctuary), the artworks and the museum contain enough for a major book. The view from the Abbey, at its grandest from the Paradise Loggia, is one of the finest in Italy.

Benedict died at Cassino in 543 according to some sources, in 547 according to the Abbey. 'You pays your money and takes your choice.' The Abbey is precise enough to claim that his passing occurred on March 21st. I think I'll go for that. The first day of spring has an appropriateness which appeals to me because Benedict certainly breathed new life into a Church much in need of renewal. Pope Paul VI visited the Abbey on October 24 1964, and while there described Benedict as 'Messenger of Peace, Unifier, Master of Civilisation and in particular Herald of Faith and Initiator of monastic life in Western Europe.' Quite an appellation.

His sister Scholastica (or Scolastica), who had joined him on the mountain, died 40 days before him. The bodies of both remain on that high ecclesiastical eminence beneath the High Altar. A black marble scroll on the tomb tells the reader that as they were together in spirit during their lifetimes, Scholastica's and Benedict's bodies are together in death. It is a very, very special place.

As you proceed further southwards into the region of Campania, a Bourbon feast awaits. Once the Sun King, Louis XIV, had substantially completed his sumptuous Versailles, early in the eighteenth century, every king of Europe wanted one. The Bourbon Charles III was one of the monarchs who coveted such a palace. He decided that his was to be at Caserta, 19 miles from Naples. In 1751, he commissioned the great Italian architect Luigi Vanvitelli to build his Versailles for the Kingdom of Naples.

No monarch since the Sun King has succeeded in producing another Versailles, but certainly Vanvitelli built for Charles one of the most beautiful palaces of Europe. Construction took twenty years, resulting in a masterpiece of balance and taste. Built on a rectangular plan, the main facade extends for 250 metres. The royal apartments are the focus of Caserta's expression of luxurious living. The Throne Room leaves you wanting to pinch yourself to ensure that it is not the mere product of a dream ready to disperse on waking.

In a sense, it's a complete room because it has no one focus. Floor, ceiling, walls, all are part of the great work of art into which Charles walked to take his royal seat. The burgundies, golds, yellows and soft reds of the floor mosaic sit in an immensely pleasing contrast with the bright crimson of the throne pedestals and seating to one side of the great hall. Creamy-gold, renaissance-style pilasters rise in pairs to lead our eyes to a richly-decorated ceiling with round-arched alcoves. The gently-curved centre is painted with a royal scene which brilliantly picks up the colours of the walls and floor below. Though the pilasters take our eyes to the ceiling, they can't deny the elegance of the walls they decorate. Motifs run in a continuous line along all sides. There is no denying that the Throne Room is regal.

It was in this Throne Room that the king received official delegations and ambassadors. They certainly would have received an overwhelming impression of majesty. But it was also the room in which court balls were held. So my mind very easily runs to pictures of magnificently gowned ladies of substance and elegantly attired gentlemen performing the intricate steps of dances long fallen from favour. I see the wine flowing freely; I hear whispered conversations as assignations are quietly made; I hear also the strings playing tunes of medieval origin; I see the king looking on in self-satisfied pleasure, looking more magnificent than them all.

The Throne Room is taste. The rest of the sumptuous meal consists of the remainder of the royal apartments, including those most private of all, the bedchambers. This palace needs time to be enjoyed, which means that you have to get there early because at the time of my visit the closing hour was 2 pm.

After the palace closure to visitors, you enjoy the garden. And what a garden! It also was designed by the Neopolitan Vanvitelli, but under the guidance of the Parisian Martin Biancour. Its focus is a 3 km-long water-and-lawn-garden featuring cascades, statuary, billiard-table greensward, and the feeder stream which tumbles down from the foothills of the Apennines to the east of the palace. About half-way along the garden, heading for the hills, there lies to the right an English garden of shade, peace, and rather gentle statues, in true English style less flamboyant. They appear in more natural surroundings and have no sense of being placed there for effect. The main garden, by contrast, is much more Italian, being obviously geometric, but not unpleasing because of it.

Horse-drawn carriages are available for those who prefer to enjoy the garden in a sedentary way, but walking is the way to appreciate it properly.

At the far end from the palace is the Fountain of Diana and Actaeon. This is surely statuary gone mad. A great mass of figures clutter the fountain, but the story is clear as you look at the main characters. In the first group, Diana is preparing to bathe. She is surrounded by nymphs who have the right to be with her, but at the edge of the group, Actaeon is casting a surreptitious glance in her direction. In the next group, we see poor Actaeon with his stag's head, having been transformed into that creature for no greater sin than gazing upon Diana's nudity. A pack of dogs surrounds him, ready to tear him to pieces. My sympathies are with Actaeon. He is being punished for being a man.

The stream which feeds into the fountains descends very steeply from a considerable height. At each side of it, there are rocks. For part of the way up there is also a winding, stepped footpath. I was determined to get to the top. Part of the way walking, part of the way running, I reached the highest point and, heart pounding, turned to look back at the garden and the palace. The genius of Vanvitelli and Biancour was immediately clear. The long straight line of the park, its geometry thrilling, led straight to what now appeared to me as a doll's house-sized Bourbon palace.

That is the view that first comes to mind when I think of Caserta.

Lying off the Sorrento Peninsula is an island which will always be at the most fertile centre of my imagination.

With spray arching out from both sides of the vessel like great albatross wings, the hydrofoil cuts its way through the blue waters of Golfo di Napoli, the Bay of Naples. I can never make this journey from Molo Beverello or Mergellina without a mounting sense of excitement as the island of Capri, with its sheer cliff faces offers another consummation of my love affair with it. I am conscious, as my craft behaves like a water-born bucking horse, that Axel Münthe, who ignited the flame of my interest in this enchanting place, first made the journey using a sailing dinghy. Alas, I have never done it that way, though I should dearly love to do so. There would be a so much slower build-up of anticipation! No matter. The hydrofoil may be second-best, but the island still beckons.

Capri is but a short distance from the western end of the Sorrento Peninsula, yet it contrives to be a world apart from any other. Were it not for the continual traffic of craft into Marina Grande disgorging armies of tourists during spring, summer and early autumn, you could easily imagine that Capri is out of touch with the Italian mainland.

How they come, those tourists! Harassed expressions, piercing shouts to friends, abusive words to local porters, garish clothing, and a search for the nearest cappuccino or beer. Mostly they are here for the day, or to be accurate, part of the day. After liquid refreshment some, if the sea is calm, will find one of the many boats departing for the Blue Grotto and after a couple of hours or less they return complaining about the price, complaining about having to pay extra to the second boatman, the one who took them into the cave, and complaining about the short time they were allowed to stay inside on the azure water.

Others may find their way to Capri town, succumbing to the taxi touts, unaware that the little bus which departs from the eastern end of Marina Grande will take them there for a fraction of the price, or that the funicular will do likewise. Some, of course, do realise these things and make the journey the sensible way. And I have to remind myself from time to time that I can sound superior, even feel superior. It is salutary and I have to make a mental note that every visitor has a right to enjoy the island in his or her way. My way is simply one.

Some, however, do stay for a day or two in one of the many hotels in Marina Grande, Capri town or Anacapri, and that means that at certain times the three major towns are crowded, or at least the waterfront of the first and the town centres of the other two are.

Capri, paradoxically, is a neglected island.

How can that be? Countless tourists visit every day. Yet neglected it is. Many visitors cram into the tiny town centres, buying trinkets, eating gelati and drinking beer or cappuccino. And if possible they visit the Blue Grotto.

There is a vastly richer experience to be enjoyed.

To start with, this island, though it bears scant evidence of it, was once the centre of Empire, its most famous resident one of the more morose and brooding of emperors. For this is the island of Tiberius, a tormented man if ever there was one. Two thousand years later old *Tiberio* still casts his shadow on the enchanted island. He had more than one palace on Capri, his residence from AD 27 to 37. Follow Via Tiberio from Capri town uphill to Villa Jovis, or House of Jupiter, the palace in which he was probably to be found when a man yet more famous, though largely unknown then, was being crucified on a hill outside Jerusalem under the watchful eye of the emperor's troops after his weak procurator had washed his hands of the affair.

Villa Jovis is in a state of ruin, but there is enough of it there on its cliff-top eminence facing the Sorrento Peninsula to make the layout clear and therefore to give some notion of the kind of life Tiberius lived there.

The Villa is a haven. Tourists rarely go there (you have to walk a quite demanding uphill route), so that even at the height of the season you can wander the ruins of the palace and feel the spirit of the strange man who was once its master. Nearby is the cliff over which, as legend has it, Tiberius cast those whom he suspected of plotting against him. Whether it was so or not hardly matters. What is important is that he was here. The man who ruled the Roman world hated Rome and chose to administer his domains from the beauty of this island where, perhaps, he could come closer to finding the peace which seemed always to elude him. I can never walk through what remains of its rooms without feeling that his ghost is hovering not far away. Nor can I avoid the attempt to get inside his troubled mind, though I have little difficulty understanding why he chose Capri for his search for peace.

The island is plentifully supplied with quiet places, including the beautiful Arco Naturale, the rock arch through which, after a short walk from Villa Jovis, you can gaze upon the wonderful blue of the sea below. I often picture old Tiberio, toga-clad, walking alone in the cool of the evening down to the lovely natural arch, his Roman sandals sliding over the rock path. I see him sitting there, deep in thought, glad to be away from the chatter of the palace. I have no chatter of a palace from which to escape, but I love to sit by Arco Naturale, watch the water and think.

What a sticky end the old Emperor came to; a year or so before his death, his reputation reached its nadir, there being rumours that he had committed numerous murders. I think of those rumours as I look over the cliff edge at Villa Jovis. He became sufficiently ill for it to be assumed that he would not recover. Rome, of course, was abuzz with gossip of the succession. Strange Caligula was named as his successor while Tiberius yet breathed, which might not have been disastrous if the Emperor had obliged by dying, but he recovered, to the great embarrassment of the Praetorian Guard who supported the nominee waiting in the wings. Panic ensued.

On March 15, in the year 37, he left the island to sleep on the mainland at Misenum. The next morning he was found dead as a result of smothering. It has long been believed that it was on the orders of the praetorian prefect Macro. Thus ended the life of Tiberius, whose last years were described by Tacitus and Suetonius as a reign of terror. His ghost is never far away on Capri.

The island's second powerful ghost for me bears the name Axel Münthe, a man of powerful personality and deep compassion who could write and dream in a way which fires my imagination. More than any other, he has made Capri alive for me.

On 31 October 1857, Axel Martin Fredrik Münthe was born in Oskarshamn, a coastal town in southern Sweden on the Kalmarsund. The cold climate of his birthplace is in the sharpest contrast with the warmth of the island which made his name as a writer, though it's of some interest that he returned later in life to the country of his birth, there to die, in Stockholm, on 11 February 1949 at the age of 91.

One of the more colourful parts of his kaleidoscopic life was his time in Paris, where he studied under the somewhat eccentric, but massively influential, Jean-

Martin Charcot. Paris remained a favourite haunt for him, especially the Jardin des Plantes where he nourished his life-long love of animals, and Montparnasse where he befriended so many down-and-outs.

Practice in Paris and Rome funded his dream of building a villa on the site of one of Tiberius' earlier palaces at the head of the 777 steps from Marina Grande to Anacapri. His major book, *The Story of San Michele*, written in 1929, describes what can only be understood as his extraordinary adventures in working towards the dream and its realisation in the beautiful villa which stands in Anacapri today with its charming garden.

It is not my task to précis the book, but I do have to say that for me it is a reading exercise in the most exhilarating English—amazing for an author whose first language was Swedish. It is a book of fact, of imagination, of humour and of pathos, but above all it is a work which captures you with the humanity of the author. His compassion and his love of the natural world and of poor people, so many of whom became his friends for life, none closer to him than old Maria Porta Lettere, the post lady of Anacapri whose illiteracy meant that she had to ask others to whom the letters in her bag were to be delivered, permeate the book.

As I crossed the Bay of Naples on my first visit to the island, my heart was pumping with the excitement of seeing Münthe's dream. It was late in the day so I knew that I could not go to Anacapri until the following morning. In the meantime, the deep blue of the bay and the enlarging profile of the island filled me with pumping anticipation.

How difficult it was to get to sleep that night! And I was not lacking in weariness. My daughter and I had checked out from the Regno Hotel in Rome's Via del Corso that morning, been conveyed by taxi to Stazione Termini, taken a stopping train by the inland route to Napoli via Cassino and Caserta, taxi again to Molo Beverello, the hydrofoil across the Bay, then the little bus up the winding road from Marina Grande to Capri town, wondering how on earth the bus driver managed to avoid hitting the tiny 'trucks' and cars on the narrow carriageway of S-bends.

The hotel was not the finest on the island, but I should have been able to sleep on a bed of nails that night after so long a day's travelling. I have slept in many finer hostelries on Capri in the years following, but the quality of the establishment was not the reason for my wakefulness. The next morning I was planning to 'make contact' with Münthe, a desire which had burned within me since I was ten years old. I simply couldn't get San Michele out of my mind and I was never more awake.

Morning came and it was time to make the ascent to Anacapri. The island consists of two massifs, the larger, western, containing Anacapri and Monte Solaro, the lower, eastern, surmounted by Villa Jovis, and saddle between, upon which the town of Capri is built. Our journey was to take us upwards to the western massif. I had noted something interesting the previous late afternoon as the hydrofoil berthed at Marina Grande, but decided to keep it to myself, and that was that the road up to Anacapri is at one point attached to the outside of the cliff-face. It's quite an experience of a bus ride, and perhaps not one for the fainthearted.

In subsequent visits to Capri, I have become used to the skill of the bus drivers on the narrow roads, but on the journey to Anacapri on that bright, sunny morning, the Capri traffic was new to me. As we moved out onto the part of the road attached to the outside of the cliff-face, another bus approached from the opposite direction. Our bus driver stopped the vehicle, reversed for a few yards, and as I looked out of the window, I could see that we were no more than a few inches from the edge, with nothing but the ocean below us. The descending bus eased past us, with the tiniest of spaces between the two vehicles. Such driving is every day on the island. Nowhere else have I seen such driving skills.

As well as the skills of the bus drivers, I have also become used to the fact that it is rare to get a seat on these small buses. Far more people stand than sit. There is luggage squeezed in all around them.

Arriving in the town of Anacapri, I went straight to Villa San Michele, set back a short way from Piazza Vittoria where the little bus puts you down. Following a footpath lined with souvenir sellers, I came to the villa and entered the world of Axel Münthe.

He dreamed of building 'a sanctuary to the Sun' and in that respect as in others his dream was realised. The house is not large, though the layout suggests more space than there is; the architecture would receive no award, but the artifacts, some of which date from Tiberius' time, make the villa immensely interesting; above all, the light floods in and that surely is what Münthe was intent on achieving. My daughter and I walked from room to room, absorbed by the elegant furnishings, tasteful appointments and charming layouts. It was not difficult to see that the Swedish doctor liked comfort.

Wandering through the garden, we made straight for the little gate which leads out to the 777 steps. I was anxious to see it for two reasons: First, because prior to the building of the precarious cliff road, the steps were the only connection between Capri and Anacapri; second, because it was by these steps that Münthe made his ascent to the town on his first visit to the island and it was upon them that he met his life-long friend Maria Porta-Lettere. It was after the ascent of the steps that he quenched his thirst in the heat of the sun with Don Dionisio's excellent rose-coloured wine in the company of La Bella Margherita who was 'fair like Titian's Flora'. It was then that he gazed for the first time upon the chapel of San Michele and his dream was born. Something of the chapel can still be seen in the San Michele garden.

That he established for himself a *paradiso sulla terra* at Anacapri is beyond doubt. San Michele is truly a sanctuary. He developed the habit of putting all the letters he received into the drawer of his deal table, still to be seen in the villa, unopened. 'I had no time for the world outside Capri,' he wrote, 'there is no post in Heaven.'

If Heaven is to be found in one place above all others at San Michele, it is in the garden. Everywhere you walk, you find yourself turning a corner to a new area of colour and interest. Annuals, lawns, shrubs and the beautiful avenue of cypresses he longed for all make it a garden of tranquillity. On that first visit to San Michele, my daughter, Alison, and I ended our walk through the garden at the sphynx which completed Münthe's acquisitions. It looks out from its wall across the water to the Sorrento peninsula. Where did he get it? Münthe is as inscrutable on the matter as the sphynx itself.

It was here, by the sphynx, that I sat down, my daughter sensitively leaving me for a while to think about the man behind the beauty of the house and the garden. Before long, my imagination began to run on a course of its own. It isn't surprising, perhaps, given the fey in Münthe, that my mind lived for a while on the edge of the normal.

As I sat there, waiting for my imagination to fire, musing upon the man and his passions, drinking in the variety and peace of the garden, the panoramic splendour of the eagle's eye view of Capri, the cliffs, the rocks and the sea below me, there appeared at my side in my imagination an elderly but upright man wearing a white trilby with a dark band. The brim of the hat was pulled well down over the brow of his eyes, yet I could see that his sight was poor. He was staring, but not seeing, while, such was the paradox, he seemed content not to see, while seeing all. His shirt was crumpled, his tie awry. A check jacket buttoned high was ill-fitting. He wore white trousers and seemed altogether out of place in modern Capri.

'I know what you are thinking,' he said, 'I don't fit here on this island of bustle and buses and bars—I don't look the part.' His English was excellent, with a slight Scandinavian clip.

'Capri, bustle?' I replied. 'Even with the tourists around, Capri seems all peace and sanity to me. I come from a land of lostness and a world of commerce. My land is one of madness where no-one stops to live, but everyone, it seems to me, is running after distractions.'

He smiled, eyes crinkling at the corners, his mouth broadening over his George V beard.

'When I sat where you sit, when I dreamed my dream of San Michele, tourism had not become the rage. We were content to let the life of Anacapri revolve around Sant' Antonio. We lived without the chairlift to Monte Solaro, and most often walked from Marina Grande to Anacapri. How did you come here, by the way?'

'By bus.'

'I thought so.' He smiled indulgently.

"Why did you come here?" I asked, feeling rather impertinent.

'To find peace.'

'And did you find it?'

'I am not first to have sought peace here. This island knows the hearts of those who seek peace. Old Tiberio could stand the intrigues of Rome no longer. He felt sure that if he could find peace—if he could end his inner torments—it would be here on this beautiful island. Povero Tiberio! Not even communion with Jupiter brought him tranquillity.'

He turned his sharp face towards me.

'Tell me what you see. I have seen it all before, but even ghosts forget, and my sight in the ephemeral is no sharper than it was at Torre Materita.'

'I see all that ever man desired. I cannot believe that I am really seeing it, but it is so beyond the powers of any man to describe that I want this day never to end. It is *Paradiso* to the eyes and *casa eterna* to the heart.'

'You describe it as I remember it,' he said, sadness tingeing the kindliness of his voice. 'You have found something precious at Anacapri, Antonio Cancelli.'

'Antonio Cancelli! But I am not Italian,' I protested.

'You have an Italian heart, or at least, the deepest possible love for this country. How else would you have found *Paradiso* at Anacapri? But beware. I sought peace at Anacapri, as old Tiberio did. If you seek it, don't expect it to be provided for you.'

'I don't know what you mean.' The sun shone brightly and I glanced down at the rocks and ocean a million miles below.

'Peace is fragile. When you find it, you must hold it together from within. If you do not, when it fragments it will dash you to pieces with it.'

Somehow, we found ourselves at the summit of Monte Solaro. Below was the whole green island, the lesser massif of Villa Jovis to the east, and away stretched the blue Bay of Naples and the Sorrento Peninsula. To the south, Calabria shone in the sunlight. We were higher than the eagles which circled far below us and the breaking of the sea against the rocks was a mere whisper on the breeze.

'How shall I remember all this?'

'Write.'

'Can I write?'

'You can write if you will.'

'What shall I write?'

'Write about yourself.'

'How shall I write?'

'Let the people you write about, including yourself, speak. Don't let precision kill them.'

'Why should I write?'

'Because you have something to say.'

Like a dark cloud coming between me and my Paradise, the thought of leaving the island and returning to a place too many thousands of miles distant captured my consciousness.

'What shall I do with my life?'

'Do with it what you must.'

'Will I come back to this beautiful place?'

'That was my fear too—that the beautiful dream might fade. And I was much younger than you—younger than anyone has ever been. And you? In you, the dream must stay sharper and more urgent. You have found your dream. Today, it is real. Take Anacapri with you. Take Monte Solaro with you back to your land of lostness and bustle. But your heart is here. You will return to where your heart is.'

'How will I return? I am not rich—not even well off.'

'You, and you alone, must make it happen.'

'Can you give me no clue to how I can make it happen?'

'Only this—your pen must write your dreams.'

Then I was left alone on the mountaintop.

The dream has never faded for me. I brought Anacapri, Monte Solaro, Villa Jovis, Arco Naturale and every other beautiful picture of Capri home with me— not in photographs, though I have plenty of them, but in a mental picture gallery unequalled by any great building housing pictures. And when I visit that internal picture gallery, as so often I do, my heart is warmed—but with it there is an undeniable ache. I have been to Capri many times since then, but the dream endures, with colours heightened rather than diminished.

A third ghost? Even for ghosts this one lacks reality. For he comes to us through the medium of legend, and especially through the writing of Homer. We know him as Ulysses, its Latin form of his name. This confuses us a little because Ulysses is a Romanised form of the Greek Odysseus, its Romanised version meaning 'wolf'.

However, Odysseus, by which he is also known, means 'son of wrath'. Greek legend makes him the son of Laertes, ruler of Itheca, and gives him a wife Penelope and a son Telemachus. Ulysses sailed with the Greeks on that famous voyage to Troy with its bloody conclusion. Though not an enthusiastic member of the expedition, he took a leading part in the siege. After the fall of Troy, he spent ten years sailing the oceans, a decade of voyaging expounded by Homer in his 'Odyssey'.

What has Ulysses to do with Capri? Close by Münthe's San Michele is the Anacapri station for the chairlift to the summit of Monte Solaro, the highest point on the island. The silent ride up the mountainside is an experience of peace as the breeze brushes my face and the whole island falls away beneath me. To the right and below is the road that leads to the Blue Grotto and stark old Torre Materita, of which more in due course. The terracing of the green hillside lies to the left and the scene is magical.

Now I arrive at the top, slip nimbly from my moving chair and walk purposefully to the southern side of the summit. To the east, rising from a sea too blue to be true, are the razor-sharp Faraglioni, popularly seen as the Capri sirens of Ulysses, who caused him to demand being tied to the mast of his ship so that he could resist their temptations. They are three saw-tooth islets soaring from the water, spectacular and a photographer's dream. Between them can be seen from time to time the launch that takes visitors round the island's coast, leaving behind it a wake whose whiteness is heightened by the blue of the sea. And there are dozens of smaller craft hired by tourists.

To see the Faraglioni from a quite different view you take the lovely walk from Capri town down to Marina Piccola, immortalised by Noel Coward's song 'The Piccola Marina'. Once you could go down to Marina Piccola by taking the steps and slopes of Via Krupp down to the village from Parco Augusto (the Emperor Augustus also spent some time on Capri), but the route is now considered too dangerous and is wired off.

Marina Piccola is well-named. It is tiny, yet in addition to a small pebbly beach, a few small boats and a boat-hire office there is, in the tourist season, a very busy restaurants area that is packed with minimally clothed, not everyone beautifully bodied, sun worshippers. But the tourists can't take away its prettiness. And it *is* a good place to relax and think. As you stand on the beach (the base of your spine will soon object if you sit on it), you look out at the Faraglioni towering above you and their immensity is irresistible. They demand attention. It is a very different experience from gazing down upon them from Monte Solaro.

If you have any familiarity with Noel Coward's wit, you can't sit at Marina Piccola without thinking of Mrs Wentworth-Brewster, released from her dull life by the death of her husband, completely losing her head in inebriated visits to the marina. It isn't hard for your imagination to hear her, more than a little under the weather, singing, after her distressed relatives had pleaded with her to give up the Caprese men who so enchanted her, unceremoniously to remove themselves to some other place. Who, having heard the song, could ever forget Mrs Wentworth-Brewster?

Returning to the matter of Torre di Materita means returning to Münthe. San Michele was a dream realised, but it was not a dream which could last. The sunlight which bathes the island is not kind to human eyes and the time came when Münthe's sight was seriously threatened. Disillusioned, he had to leave his beloved villa for the sake of preserving his vision. He found another residence at Anacapri, a few kilometres from San Michele, namely the old tower of Materita.

It is situated on the western side of the village and became the object of my search during my first stay on Capri.

My heart leapt when I saw on a gate, 'Torre di Materita'. Not knowing if I was trespassing or not (I have discovered since that it is in private ownership), I wandered through the gate to search out the tower. When I came to it, I could see why Münthe chose to move there. Its windows are small. Very little light can enter. The tower is substantial, but it must have seemed like a prison after San Michele. I have returned to the tower a number of times since then, always feeling the sadness of the man who had to leave his dream behind him.

There are two ways of visiting the Blue Grotto (not the only grotto on the island's coast, simply the only famous one). The most usual is to take a launch from Marina Grande, the least usual to go by road from Anacapri and descend the cliff track to a jetty close by the entrance. The launch leaves Marina Grande only on calm days. Not far from the entrance you transfer to a small rowing-boat (paying again) for the visit to the cave. This is not for the claustrophobic.

The entrance to the cave is narrow and low, so that the occupants of the boat have to lean backwards, almost to a lying-down position—not the moment for panic! There is no possibility of describing the colour of the water. It has to be seen to be understood. I simply know of no other blue like it, and when I first entered it, I tried to put myself into the costume of the swimmer who was the discoverer of the cave and who must have wondered at the unreality of the world into which he had swum. Alas, we can't have his experience.

Every boatman is convinced that the occupants of his small vessel are there to be entertained and he 'obliges' by singing off-key songs until the cave is filled with the most dreadful cacophony when all that I want is the quietness which will allow me to listen to the lapping of the water. Go to the Blue Grotto if you have nothing better to do or if you want to say that you've done it.

One of the more interesting places on the island to enjoy the coastline while enjoying a drink or food is Pharo, also westwards from Anacapri. It is where young people in great numbers gather in the summer, some so swim, more just to be there to talk excitedly about whatever there is for those strong of limb, young of heart, hormones racing, to discuss. I think I have enjoyed Pharo mostly because the young faces to be seen there in numbers are almost all happy faces. I don't yearn for my own youth; I value age a good deal more. But I can still rejoice in the bursting life that I see in those who are still experiencing the salad days. Pharo is such a place for feeling again the pulse of youth in all its celebratory life.

There is a regular bus service to and from Anacapri. When you alight at Pharo, you have some walking to do as you descend to the café among the rocks, within sight of the lighthouse which, of course, gives Pharo its name. It is in an especially impressive part of Capri's coastline, and I found it a lovely place for relaxing with Ruth, my second wife, for a while.

Another opportunity for taking in the life of young people occurs in Capri town. One of the truly enjoyable experiences is to join in the *passeggiata* on Saturday night. From approximately six o'clock onwards, Piazza Umberto I is filled with young people, many of them over from Naples on the ferry, to wander, talk and drink. Their chatter is lively, and often centred on the fortunes of Napoli, the local football team. They go into the cafés around the piazza for coffee, but bring it out with them so that they can continue their strolling and talking. This is one of the great Italian customs.

In the evening, people go out to walk and talk, to meet and greet, to enjoy the sheer pleasure of people and conversation. It's a lovely thing to get out into the piazza and join them in the strolling and chatting. It provides perhaps the best of all memories of Capri.

I can't leave Capri before mentioning a visit which consisted of ten days on the island with Ruth in a B&B high above the town of Anacapri on the wooded slopes of Monte Solaro. It lies on a narrow road, Via Migliara, which runs westwards from Anacapri's Piazza Vittoria. When we arrived on the island, we took the bus to the little Piazza Caprile, which lies between Piazza Vittoria and Pharo. From there, we were picked up in his car by our host and taken by the narrow road to the B&B. Its location is stunning. As he took us to our room, the best in the property, with a veranda looking out over the Bay of Naples he made sure we felt welcome. 'Welcome to my part of Paradise,' was his greeting. A part of Paradise it certainly is. Ten days in that beautiful place! What more could we want?

Very quickly, we discovered our bearings and began to feel at home. Our first familiar location was the café in Piazza Caprile, where we enjoyed simple lunches among the locals and watched the fascinating interactions of the Caprese who used the lunch venue every day, perhaps during the break after the morning's work, perhaps as a social centre no matter what the time of day. The real joy was seeing the easy camaraderie of those long at ease with fellow islanders.

We also discovered very quickly the magnificence of our location, away from the crowds and with a grandstand view of the island, yet so conveniently placed to walk along Via Magliare, including a dog-leg where it becomes via Caposcuro, to the Monte Solaro chairlift and Piazza Vittoria. In the other direction via Magliare took us to a restaurant to dream about. From its tables, it was possible to look across the bay to Ischia. At night from the same tables, we could see the lights of Capri and distant Naples impressing their patterns upon the darkness. And to add to that, the food was magnificent.

It also became our habit to enjoy a coffee and an ice cream at a café in the grounds of an outdoor sports centre as we walked the climbing narrow road back to our B&B. Yes, we felt at home. It was so beautiful and we were so welcome at our B&B, the view so beyond description and the island below us enchanting to the point that I could easily have hoped that it would not turn out to be a Neopolitan variety of Brigadoon, that magical place of enchantment that in the story appears once in a hundred years, then disappears for another century. From our location where in the peace of a warm morning, I could paint to my heart's content, I had to pinch myself on occasion to ensure it was real.

Perhaps one more experience should be added to these words about Capri. Running from Piazza Vittoria almost to Piazza Caprile is a dog-leg street called Via Giuseppe Orlandi. It is a shopping street that provides human interaction. We entered a number of shops in the street and each one was an experience of human contact. It was more than a commercial transaction. We got to know something of the life of the person who served us, and they learned something of us. We loved every meeting. One person who served us shared some personal unhappiness; others shared their family backgrounds; others shared moments of joy. Yes, we shopped in Via Giuseppe Orlandi, but it was so much more than shopping. On many of our ten days at Anacapri, we walked that fascinating street.

Who was Giuseppe Orlandi? He was born in 1713 at Lecce and took priestly orders in 1736. Two years later, he was appointed to the chair of experimental physics at Naples' Royal University. He was, it seems, a brilliant teacher with an active, enquiring mind concerned especially with general and particular properties of bodies and the motion of solids and fluids. He also changed the teaching language of his department from Latin to Italian at the request of the students.

He was, it seems, a teacher who listened to his students and their concerns. He became a member of the Academy of Sciences which had been founded in 1732. In 1752, he was appointed Archbishop of Giovinazzo and Terlizzi. He died in 1752 at the young age of 38, yet in the 16 years of his major work, he achieved a great deal and established a reputation as a fine teacher of physics and mathematics, an academic leader, a motivator of young people to develop fine discernment and to respect arts and sciences, and to promote welfare in society. He is remembered with honour in Naples and the towns around its bay.

Such a man is commemorated in Via Giuseppe Orlandi.

Dominating the Bay of Naples is its most infamous resident, Vesuvius. Has there ever been a more cruel mountain? How it flatters to deceive! Its hillsides are the most fertile in the Naples area, ever luring those who live off the land to its slopes. Like the harlot of the streets of Napoli, the very attraction of that fecund soil hides a menace waiting to strike at all who would enjoy its delights. While *le donne delle note*, the women of the night, in Napoli might lure you with the very body which could give you an unwelcome reminder of your visit, Vesuvius is more straightforward with its counterpunch. Those it attracts to itself run the risk of death. Pompeii, Herculaneum and the Naples Archaeological Museum offer all the evidence required. They stand in ironic contrast, these two: Vesuvius, giving life to the most wonderful fruit and vegetables, standing as a giant fertility-goddess over all around it—yet surrounded by the debris left from its destructive, fatal anger.

Don't go to the museum in Naples unless you are prepared for a heart-rending experience. The exhibits, many of them casts of those who perished in their final death-throes of agony and terror—casts made possible because the volcano's mix of gases and heat left in many cases only their impressions in the solidified ash—are not pretty sights.

Don't go to Pompeii or Herculaneum without first familiarising yourself with what went on during those dreadful hours in AD 79 when Vesuvius threw its lethal contents in merciless fury over the Sorrento peninsula. You will find it difficult to comprehend the terror of the victims. But you must try to do so, otherwise what you see will not be the Roman towns which were buried for so long in their lava coffins, but 'cleaned up' tourist attractions where guides will tell you of the pleasant life lived there, tease your prurience by showing you

179

brothels, enlighten you on the fine baking facilities used by 1st-century Romans, and many other things which, if not unimportant, nevertheless give you no insight at all into the hell that once, briefly, was Pompeii, Herculaneum and Stabiae. And of course, you will be offered cute trinkets to take away from the excavations. All of this will insulate you from the immediacy of the fact that where you are, Pompeii or Herculaneum, is a vast tomb, but unlike other tombs, the inmates were buried alive.

Pompeii was an ancient town. According to Strabo, the Greek geographer and historian, it was occupied in turn by Oscans, Etruscans and Samnites, indicating a rich pre-Roman history. Herculaneum and Stabiae shared the same history of settlement, beginning their days as villages of the Oscans, the local descendants of Neolithic peoples. The area received important further civilising influence in the 8th Century BC when the cultured Greeks came to the Campania region.

All of them—Greeks, Oscans, Etruscans and Samnites—were attracted by the fertility of the Vesuvian slopes. What they were presumably unaware of (or perhaps they were aware of it and decided to live with the fact) is that the promontory upon which they settled was formed by a vast stream of lava which, in very ancient times had flowed down from the volcano into the valley of the Sarno, providing an explanation, incidentally, for the irregular shape of Pompeii which is built upon it.

Solidifying, the lava laid the foundation for the rich agriculture which followed. Vesuvius had already demonstrated its danger for human settlement. The macabre relationship with the mountain continued under Roman rule, the main industries being winemaking from the grapes grown on the slopes, and millstones fashioned from lava. Did they believe the gods were going to behave themselves in future? If so, they received warning enough that their perceptions were wrong in AD 62 when an earthquake devastated a great deal of Pompeii and Herculaneum.

On 24 August AD 79, the people of Pompeii were still repairing parts of the town damaged by the earthquake. They had no idea that they were living their last day. The volcano was, I imagine, looking to them approximately as it looks today. The shape was a little different, because what was about to take place had its impact upon Vesuvius as well as upon those citizens of Rome going about their daily activity in its shadow. There is evidence that the mountain contained one crater, not two as it does today. Wisps of steam were floating from its summit, forming the long, thin cloud so familiar today.

Shopping was going on in Via dell' Abbondanza; provisions were being bought in the market where, no doubt, the gossip was flowing about who was up to what with whom; bread was being purchased from the grain-to-bread establishments which undertook the whole process of converting the product of the field into baked bread; wine was being purchased and the grapes were looking luscious and inviting on the vines close to the amphitheatre; informal business was being conducted in the forum, where, no doubt, there were also those whose bent it was to engage in philosophical discussion; the gods Jupiter, Juno and Minerva were being worshipped, as no doubt were the guardian deities of the town; fulling was continuing in the many fulleries in Pompeii, the brothel had customers enjoying the pleasures offered for a price; the sculptors were at their work and the gem cutters were absorbed in their artistic trade; the rituals of family life were being played out as always in the pleasant homes of Pompeii. An ordinary day. Or so it seemed.

Yet not entirely ordinary. For four days, earthquake tremors had been felt in Pompeii, Stabiae and Herculaneum, but they failed, it seems, to interrupt the ordinary, everyday life of the towns. In Rome, on August 23, the day before Vesuvius vented its anger upon the countryside, the annual festival of Vulcan had been celebrated, a fact which appears in retrospect to be an ominous coincidence. The following day, the mountain split itself apart as a new crater was forced open.

We have some detailed knowledge of the events because, fortunately for us, the historian Tacitus required information concerning the death of Pliny the Elder who, as commander of the Roman fleet at Misenum had sailed with haste across the bay to aid the endangered populations of Herculaneum, Pompeii and Stabiae. Pliny had died at Stabiae, perhaps because he was the kind of enquiring man who wanted the closest possible view of the phenomena which were destroying all life within lava-and-pumice-throw of Vesuvius. Pliny the Younger wrote two letters of explanation to Tacitus, containing vivid eyewitness reports.

The first warning to the population of Pompeii was a light hail of volcanic fragments from the sky, which soon became very much heavier. Many people ran into their homes to join those already there, in the belief that strong beams and fine stone would provide their security. The debris included fragments of pumice and lava which continued to build up on every roof in town. As people huddled together in terror, praying to the gods, the last moment for most of them was looking up to see the ceiling collapsing upon them.

As I place myself in their sandals, I feel their terror. Yet as I walk through the ruins of Pompeii today, it is hard to make the transfer from the calm of the ruins and the chatter of the camera-operating tourists to that night of terror. I look up at the smoking peak of Vesuvius, my imagination returns to the terrible events and I am again in those awful hours. Yes, that is the secret of realising the events; look up at Vesuvius with its reminding smoke.

At Herculaneum, the terror was just as great, though the destruction of the town was different. Here, the lava flow was the major danger and the medium for bringing life there to an end. People ran, in their fear, from the lava towards the water's edge, but there was no escape. The terrible mountain showed no mercy. The young Pliny describes in his correspondence to Tacitus a great black cloud which ascended to an enormous height over the southern part of the bay, eventually taking the shape of an umbrella pine. How easily it reminds us of that terrible shape we have come to call a 'mushroom' cloud produced by an atomic explosion.

I can never look at Vesuvius, with its dual craters emerging from one chimney, smoke languidly floating from it, without seeing that terrible day of black cloud and scarcely-imaginable human suffering. Once the events of AD 79 are understood, Pompeii and Herculaneum become real places of human settlement and human tragedy, rather than mere tourist attractions. It also makes clear why it is that the buildings in Pompeii are mostly roofless, while those in Herculaneum mostly still have their coverings. The effect of the pounding from the skies was different from that of the lava flow.

If possible, you should visit both sites. Pompeii is larger than its companion-in-death, and excavation still continues. Much of Herculaneum lies beneath the modern town, and might therefore never be unearthed, but there is enough of the excavation to make a visit an experience of fascination. It will be evident immediately that it is a very different site from Pompeii.

The most interesting way to travel to the sites? By the Circumvesuviana railway. The articulated electric trains leave from Piazza Garibaldi, below Napoli Centrale station and connected to it by walkways. The journey from Naples to Sorrento takes approximately an hour and the trains are frequent, stopping at Herculaneum, Pompeii, Torre del Greco and Stabia on the way.

Sorrento is the end of the line. It's a large, attractive town with two marinas and an alluring main shopping street. You can take the hydrofoil from Sorrento to Capri, a short twenty-minute journey.

The town is best-known for its inlaid wood decoration. There are many workshops where exceptionally fine products, large and small, ornate and simple, can be purchased. Only the strongest wills can resist the kind of shopping the workshops offer.

Sorrento is also home to one of the finest gelaterie in Italy, *Davide*. *Davide* produces ice cream of such creaminess, and in so many flavours, that you just keep returning for more. Those for whom trim figures are important are wise if they never go near *Davide*! Italians produce ice cream to beat all ice creams, and in a country of masters of the craft, *Davide* is up among the best.

Among the attractions of Sorrento is the small church of San Francesco and its delightful cloisters. It can be reached in a few minutes from the main shopping street or by climbing up the cliff-face from the marinas. The path of steps is steep and at one point is cut into the cliff in order to achieve a hairpin necessary for continuing the ascent.

The church is a haven of peace. My most enduring memory of it is of sitting in a pew towards the front with my late wife Ann, enjoying its simplicity after wandering through the cloisters. A short, rather rotund man came in and sat down at the small organ. Shortly, he began to play. I do not know what the piece was called, I only know that I have rarely heard such beautiful music or such compelling playing. Ann and I looked at each other, moist-eyed. She, also, was deeply touched by what we were hearing.

When the organist had finished playing, I walked over to the organ and asked him who wrote the piece. 'I did.' I thanked him for something beautiful. In those moments, the music was an insight into a beautiful man—only a beautiful mind could have produced it. It was music moving somewhere deep within me. In that little church, we knew an experience of grace.

So many precious experiences provided by the Bay of Naples.

Chapter 13

Greeks, Romans and Invisible Mafia

What thoughts came to mind as I walked onto the platform at Roma Teremini station?

There is no station quite like Rome's central terminus. For a train fanatic such as I, it's truly a heaven on earth. Excitement unlimited. Trains on the departures board offer imagination-galvanising journeys to just about everywhere in Italy, and some places beyond. As I read the boards with my romantic perspective, I was emotionally bonded to every train mentioned. Florence, Venice, Ventimiglia, Naples, Milan, Bologna, Palermo, Syracuse, Vienna, Lyon, Paris, Cologne, Linz and a host of other places are there, all producing exotic pictures in my mind. I am on a magic carpet. That's what great railway stations do to a man in love with trains. The wider canvas of Europe, continent of enduring fascination, appears on the boards. Only a major railway station can open up a magnetic world to enjoy while sitting in one place.

My own train was shortly to leave for Sicily. It would be shunted into a number of sections, all of which would be accommodated on the ferry's onboard tracks. Once across the Strait of Messina, it would divide into two; one part to terminate in Palermo, the other, my part, would head south to Syracuse, though I would leave it at Taormina. My heart was beating with a kind of metronomic excitement. It wasn't just that I would be visiting Taormina, with its Greek and Roman history, delicious as that thought was. Just as important, the train itself would be making the crossing of the Messina Strait on a ferry supplied with railway tracks. Who could not be intrigued by such a prospect? I didn't expect to see a great deal, The crossing would be at night. It was the *fact* of it that mattered!

I might point out that I have since made the crossing in daylight and enjoyed every moment.

Yes, it was a night train and I was heading for my sleeping car. As a man who has an incurable addiction to trains, there is something especially captivating about a night journey, tucked up in my private sleeping compartment.

This was even more special, because I was about to commence my first journey to that island of many faces.

What images Sicily threw up in my mind! Could any place on earth contain so much evocation? The civilisation of Greece, which has left such a deep impression in southern Italy—and in the case of Sicily, those wonderful temples at Agrigento, at Selinunte, and at Segesta! I would see those at Agrigento on this first journey, and see them all, as well as Greek remains at Syracusa on my second visit.

Some of the pictures that appear in my mind now when I think of the Mediterranean's largest island are fuller than those of my first setting foot on the island. My imagination leads me immediately to a combination of the connected narrative of the ongoing human story in the Greek temples, the Greco-Roman theatre at Taormina, the Benedictine abbey at Monreale and the city's superb Moorish and Norman—influenced cathedral. Pictures also come to mind of wine production at Marsala and Garibaldi and his Thousand landing on its shores, the vines of here, there and everywhere, the 1282 revolt in Palermo known as the Sicilian Vespers, occupation by Swabians, Angovins, Normans and a seemingly endless stream of other colonisers.

And I think of small country villages and towns still bearing both their marks of age and their country life, the baroque cathedral of Ragusa and a delightful country hostelry between Ragusa and Modica where my wife Ruth and I stayed for all-too-short a time, the 13th century Castello Ursino at Catania with its sense of impregnability, an idyllic hotel on the slopes of Etna that I could have stayed in forever, the evocative Sicilian writings of Leonardo Sciascia and Giovanni Verga, and the one non-ignorable presence that stands outside the human story as a reminder of a permanence we don't attain, Mount Etna, the multi-cratered, regular donator of larva to the surrounding countryside, prodding us to acknowledge that there are some things we can't control.

Yes, Etna dominates, Monarch of the island. You are always aware of its presence. Such are some of the images that transport me when I think of Sicily.

Fiction adds spice to my understanding of Sicily. In addition to the works of Sciascia and Verga, Inspector Montalbano never seems far away, especially when I'm in a seacoast town. And how could I ever forget *Il Cinema Paradiso*, one of the most moving films I have seen, and the beautiful friendship between Alfredo and Toto? And then there is *La Stazione*, a film of an unimpressive man's one night's adventure while on duty at a Sicilian country railway station. Sicily is a mix for me, fact and fiction, land and people. It is a *spirit*.

Of course, the Mafia can't be ignored.

Yet perhaps they can be. Paradox?

To return to my first visit to Sicily, thoughts of adventure occupied my mind as I sat in my private cabin while it was still a sitting room before the bed was pulled down. It was impossible not to think excitedly. The adventure begins on the Italian mainland when the train arrives at San Giovanni from Rome. The whole train, in sections, crosses the strait. On the Sicilian side, the train is reassembled, generally into two sections. There has been talk from time to time of constructing a bridge across the strait. Fortunately, the talk has always come to nothing. How boring to be crossing a bridge when you could be crossing the water in a train on board the ferry.

Where does Sicily fit in the geography of the Mediterranean? Nearer to Africa than to, say, Milan, its climate might be expected to reflect that. And might it mean that Sicilians have developed a psychology different from much of mainland Italy? I remember a line from *Il Cinema Paradiso* where a Sicilian refers to a man from Naples as a northerner. What, then, should I be expecting on this isle that promised so much? I was certain of one thing only: I was going to enjoy myself. And I was going to learn a great deal. This was, after all, an island in a sense linked to two continents, many civilisations and perhaps a little more tenuously to Italy than some other Italian regions. It would be reasonable to expect a strong Sicilian identity.

Sicily is rather neatly shaped. It's broadly a triangle, dominated by volcanic Mount Etna and its slopes in the east, and rather lower country in the west. At its widest point, it is about 250 km and at its greatest depth (the eastern coastal region), about 160. It's bounded by the Ionian Sea to the east, the Tyrrhenian Sea to the north and the Mediterranean to the south.

After the night-time fascination of the train boarding the ferry, I was on my way down the Ionian Sea coast, heading for Taormina. Daylight was flooding through my window when the train's PA system informed passengers that we'd be arriving in Taormina in 30 minutes. I was not aware that I was about to discover one of the most beautiful places in Sicily.

The station for Taormina is Naxos, the oldest Greek settlement on the island. Founded in 736 BC, it is one year older than Siracusa. There seems to be near-

186

universal opinion that it bears its name because it was colonised by people from the Greek island of Naxos.

But my objective was the top of the cliff overlooking Naxos and the town of Taormina. A bus ride up the hill, followed by a short walk to my hotel, the superb San Michele in Via Damiano Rosso, and I had begun my all-too-short experience of the Roman-Greek town that was to capture part of my heart.

What followed were a few days of delight in a world high above everything I could see around me, with the one exception of the rarely quiescent Etna, a mountain that likes to make its presence felt. Yet Etna was far enough away for it not to disturb the sense of 'overlooking all' that Taormina provides.

The town was known as Tauromenion to the Greeks, Tauromenium to the Romans, indicating at least that it has been around for a long time. However, before the Greeks arrived, it was already occupied by the Siculi, an Italic people who inhabited eastern Sicily as far back as the Iron Age. It nestles high on the fell at 250 metres (800 feet), the escarpment falling as cliff face to the Ionian Sea. The position is spectacular.

The most interesting structure in Taormina for me, and I think for anyone who is intrigued by the past, is the Greco-Roman theatre, known locally as the Teatro Greco. The age of the oldest parts of the theatre are not known with any precision, but the major structures are certainly Roman. The lack of clarity is due to a Roman theatre being built on the site of an older Greek one.

The site speaks Greek, the later structures speak Roman. The most obvious Greek feature is the nestling into the hillside of the site. Greeks generally built their theatres using excavation into a hillside. In that way, no major supporting walls were necessary. Romans, on the other hand, built freestanding theatres, usually on flat land.

It is the second largest ancient theatre in Sicily. Siracusa has the distinction of possessing the largest. That at Taormina has a diameter of 109 metres, or 385 feet. The Siracusa theatre measures an extraordinary 140 metres by 119.

I never cease to be impressed by the acoustics of Greek (and for that matter Roman) theatres. At Taormina I stood on the stage area and declaimed, as I have done in many ancient theatres, just for the fun of it. I recited the 'Once more unto the breach' speech from Henry V. My wife, a long way off at the highest part of the terraces, heard every word. It's clear that both Greek and Roman theatre builders brought a great deal of engineering and acoustic expertise to their work.

Much of the charm of Taormina lies in its small cafés, the best ones being off the main street through the town. One of the most charming I remember, 'The Hanging Garden', was discovered when Ruth and I decided to explore a steeply-descending lane from the main street. It had tables in the lane, looking over a valley way below, as well as inside. We chose to sit outside. We didn't want to move one moment before we had to. Sitting under vines, looking at the steps of the lane falling away below us, we had no desire to be anywhere else—ever. The sun ran it gentle fingers of drowsiness over us, the wine persuaded us not to resist. It was a long time before we summoned up sufficient resolve to leave. Time determined that we must. The memory is sharp still. It was Sicily *par excellence.*

It was during my first stay in Taormina that I made my initial visits to Catania and Agrigento.

The journey from Taormina to Catania is noteworthy for the volcanic rock to be seen as the journey proceeds southwards. Some is by the road and rail sides as a reminder that the monarch of Sicily is alive and well. But that was not my purpose in going to Catania. It was to find the home of Giovanni Verga, writer of the so-Sicilian short story, Cavalleria Rusticana, the basis of Mascagni's one-act opera of the same name. Catania is not a pretty town by any means, but I was not there in search of a pretty town. I had studied the short story in Italian at Perugia, and so had developed a strong interest in Giovanni Verga.

Born at Vizzini, in the Kingdom of the Two Sicilies in 1840, his life of 81 years encompassed the unification of Italy and therefore Garibaldi's landing in Sicily. In short, he lived through momentous events, yet focused his writing on rustic Sicilian scenes and activities. His best-known works are Cavalleria Rusticana ('Rustic Chivalry') and I Malavoglia ('The Malavoglias' or 'The Reluctants'), both thoroughly country tales and both are narratives of tragedy. Perhaps that is reflective of Sicilian life in an island historically associated with poverty and perhaps unfulfilled dreams that too often accompany lives of deprivation.

I Malavoglia is the best-known of his literary works, though Mascagni made Cavalleria Rusticana part of opera lovers' vocabulary.

I Malavoglia was published in English in 1890 under the title, *The House by the Medlar Tree*, an appropriate title given that the novel focuses strongly on the desire of the Toscano family to reclaim their lost residence, Casa del Nespolo, lost in a time of family financial crisis. It is a story of family fortunes going from bad to worse to ruin. Even a recovery at the end of the tale is tinged with sadness as Ntoni, the family head, now old and having served a prison sentence for murder, finds that he is unable to return to Casa del Nespolo, now back in family ownership, because he has betrayed all that the Toscanos stand for. It is a moving epic of family misfortune that rightfully has an honoured place in the finest Italian literature.

The house by the medlar tree is situated in the village of Aci Trezza, a little to the north of Catania, where la Provvidenza, the family's fishing boat and source of income, is based. Today Aci Trezza is no longer a village, but a rather scruffy suburb of Catania. My stay there was disappointing, but I was nevertheless conscious always of the fictional Toscano family and its fishing boat and tragedy. Less-than-attractive as Aci Trezza is, I am glad that I visited it. I was there to paint, and while doing so my mind could range over the work of Giovanni Verga, a man who intrigues me. I Malavoglia is a read that immerses me in a Sicilian culture now probably gone and a family disaster that is always contemporary.

Cavalleria Rusticana is a different kind of tale, though utterly Sicilian. Turiddu, returns to his Sicilian village from military service, and peacocks in his colourful uniform to impress the girls. If one becomes involved with a woman who belongs to another, country chivalry demands a dénouement. This one which takes the form of a knife fight, costing Turiddu his life. There is a good deal more to the story, but it's the dénouement which carries the emotional content.

Pietro Mascagni's one-act opera captures the story, though his librettists Giovanni Targioni-Tozzetti and Guido Menasci might have taken a liberty or two with Verga's tale.

Why is it a one-act opera? Edorardo Sonzogno, a Milan music publisher held a competition for young composers. They had to have two principal qualifications: They had to be Italian and be composers who had not had work performed on stage. The competition required composition of a one-act opera. The most impressive three of the works submitted were to be performed on stage in Rome. Macagni's Cavalleria Rusticana was one of the three out of 73 works submitted.

The first performance hardly indicated a future for the work. It was put on in Rome's Teatro Constanzi, and it must have been hard for the performers to be motivated because the theatre was around half-full. However, the most important critics were there. Queen Margherita, a lover of fine music, was present. She, and the critics, certainly gave the occasion, theatre less than full or not, some prestige. As it happened, the opera was received in great enthusiasm with a standing ovation that was apparently close to deafening, despite the empty spaces Mascagni might have been exhausted by the curtain calls alone—he had forty. Not least importantly, he won the prize.

At the time of his death on 2 August 1945 in Rome, Cavalleria Rusticana had achieved in excess of 14,000 performances in Italy. That is success.

Mascagni was not Sicilian, having been born a Tuscan at Livorno in 1863, The tale, however, is totally Sicilian and might happen at any village on the island.

At Arci Trezza and at Catania, my mind inevitably turns to Giovanni Carmelo Verga.

To continue southwards is to reach the end of the line at Siracusa (Syracuse). I always find great delight in following a railway route to its terminus. Alas, I have arrived in Siracusa only by bus. That does not take away one jot from the attraction of the city, nor the opportunity to explore. Nevertheless, I should like one day to take the train all the way from Rome to Siracusa.

The city has an important claim to classical fame.

Somewhere around 368 BC, no less a figure than Plato, a native of Athens, set sail for Siracusa. He was 59 or 60 years old, with about 20 years of life left It wasn't his first visit to the island, but it was the one historians are most interested in because this one involved the great philosopher, not necessarily willingly, in politics. This is interesting on the ground that Plato, who had once thought about entering political life, was put off by the oppressive rule he experienced in Athens and became one for whom politics was close to being anathema.

He believed that the best citizens could hope for from politicians was moderate government which accepted and lived by the rule of law, perhaps an unrealistic expectation, even though such a limited aspiration. A much later thinker, Henry David Thoreau, would have had no argument with Plato on that score. Thoreau believed that the government to be preferred was one which governed very little, and the best government was one which governed not at all.

So why, in about his 60th year, make the journey to Sicily?

He was not sure of the wisdom of making the journey, not because there was any uncertainty about the attraction of the island, though he was suspicious of what he saw as the culture of sensual gratification there in his day, but rather for political reasons.

Sicily was under the tyrannical rule of Dionysius the Elder, a fact which was wholly unattractive to Plato. However, a young nobleman had been attracted to the teaching of Plato and felt that the great philosopher might influence change in the ruler by direct speech with Dionysius. It isn't difficult to understand why Plato was unsure of the wisdom of the visit. He wrote in his seventh letter that he went because he felt that not to accept the invitation would have shown him to be a man satisfied to remain a person of words rather than to get involved in practical issues. It became obvious very quickly that the invitation and the visit were not wise. Plato's efforts resulted in failure and he left Sicily regretting the visit.

Even so, the streets of Siracusa can be walked in the knowledge that in the 4th century BC, Plato walked on that soil. That is no small sense of history.

Something of the feel of Plato's time in Siracusa can be gained by visiting the Greek theatre, now a world heritage site. It was built during the 5th century BC and therefore was standing at the time of Plato's visit to Sicily. It received some rebuilding, however, in the 3rd century BC, so is not exactly as Plato would have seen it. It is thoroughly Greek, having been carved into the hillside, rather than being free-standing which, as has been noted, was usually the form of construction employed by the Romans, though the Roman amphitheatre is partly carved out of the rock.

Ancient remains, of which there are many examples in Siracusa, confirm that it is a very ancient city, its founding having occurred 2,700 years ago.

Archimedes was one of the famous names of Sicily. Born in Siracusa in circa 287 BC, he died in the same city about 212, killed by a Roman soldier during the siege of Siracusa. This is no place to discuss all his achievements as a Greek physicist, astronomer, mathematician, engineer and inventor. Sufficient to note that they were considerable.

His major discovery that excites me is that which has become known as "Archimedes' Principle", which is expressed as 'a body immersed in a fluid experiences a buoyant force equal to the weight of the fluid it displaces.' It's occasionally popularly known as 'the Eureka principle' because Archimedes, it's said, was so excited by his discovery that he (perhaps forgetfully?) ran naked into the streets shouting 'Eureka!' It translates as, 'I have found!'

I have also admired for years his invention of the Archimedes' Screw. It is its simplicity that is so compelling. It consists of a continuous screw of whatever length is required, inside a tube. When the screw is turned, it very effectively lifts water. The simplicity is beautiful. It is said that the invention was first used to raise water from the bilges of a large ship. Appropriately, the world's first ocean-going, steam-powered, screw-propellered, ship was named 'SS Archimedes'. Archimedes' Screw principle is still used today in engineering.

Another famous visitor to Siracusa was the Apostle Paul, who, on his way to Rome in the second half of the 1st century AD, called in at Siracusa. He was under guard on his journey to the Empire Capital for trial as a Roman citizen. He had claimed the privilege of a hearing in Rome as the right of a citizen, rather than have his case dealt with in Jerusalem. He had in effect been accused of being a disturber of the peace, and having been born a citizen, had appealed to Caesar and so claimed his right to be tried in Rome rather than by a local tribunal.

The previous port of call on the way was in Malta. There Paul and his guard took a ship which had wintered there, a fact which tells of the hazards of winter sea voyages in the craft of the day and perhaps also of the limited navigational aids available.

What did Paul do in those three days in Siracusa prior to setting sail for Italy? Knowing his habits wherever he went, we can be certain that he would have taken whatever opportunities came along to spread his Christian message. Paul was a focused man who used every moment to maximise his impact.

Santa Lucia, already referred to in the Venice chapter, was a native of Siracusa. Her birth there was about AD 283. Only 21 years later, her martyrdom occurred in the same city in 304, during the Diocletian persecution.

The persecution, lasting from AD 303 to 313, when it was ended by Constantine's and Licinius' Edict of Milan, was the last and most severe endured by Christians. The Emperor Diocletian issued an edict which rescinded the legal rights of Christians. This in itself was difficult enough, but more seriously, Diocletian required Christians to comply with Roman religious practices, something a faithful follower of Christ could not do. Sacrificing to Roman gods was out of the question. Death, torture and imprisonment were all used as punishments for dissenting Christians.

Lucia had consecrated her virginity to God and was noted for her distribution of whatever she could to the poor. She was much loved in Siracusa. Her end came when she refused to burn a sacrifice to the emperor's image. She accepted one Lord only. The refusal made her death inevitable.

Her post-mortem peripateticism has already been noted, as has the current resting place of her bones in the church of San Geremia in Venice. She is mentioned in Dante's 'Inferno' and in John Donne's poem, 'A Nocturnal upon St Lucie's Day', seen by Donne mistakenly as the shortest day. Santa Lucia's feast day is December 13, a week before the solstice.

On that day, the statue of Santa Lucia is paraded slowly through the streets from the cathedral to the Basilica of Santa Lucia Outside the Walls, where it stays for a week before being paraded on the return journey. Not surprisingly in a country of Catholic devotion, considerable crowds watch the procession.

What is my most enduring memory of Siracusa? Sitting by the waterfront sketching a craft tied up at the wharf on a sunny, but not hot, day in late spring. Modern Siracusa is not lacking in places for relaxation.

The northerly rail route from the ferry takes the traveller to Palermo.

It is not the most important city to me, nor necessarily the most interesting part of Sicily, though interesting it certainly is.

For those who fly into Sicily, Palermo is likely to be the airport of arrival. Those who arrive in Sicily by train are as likely to choose the northern rail route to Palermo as the southern alternative to Taormina, Catania and Siracusa. For my part, though I have flown into Palermo, I prefer the rail alternative. But then I am a rail enthusiast.

Palermo, on the Tyrrhenian coast, is the main port of Sicily, so there is an opportunity for the romantics who love to gaze upon ships tied up at wharves and wonder whence they came and where they might be going to stir their imaginations. Whenever I see a ship in port, my internal movie screen takes me on a voyage with her, as part of her crew, to the most romantic and exciting places imaginable, even though the reality is that she will be heading for places with prosaic names such as Genoa, Hamburg, London, Sydney or New York. No matter. A ship in port is an imagination exciter. In any case, those places, and ports wherever ships go, have their captivating tales to tell, as I discovered during my young years as a seaman.

Palermo lies on the edge of a very fertile plain, backed by a dramatic range of hills to form an embraced enclave known as the Conca d'Oro, or golden shell. The backdrop hills certainly do suggest a shell and the name supplies a very accurate notion of a fertile place. It is a horn of plenty, a cornucopia of vegetables, citrus and vines.

I love the name the Phoenicians gave to the city when they founded it in the 7th century BC. They called it Ziz. Besides being easier to spell than Palermo, it has the lovely meaning of *Flower*. It is sad that the name was changed. Were I a resident of that city, I would take delight in living with such a name. It is gentle. It is appropriate because Palermo has an abundant share of beauty.

But alas, the name did not last. Along came the Romans who decided to call it Panormus, meaning large port. Well, it has at least the virtue of being descriptive. However, Sicily has never long been without Arab influence. Palermo, after all, is nearer to Africa than it is to northern Italian cities such as Turin, Milan and Venice. Panormus was therefore corrupted by the Arabic name Balharm during the area's golden age of the 9th century AD under Arab domination, and today the map declares the city to be Palermo.

The ancient city of Palermo is focused in the intersection of two perfectly straight roads, Via Vittorio Emanuele and Via Maqueda. They cross at the delightful small baroque Piazza Vigliena, known locally as the Quattro Canti. It is effectively the charming centre of old Palermo. At each corner, a concave-façaded building stands. Each building contains in its concavity a fountain and a statue symbolising one of the seasons. When I first saw the piazza, I was strongly reminded of the four fountains of Via Quattro Fontane in Rome. The façades also contain statues of four Spanish kings of Sicily, Charles V, Philip II, Philip IV and Philip III, in the order spring to winter.

Piazza Vigliena is as pleasing and elegant as the nearby Piazza Pretoria is (to my taste) vulgar and over-the-top. The latter piazza features a very large fountain over-populated by sculpted figures, the work of the Florentine Michelangelo Naccherini. While it is too much of everything, it's important to see it if only to witness what enthusiasm can do.

Though Fontana Pretoria is too gaudy to work very well as an artistic work, if you are able to gain access to a window in one of the buildings on the second or third level, you'll see the piazza and fountain at their most acceptable. The plan view is quite attractive with its four staircases leading up to the central pool within the great circle. It's the excessive detail at eye-level on the ground that seems all clutter.

For me, the most interesting thing about the fountain is the offence it caused at its 16th century 'unveiling'. The nude statues, seen today as a routine art form, were the cause of great shocks felt by many of the respectable persons of Palermo. I think they must have been the cause of much gossip while, perhaps, enjoyed by the more prurient. It should also be admitted that there were probably genuine art lovers who loved the statues as individual pieces while not necessarily approving of the whole, huge collection of *dramatis personae* on the fountain stage.

To move to a quite different mood, I have mentioned already the Sicilian Vespers. What on earth could they have been?

Well, it all started in 1266, a fateful year for Sicily. At that time, Charles of Anjou, the French king of Sicily and Naples, appeared in Palermo. His arrival was supported by the Pope of the day, Clement IV, a man not, it seems, at that stage of his life at least (he was 75), the best physical specimen to look at. A Frenchman, born Gui Foulques, he was also known as Gui le Gros (Guy the Fat). He was a man of mixed background, having fought against the Moors in Spain, studied law in France, and been Secretary to Louis IX of France. Gui was married with two daughters. It was after the death of his wife in 1256 that he decided to enter the Church. Thus, he entered the Church at the age of 65.

His rise was so rapid that three years later he was appointed Archbishop of Narbonne. He enjoyed such a rise to prominence that he became Pope only nine years after his entry into the Church. One might imagine that other clerics would give a great deal for such favour in the Church.

His election to the Papal office occurred at Perugia on February 5 1265. It was a rather drawn-out affair because at the time the Church was at war with the Hohenstaufens, Swabian rulers who wielded considerable power in the 13th century and who cherished claims to the Holy Roman Empire. An interesting curiosity is that the name Hohenstaufen appears to mean 'high chalice'. Given the conflict with the Church, the name is intriguing.

Much of the Perugia conclave was taken up with the matter of Foulques' election to the papacy. Charles of Anjou was involved indirectly at Perugia as the cardinals debated whether to enlist him in their Hohenstaufen war.

A decidedly political Pope, his encouragement of Charles to set foot in Palermo suited his own political ambitions of an alliance to remove all Hohenstaufen empirical influence from the Italian peninsula. Charles, a Papal supporter, as the French king of Naples and Sicily, would suit Clement's purposes very well.

Was French rule in Sicily benevolent? Not if the Sicilian Vespers rebellion is evidence. French forces were hardly popular before the rebellion. To take the trouble to pronounce local words properly was not one of their aims and because of their atrocious pronunciation the Palermo population called them *tartaglioni*, stutterers.

On 31 March 1282, as the bell of Santo Spirito was ringing for Vespers, a French soldier verbally insulted a Sicilian woman in front of the church. The insult brought an immediate angry response from the crowd. It developed rapidly into a revolt throughout Sicily. Rarely can an insult have had such great costs. One of the costs was an island-wide massacre.

The Sicilian Vespers are remembered as one of the bloodiest episodes of the history of southern Italy.

The church of Santo Spirito is in the cemetery Santa Orsola outside the gates of the old city. Any serious interest in historical church architecture will put Santo Spirito on the list of places to see in Palermo. Built in 1178 during the reign of Roger II, it exhibits the expected Norman influence of the time. It also has influences of early Gothic. The façade is incomplete, austere, but interesting. Its double colours are reproduced throughout the building, giving a harmony which unites the Norman and Gothic elements. More importantly, you can stand before the façade and imagine the event that took place there, initiating the rebellion that drove the French Angevins out of Sicily. That alone makes the church worth visiting.

It isn't a long journey from Palermo to Marsala, heard of by most people for its fortified wine of the same name. These days the name Marsala as an appellation for the wine is limited to products from the Marsala area.

That leads into a little-known fact of Marsala. That fact is that twice the English have had a significant role at Marsala.

The first concerned the wine itself. In 1773, an English merchant with a keen eye for business opportunity, John Woodhouse, landed at Marsala, and among other things in the town discovered a local wine, which was, he felt, a little like some of the fortified wines drunk in England. I was unaware of this until I was enjoying a wine producing establishment in Marsala, and was told the story, which I have since verified. Woodhouse became convinced that fortified Marsala would find a viable market in England.

True to his conviction, he returned to his homeland with a consignment which sold so quickly that he returned to Marsala and in 1796 began mass production of the wine. He had established a market in England and shown himself to have a good instinct for a business opportunity.

In 1806, Benjamin Ingham, a Yorkshireman, voyaged to Sicily and saw more possibilities for Marsala. He set about establishing good markets for the wine in continental Europe and America to supplement that already being exploited in England. His success led to his making considerable 'brass'. And so Marsala became large on the world stage due to the efforts of two Englishmen. I, for one, am glad that Marsala moved out of Sicily and became a sensual pleasure for my palate and for inward warming.

The other English influence concerned the Royal Navy.

On 11 May 1860, Giuseppe Garibaldi landed with his 'Thousand' at Marsala. They were momentous times as the *Risorgimento*, the movement to unite Italy, gathered pace. As I walked Marsala, I could not help being aware that extraordinary things had happened in that place. Five very disparate people with different agenda, but having in common the unification of Italy, Giuseppe Garibaldi, Francesco Crispi, Camillo Cavour, Giuseppe Mazzini and Vittorio Emmanuele II, had marshalled popular sentiment for freedom from occupying powers and given drive and soul to the unification movement which was ultimately to prove successful.

Garibaldi's task in Sicily was to liberate the island from French Bourbon occupation, and after that to drive the Bourbons from the south of the Italian mainland. He had 1,089 volunteers with which to achieve his purpose, a very small force indeed. They were minimally uniformed, with red shirts and grey trousers; more importantly, their muskets, their only weapons, were dated. Any reasonable assessment would have forecast failure. As it was, Garibaldi's troops had success after success in Sicily, gathering numbers as the campaign progressed.

The landing at Marsala was tricky. The Bourbons could not be expected to do anything other than oppose the redshirts with considerable force. Enter right the British Royal Navy. Under the command of Admiral Rodney Mundy, HMS Hannibal and two gunboats, Argus and Intrepid, accompanied Il Lombardo and Il Piemonte, two steam vessels carrying the red shirts, into Marsala harbour, thus keeping Bourbon vessels at a distance from the action.

I think of Marsala in a good many ways, not the least of them as the place where the liberation and unification of Italy had its military beginning. And I enjoy the thought that the Royal Navy was there in the early days of the action.

What was in the minds of those redshirts, as they marched across Sicily, celebrating one success after another under Garibaldi's leadership? On balmy Sicilian May nights did they talk about the details of the victories, perhaps each person making sure that the group heard about his own contribution? Did they sing during their evening gatherings, songs patriotic, songs military, songs bawdy? Did they look at the red shirts around them with pride? They were a successful army who had begun the enterprise when only a little over a battalion and a half strong, extraordinarily under-armed for the task. A successful army celebrates. Perhaps they enjoyed some of that delectable Marsala.

Admiral Mundy could count his own Royal Navy contribution a job well done.

On the south of the island lies Agrigento, one of the most fascinating Greek archaeological sites in Italy.

The archaeological area is extraordinarily named Valle dei Templi, the Valley of the Temples. The name is odd because that which is called a valley is a ridge which rises above its immediate surrounds. The glory of the large area, at 1,300 hectares the largest archaeological site in the world, and since 1997 having UNESCO World Heritage listing, consists in seven Doric Greek temples dating from the 6th and 5th centuries BC, the former being the century of the founding of Agrigento.

My first visit to Agrigento was by road from Taormina, a journey which took me under the ominous gaze of Mount Etna, always a sombre, yet magnificent presence. I remember well my arrival at the Valley of the Temples as I gazed in amazement at the sight of the so-intact, huge Temple of Concordia. It seemed to be declaring my own brief presence on the earth by its own longevity, still standing proudly after two and a half millennia.

The base is almost 40 by 17 metres upon which are built a peristatis (supporting outer rectangle) of 6 x 13 columns, giving a total of 34. The columns of elegant Doric are characterised by the wonderful technique of entasis, that is, a minimal convex curve which deals with the illusion of a straight column having a concavity. The technique, used so well at Agrigento, can also be seen in the temple at Segesta, also in Sicily, and in Egyptian pyramid building.

Its fine state of preservation is largely due to its having been used as a church in the 6th century AD, a thought quite staggering to me given that it was already about a millennium old, having been built in the 5th century BC. It received its name from a Latin inscription discovered in the temple's vicinity.

That it was used as a church, when already an aged building says something about the construction skills of its builders, but also about the pragmatism of *homo sapiens*. If a building exists, and no one else is using it, why not utilise it? Those 6th century Christians saw no point in reinventing the wheel. In choosing to do the sensible thing, they aided the temple's preservation, contributing to the pleasure visitors to Agrigento have today at the sight on the magnificent temple of Concordia.

There are six other temples in various states of repair, to Juno Lacinia; Heracles; Zeus; Castor and Pollux; Vulcan; and Asclepius respectively. One of the temples in that list will bring to mind for some the temple of Castor and Pollux in Rome and perhaps also the ship in which the apostle Paul made his journey from Malta to a landfall south of Rome, the vessel whose figurehead was the Twin Brothers.

The most important of the six from a state of preservation point of view is the temple of Juno Lacinia, also constructed in the 5th century BC, but damaged by burning at the hands of the Carthaginians in 406 BC. It is only very slightly smaller in area than the temple of Concordia and has the same number of Doric columns forming the peristatis. Though only fragments of the architrave and frieze survive, nevertheless the temple has more than a suggestion of the grandeur it once possessed.

To visit Agrigento is to immerse yourself in the religious life of an age well past, but which somehow has the feel of the spirits of its gods still in some way on the site. Could I detect the spirits of a culture, a civilisation, now passed? It certainly felt that way as I allowed my imagination to enter into the life of the Valley of the Temples. A person interested in culture and religious history will not be disappointed in Agrigento.

Mt Etna is a fascinating place to be.

I first saw the volcano from a distance, on my way by road from Taormina to Agrigento. More recently I have had it rear up before me from its foot, traversed its slopes of black, hardened streams that appear as the legs of a giant spider, by walking on them, and have seen it from another slope, just a few kilometres away to the south. It doesn't matter where you are, Etna dominates with a threatening look.

Its height at the time of writing is 10,912 feet (3,326 metres). It won't remain at that height. Frequent eruptions modify the height from time to time.

It is an active stratovolcano, which means that it has a steep, conical shape caused by many eruptions laying stratum upon stratum of lava, ash, tephra and pumice. A stratovolcano is sometimes called a composite volcano. The major crater is at the summit, but it is not unusual to see, as in the case of Etna, a number of smaller craters at various elevations of the slopes. In fact, it's one of the aspects that makes a visit fascinating. You don't have to go to the summit to see the volcano's workings.

Given that it is one of the most active volcanoes in Europe, it might be expected that it would be extraordinarily destructive. That, however, is not the case. Eruptions are frequent, but the extruded material cools quickly and hardens, due to its high viscosity. Most of the time, therefore, settlements around the mountain are not threatened by it. In fact, agriculture, orchards and vineyards are part of the life of Etna's slopes.

It's the highest active volcano in Europe and the highest mountain south of the Alps. That might add to the pull of Etna for potential visitors.

Its attraction for me, though, is more romantic than facts and figures. In Greek mythology, Zeus dealt with the monstrous Typhon by trapping him beneath the volcano. Zeus, besides being king of the gods was thought of as the thunder god, so it can be understood why he has this association with Etna.

It doesn't end there. Hephaestus, the god of fire and of workers in metal, among other accreditations, was the son of Zeus. It was believed that the forges of Hephaestus were beneath the mountain. How much more the experience of Etna can be when allowing our minds to imagine trapped Typhon the monster writhing in his subterranean world, causing lava to thrust out of the mountain from time to time, and to imagine the forges of Hephaestus heating it up in a within-the-volcano world of incredible temperatures.

That's how I like to let my imagination run when I look at Etna.

It also has its beauty. One of my most precious memories of the mountain is staying overnight at an isolated hotel on a slope just to the south of it. The situation is idyllic.

Ruth and I were part of a watercolour painting group visiting Etna. We had called in to use the grounds, with the permission of the owners, to paint the wonderful view in almost every direction. We were due to return to Aci Trezza that day. Late in the afternoon while I was working with watercolours, Ruth came to sit beside me, and said, 'What do you think of this idea? I've spoken to the manager, and he said we can stay here for tonight. We could get a car to come up from Catania to collect us tomorrow for   100.'

What idea could be better than that? I agreed, of course, and we had an evening of luxury in a bed to dream about, waking in the morning to sun streaming into our room, then a fine breakfast and a morning outside in crisp Etna air. I used the morning painting in a pine forest, as contented as a man could be. Who could end a visit to Etna in a finer way?

As I think now of Sicily, and as I know I shall continue to think of that magical island, I shall think of many places, many experiences, but especially of Etna, threatening as it might look, lovely as it is.

Chapter 14

Popes, Caesars and the Piazza Navona

There are many popular images of Italy. Spaghetti seems to be one of them. Like most popular images it is a false one. Italy is a land of many cuisines, almost all of them exciting, so that no one style of food preparation can be said to be 'Italian', unless they all are. I remember so well inviting two very good friends to join my late wife and me at our home for an Italian meal. I cooked for them a Tuscan meat dish with fresh vegetables, and I can still hear the surprised tone of one of my guests, 'Do Italians eat meals like this?' He, like so many, thought pasta when he thought 'Italian'.

The 'Latin lover' is another popular image of Italy. If nothing else, it has a touch of romance to it, though it probably lacks the substance that characterises the genuinely romantic. I admit that the Italian male can seem to have a propensity to strut before his females like the peacock showing off his splendour to the hen. I have to concede too that Italian men of most ages can give the impression of talking a great deal about their sexual prowess and are not at all shy of sharing with other men at a bar their plans for the evening's conquest. But is that so different from the habits of young men of other countries? I have certainly observed young men in Australia who appear to see themselves as beautiful as rainbow lorikeets.

I must also yield to the truth that a pretty girl in Rome, or anywhere else in Italy for that matter, will have male eyes turning to her with a suggestive invitation in their look. no matter what rings she has on her finger. No matter either that she is already in male company.

The Italian male, however, is supposed to be full of bravado, and fortunately for the female population of the country, who would otherwise be in a state of perpetual exhaustion, it is likely that there are a million words for every action.

The roots of the 'Latin lover' myth might lie in the celebrated status the male is thought to have in the country. When a wife gives birth to a son, she is said to become a proud mother indeed. It is suggested that she will spoil him and ensure that other mothers know that her body has produced male issue. It is supposed that from the earliest age he will be regarded as a jewel in the family, shown off to all who care to admire, pampered and flattered and made to feel that he is privileged and fortunate to be of the sex he is.

When he eventually discovers the girl he wants to spend the rest of his life with (or she is discovered for him), it is said that his mother will spend time training the betrothed to understand what her beloved's favourite foods are, how he likes his clothes laid out for wearing and in short how to please him by meeting his every preference. He is made to feel important from birth, and it's not surprising, therefore, if he believes the myth himself, and like Turiddu of Cavalleria Rusticana, 'peacocks' before the girls so that they can have the pleasure and privilege of gazing upon him.

My observation is that in Rome, the male 'peacocks' for all he is worth. There are, after all, perhaps more female visitors to Rome than to anywhere else in Italy. You can see him at his feathered best in Piazza Navona while you sit at an outside table with a fine wine, perhaps also to taste something from the best of Rome's cuisine.

Piazza Navona, close by the Tiber and the Parthenon, is one of the relaxing places of Rome. Outside tables, the three fountains and the lack of traffic make it a kind of resting aural oasis midst the cacophonic din of the city, for Rome produces a volume of noise far out of proportion to its size, due as much as anything else to the habit of Roman drivers of using their vehicles' horns as self-expressions, and the compulsion felt by the police to use their sirens to advertise their presence. Via del Corso and Corso Vittorio Emanuele are just far enough away for their noise to be reduced to a soft background by the sound insulation of the buildings lining the piazza.

Had Turiddu been a Roman instead of a Sicilian, this is where he would have 'peacocked' before the girls. His brothers-in-spirit do it every day. They parade past the fountains, clearly dressed to impress, their eyes feigning disinterest in the female sex, so that we see a kind of acted lie. The girls watch them, though they also engage in the theatrical by making their gazes as covert as possible. It's all quite delightful to the observer of the play. I make my own observations from one of those outside tables with a glass of red, which adds more than a little to my pleasure. From my table, I also enjoy the clear indications that Piazza Navona is a place for lovers. Couples with arms entwined and obviously in love are to be seen at any time of the day, reminding me that, to use Roberto Benigni's famous line, *Life is beautiful*.

Piazza Navona is not the shape you might expect it to be, even though a piazza in Italy can be almost any shape. It is unusually long and relatively narrow for a public space. It was, in the days of imperial Rome, a *circus*, or track, used chiefly for chariot races, like its more famous Circus Maximus close under the Palatine hill. Built by Domitian, Emperor from AD 81 to 96, it must have been an arena of deafening noise.

As I sit today, sipping my red, I let my mind contrast that noise of crowds roaring on the chariots which carried their wagers, the crescendo building as the competitors neared the finishing line, with the peaceful space that is today one of the quieter parts of Rome. What a delightful paradox that the place of overwhelming noise has become a refuge from din.

The excitement in the city must have been great when, in the year AD 86, the *circus* was dedicated for athletic contests. It was part of an extensive building programme which followed the destruction by fire in AD 79 of a good deal of the area where the piazza now exists, known then as the Campus Martius. That was also the fateful year for Pompeii and Herculaneum, when Vesuvius made its own fiery presence felt as it went about its massive destruction of buildings and human life.

The structure was Rome's first permanent field of contest for competitive athletes. It was known as the Circus Agonalis, the circus for public games. A form of the name is preserved in the church of Sant' Agnese in Agone which stands on the long side of the piazza nearer the Tiber. In an obscure way, the name of the *circus* is also preserved in the title of the piazza itself. One suggestion is that the name of the circus evolved into *in avone,* which eventually became *navona.* Thus the name itself takes us back to the athletes of Domitian's day and the chariot races which were part of the arena's entertainment.

So as I sit in Piazza Navona, I gaze at the many people who provide endless fascination. I never fail to hear the roar of the crowds, never fail to see the charioteers who are risking serious injury, never fail to see the horses stretched to their limits, never fail to see the dust as the chariots slide around the sharp ends of the *spinas* on their competitive course to the finish line. Were there instances of foul play during the races? Probably. In any case I see them, as a charioteer veers his chariot to force another into the barrier, and another moves his chariot across the path of a horse rapidly making ground on him. I feel the excitement. I am in Domitian's Rome.

Who was this Domitian? He was born Titus Flavius Domitianus on 21 October AD 51. He was to become the longest-serving emperor (AD 81-96) since Tiberius, and like Tiberius, his reign ended in assassination.

The stadium was not all that Domitian commissioned in the Campus Martius. Almost adjacent to the stadium on the southern side stood his other major building on the ancient greensward, the Odeon, used for musical performances and poetry readings. If you are walking to Piazza Navona from Corso Vittorio Emmanuele via Piazza di Pantaleo, you are walking through the site of the Odeon, which also occupied the land on which, to your right, Palazzo Massimo now stands. Once, Romans who sought refinement of spirit gathered in the area you are passing. Knowing that, the Campus Martius comes to life for you.

As I stroll through it, I see Romans of high rank coming to the Odeon for cultured stimulation and I am reminded that while Rome catered for the tastes of *hoi polloi*, it also made provision for citizens of refinement.

That takes us to a consideration of the Campus Martius as a whole. It lay approximately between Tiber Island northwards to the modern Piazza del Popolo and between the Tiber and the western end of the Quirinal hill. It was lawn covered and green throughout the year (so different from the concrete of today). Strabo, the Greek philosopher admired the Campus Martius when he visited Rome in 7 BC. I would love to have admired it with him. Sadly, we have to use our imaginations now to reconstruct the Campus as it was, the stadium as it was, the Odeon as it was and the milling of Romans out either for the excitement of the Circus Agonalis or performances at the Odeon to nourish the cultured spirit.

East of Piazza Navona lies the Pantheon, a glorious building by any standards. I usually visit it after a three-flavoured gelato from Giolliti, the irresistible gelateria approached via Piazza Colonna from Via del Corso. If there is a finer gelateria anywhere, I have not yet discovered it. For all the historical and cultural significance of the area, I cannot resist a visit to Giolliti. Don't miss it. It makes even the hottest day in Rome pleasant. It is two minutes' walk from there southwards to the Pantheon.

The Pantheon does not stand in its original condition. It was built as a temple to 'all the gods' in 27 BC by the town planner Agrippa. Those visiting it today might be surprised to know that it originally faced south. How can that have been?

It suffered severe fire damage in AD 80 and was restored by Domitian (Yes, Domitian again). However, it was Hadrian (Emperor from AD 117 to 138) who made the greatest changes. He rebuilt it with its major façade facing north, a reversal of Agrippa's orientation of the building. So today, perhaps with your Giolliti gelato still in your hand, or some of it, you approach the Pantheon from that place of homage for all ice cream lovers, across Piazza della Rotonda, straight to the major façade.

It seems a little strange today to see on the porch cornice the name Agrippa, given that his orientation was reversed. We are also reminded by an inscription that Septimus Severus and Caracalla were involved in restorations.

The first time I walked into the Pantheon via the *pronaos* (the multi-pillared porch), I was treated to an interesting ceremony. One of the chapels contains the tomb of Vittoria Emanuele II, the first king of united Italy. It was immediately apparent that something important was happening at that chapel. An almost military function was taking place, with representatives from various groups moving forward towards the tomb.

It became apparent that I was watching an assembly of fascists keeping their movement alive and claiming Vittorio as their own. It was a fascinating addition to my visit. I have to admit, too, that there was, for my sense of humour, a little comedy in it; the participants were taking themselves very seriously. But then, if you feel strongly enough about a cause, why wouldn't you take yourself seriously? Even so, my detestation of fascism gave way to amusement, but I was glad to have witnessed the event.

There is another important presence in the Pantheon. Between two of the chapels lies the tomb of Raphaël, painter of extraordinary talent who lived only to the age of 37, dying in 1520. On the sarcophagus is an inscription by the poet Pietro Bembo (1470–1547), which Alexander Pope translated as:

Living, great nature feared he might outvie
Her works; and dying fears herself to die.

It might be an exaggerated estimate of Raphaël, but perhaps not an inappropriate recognition of his artistic genius.

To gaze on his sarcophagus takes me to the Palatine Gallery of the Pitti Palace in Florence, which houses no fewer than eleven Raphaëls, including the two beautiful *Madonne*, Madonna of the Chair and The Grand Duke's Madonna. It takes me also to the chapel of San Severo in Perugia where it was my joy during the brief time that I lived there, to gaze upon the Raphaël fresco which depicts a number of saints and the Trinity and is one of the gentlest, most charming pictures that I know. It makes great use of white amongst light shades of other colours, including a pale pink which reminds me so much of the pink that for me is almost the trade mark of another artist, Piero della Francesca.

I get the impression, perhaps falsely as I look at the fresco, that Raphaël confined himself to quite a limited palette in executing the work. The artist completed the upper part of the wall in 1505. The lower part had to wait 16 years for completion by Perugino. So in the chapel it was my delight to share the work of Raphaël and the local artist Perugino, one of Perugia's favourite sons. There is a niceness to this work in the chapel when it is remembered that Perugino (Pietro di CristoforoVannucci) was the teacher of Raphaël. Thus the work was begun by the taught and completed by the teacher. The local artist was born at Città delle Pieve not far from Perugia and died from the plague at Fontignano, also close by Perugia, in 1523.

These are the thoughts that come to mind as I gaze at Raphaël's sarcophagus in the Pantheon.

The Circus Maximus lies a not-too-demanding-walk from the Pantheon, close to the Forum and consists of the earthworks which show the track, the spina and the slopes of the Aventine and Palatine hills between which it lies. It is bordered by *Via del Circo Massimo* (Road of the Circus Maximus) and *Via dei Cerchi* (Road of the Blind). The measurements of 2037 feet (621 metres) x 387 feet (118 metres) give some impression of its enormous size. It is not difficult to imagine the speed attained by chariots on those long straits and the dangerous concentrations on the tight corners at the ends of the spina. The excitement of the crowds must have been considerable.

Speaking of the citizen of his day, Juvenal (c.60-c.180 AD) wrote:

Duas tantum res anxius oplat,
Panem et circenses

(Only two things does he anxiously wish for—bread and circuses)

One of those wishes was certainly realised at the Circus Maximus.

While its purpose included staging other athletic contests, the chariots were the star performers at the Circus.

Come with me from the Circus Maximus past the Baths of Caracalla (familiar to all who saw and heard the 'Three Tenors' performance there many years ago by Jose Carreras, Luciano Pavarotti and Placido Domingo) to the *Porta San*

Sebastiano (the Saint Sebastian Gate) in the Aurelian walls, the exit of *Via Appia Antica* (the Old Appian Way) from Rome.

We are now on one of the most famous and most important Roman roads of all. Not least it had great strategic value for the movement of troops and supplies and therefore made a major contribution to the immense power of military Rome.

In fact, it had its birth in a time of great military importance. One Appius Claudius Caecus, after whom the Via Appia is named, completed the first section, specifically as a military road during the Samnite Wars in 312 BC. When completed, the road connected Rome with Brindisi (Brundisium), today a distance of 475 miles (765 km) by roads which do not divert seriously from the Via Appia route.

Who was Appius Claudius Caecus? He was a Claudian and therefore part of the family of patricians descended from the Sabines who became part of the Roman state early in its life. Was Caecus originally part of his name? There is a belief that he gained the name after losing at least a degree of his sight, and so became known as Caecus ('Blind').

Be that as it may, he was a man greatly respected in Rome, twice becoming Consul. Though he might have been partially blind he had great vision of mind, as the Appian Way, probably Rome's most important road, demonstrates. It is a lesson to modern roadbuilders that the first major portion of the Appian Way, Rome to Capua, a distance of 132 miles (212 km), was both started and completed in the year 312 BC.

Its construction, without any of the machinery we are used to seeing in road work, was meticulous. An earth roadway was levelled and tamped. Then small stones and mortar were laid on top. The next layer was gravel, upon which were laid tight-filling stones with flat upward faces. It provided as smooth a surface as stone-built roads could supply, and was considered, rightly, to be a major civil engineering achievement of the age. Appius Claudius could claim great credit.

It is a road which has seen terrible days. One of the most horrific followed Rome's defeat of Spartacus' army in 73 BC. The defeated army consisted mostly of ex-slaves. In 71 BC 6,000 of them were crucified, dying on their crosses along the 132 miles section of the Appian Way between Rome and Capua.

As I walked the Via Appia Antica from Rome's outskirts to the Catacomb of San Calisto, I imagined those crosses on both sides of the road, and the imagining was not pleasant. Could I hear their groans? Could I smell their sweat? Could I see the agony in their eyes as they fought for breath as well as endured the pain of Rome's cruel execution apparatus? I really think I could.

My mind easily turned to another crucifixion, that of a Galilean Jew, Jesus of Nazareth, who fell foul of the Jerusalem authorities, then suffered the usual death penalty at the hands of Rome. His crucifixion was one of multi-thousands; Rome had no cause to see his execution as any different from the thousands of others.

While on the subject of Christian faith, my other *feeling* while on the Via Appia Antica, was the strong excitement that the Apostle Paul walked this road upon which I was setting my own feet. He walked this way on the road via Three Taverns, or *Tre Taverne,* around 30 miles (48 km) from Rome. He had arrived at Puteoli, and on the way was met by believers from Rome at Three Taverns and the Forum of Appius. So Appius Claudius would find, were he alive today, his name in the New Testament. Paul arrived at Puteoli from Malta on a ship with the figurehead of Castor and Pollux, the twins of mythology, the ruins of whose temple stand in the Roman Forum.

Thoughts such as these filled my mind on Via Appia Antica on my way to visit the Catacomb of San Calisto, also known as the Catacomb of Callixtus. It is one of the largest catacombs of Rome, and quite a lengthy walk out of the city. Tourists are able to take a bus to the catacomb by a different road, and most do. But that misses the thrill of walking the ancient way and the stirring of the imagination it provides. For that reason, the Appian Way is best travelled as a solitary walker. You want your mind to concentrate on all that the road means, rather than to be distracted by conversation. Company is definitely not required on the Via Appia Antica.

The creation of this Christian catacomb is believed to be associated with Callixtus who was to become Pope. Callixtus was not entombed in the catacomb he established, but in another on the Aurelian Way.

The catacomb occupies about 15 hectares and is a maze of extensive tunnels, some of which have fine, carved examples of interesting subterranean architectural effects. Access is possible only as a member of a guided tour. It is easy to get lost in the Catacomb of Callixtus.

It is estimated that there were around 500,000 bodies interred there.

A fact of special interest is that the catacomb contains the remains of some second to fourth century popes, making it a place of special interest, perhaps veneration, for Catholics.

I had the strongest sense, as a tour leader took me through the catacomb with others, that I was in spiritual touch with the early Christian community of Rome. It was as though I could hear whispered voices from beyond, *We have lit the torch; it is for you to carry it.* In a strange way, I *felt* that I was linked in those moments, though it is beyond my ability to explain how or why.

It might be that in the catacomb I was in a place which marked more clearly than any other the spiritual separation of Christians from other Romans. Though the Catacomb of Saint Callixtus originated in the second century AD, from the first century Christians did not have their own cemeteries; they had no consecrated ground for members of the Faith. There were Christian landowners, and many of them buried their dead on their own properties. Yet it was strongly felt that Christians needed their own consecrated land for inhumation of their own, and from this conviction the catacombs were born. Thus, the catacomb of Saint Callixtus is more than a tourist attraction; it is an experience of early Church history.

As I walked the Via Appia Antica towards the catacomb, I felt so great a sense of anticipation of entering into the history of the Christians of Rome, that I could almost touch it. I was about to descend into the largest early Christian burial ground known in Rome, a sacred place where those of the faith chose burial rather than cremation. And I thought of the possible influence of Christian burial practices over the Empire of Rome itself. I remembered that the Greeks had introduced cremation to the Western world no later than 1000 BC with so powerful effect that it became the preferred funeral practice of Romans of high status. Could it be that Christianity had an even greater impact upon Roman methods of dealing with the dead than Greeks had achieved?

The Greeks had a very practical reason for adopting cremation. It was important to them that a fallen soldier should be interred in his own land, so those who fell in battle were reduced to bone through cremation on the battlefield. This enabled their ashes to be transported home where they were interred in the presence of their families and the proper procedures carried out.

Rome took up the Greek way of doing things with respect to their deceased military heroes. However, it didn't stop there. Cremation became a status matter, and that led to the establishment of *columbaria*, that is, vaults with niches for receptacles containing the ashes of the dead.

The time of ending cremation in the Roman Empire is subject to various estimates. Some are as early as AD 100, some as late as the early 3rd century AD.

But it is generally accepted that the ending of the practice was due to Christian influence. But why did Christians favour inhumation rather than cremation? It is reasonable to assume that the expectation of resurrection had at least something to do with it. Cremation was not encouraged, perhaps, though maybe not entirely prohibited by Christians, because it has strong associations with non-Christian peoples. I am, however, more easily persuaded by the resurrection expectation as a probable reason for bodily burial.

So I walked the Via Appia Antica with a strong sense of approaching a Christian site with empire-changing significance. If this was what Christians could effect in death, what might they have achieved in life!

I was not disappointed when I entered that huge beneath-the-surface burial maze. Even though it was not possible for me to let my imagination run in solitude, the best way to enjoy an ancient site, I felt myself in spiritual communion with those Christian adherents to early-days faith.

San Calisto is not to be missed.

From San Calisto, return to Rome. If you have had enough of walking, leave the site at the exit on the opposite side from the Via Appia Antica entrance, and you will find yourself immediately at a bus stop. You will be in Rome in a few minutes after the bus arrives. But don't go to the site by bus if walking is not a difficulty for you. The Via Appia Antica is a special experience if your imagination is not completely inactive.

Among the most impressive achievements of Rome were, and in their ruined condition still are, its aqueducts. When I saw my first one, a branch of the Aqua Claudia, while walking from the Colosseum to the Circus Maximus, my thoughts were twofold: the engineering magnificence of Rome and the city's vulnerability.

On the first score, any open-minded visitor to Rome who takes the trouble to notice the aqueducts and take note of their scale and the civil engineering involved must pause to admire the abilities of those people who established such an empire that the Mediterranean became a Roman lake and brought a great deal of Europe under its control. They were not only militarily skilled in gaining an empire, they were skilled engineers who produced the infrastructure to administer it and make its component countries operate more effectively.

That their aqueducts were fine vehicles for water flow is best illustrated by the fact that the Spanish city of Segovia still uses its Roman aqueduct. There could hardly be a greater commendation than that. The other side of the coin, it seemed to me as I gazed at the aqueduct that was cut before it reached the Palatine, is the vulnerability that Romans must have been well conscious of, that sabotage of the city's water supply was far from impossible. The city would then very easily come under siege. That is precisely what happened when Germanic enemies cut the viaducts and accelerated the end of the Empire.

That, however, does not in any way diminish the wonder of the structures. I have admired them in Rome, I have admired one in Istanbul, I have admired the wonderful aqueduct at Pont du Gard, and in many other places. Yes, the aqueducts of Rome were magnificent.

They were constructed to convey water from appropriately high elevations to the cities of the Empire. Where an aqueduct crossed a valley, it was borne by an arched structure to keep its elevation and its gradient. Pont du Gard, already mentioned, is one spectacular example, carrying out those functions in taking water into the city of Nîmes. The aqueducts were built with stone and brick, the matrix being provided by mortar from volcanic material. We might question today the material used for distribution because lead was used for some pipes to city locations. The lead pipes ran from large cisterns which were fed by the aqueducts.

The detrimental potential of lead was known, and in some cases ceramic was used rather than lead, but lead piping was not entirely abolished. At its height, the population of Rome stood at approximately one million. That placed great demands upon the supply of water. The Aqua Claudia, after a 69 miles (111 km) journey, supplied two-thirds of the city's supply of approximately a cubic metre per inhabitant.

The water moved by gravity alone, gradients being carefully calculated and maintained over the length of the watercourse. Rises in the landscape were either circumvented or tunnelled through, the choice being influenced by the material of the rise.

The aqueducts required regular inspection and maintenance. Tree roots could intrude into the ground-level or underground ducts and there could be build-up of calcium carbonate. To be in charge of such work was high-prestige in Rome. Under the emperor Nerva, there were 700 members of the aqueducts inspection and maintenance workforce. For both health and engineering reasons, such work was taken very seriously.

The city's many public baths used a very large quantity of the water, but gardens, households and every other need, including public fountains, were supplied via the aqueducts. Rome did not stint itself in water use.

Remains of aqueducts today can be seen in various locations, including the road from the Colosseum to the Circus Maximus, and the Arch of Drusus.

The forum? There is more than one forum in Rome. The major forum, known as the Foro Romano (Roman Forum), needs a sizeable volume of its own. It is a concentrated viewing of the life of ancient Rome. I do not intend to spend a great many words on it here. This is, after all, not a comprehensive guide to Rome. It is a book about *my Rome, my Italy*, and it will differ therefore from other books on Rome and for that matter all guidebooks to the city. I mention only those aspects of the forum which have made it live for me.

The Arch of Titus is the first. For those who have an interest in the Jewish and Christian stories, this is a most important monument. It stands at the edge of the Forum on Via Sacra at the foot of the Palatine Hill.

Those seeing it for the first time might feel that it looks just a little familiar. And yes, it does have a familiar look because it provided the inspiration for the huge Arc de Triomphe at Paris' *Etoile*. That is hardly surprising, for the Arch of Titus has a solidity that is appropriate for a feel of victory. That is precisely what the Arch of Titus is, an arch commemorating victory. It appeared a dozen years after the major victory it commemorates. The emperor Domitian had it constructed in AD 82, principally to commemorate his elder brother Titus' sack of Jerusalem and victory over the Jewish nation in AD 70. It was a victory which tore the heart out of the Jewish State, for it included the destruction of Herod the Great's temple, the centre of Jewish worship and its sacrificial system. Two or three generations later, the Jewish State ceased to exist when the Romans brutally put down the revolt of Bar Cochba in AD 135.

When we look at the Arch of Titus, we are looking at monument to a victory which has great impact upon both Jews and Christians, the faith of the latter having had its nativity in the faith of the former.

Sadly, restoration in 1817 and 1821 included materials not original, but no matter, the essential Arch of Titus is still there with its important reliefs.

The soffit of the archway is wonderfully coffered. There is little in architectural art that, for my taste, rivals coffered soffits, and I gaze at them when I see them until my neck aches. There is, of course, damage sustained over the years, but nevertheless, the coffered soffit of the Arch of Titus' archway calls for some extended pleasurable study.

There is one reason above all others that I gaze upon the arch and have to pull myself away and that is the depictions of the spoils taken from Jerusalem. Why do they compel me to look at them for as long as I have the time to do so? I am excited by them because there are few extant depictions of the religious artefacts used in the temple which were made at or close to the time of the temple's existence. The depictions on the Arch of Titus are among those very few, having been made only a dozen years after the temple's destruction.

The *menorah*, or golden seven-branched candlestick, is a central relief depiction. Traces of yellow ochre have been discovered on it, suggesting that the monument might well have been even more impressive in its empire days with most if not all the reliefs being painted, perhaps with a number of colours. The *menorah* is an absolutely central devotional artefact in Jewish life and worship and has had an important diaspora unifying influence. As I gaze at the *menorah*, I have mixed feelings, sensing the templeless diaspora of Jewry united in this symbol, yet a sadness that Jews of the modern state of Israel have declined to walk under the arch, apparently because of an ancient ban placed by the Jewish authorities of Rome, a ban which was cancelled in 1997.

It may be that Jews are less reluctant to walk under it now. Nevertheless, the ban indicates the depth of the tragedy of Titus' sack of Jerusalem, and as I stand by the arch I feel the depth of that catastrophe, a disaster almost certainly seen as inevitable by Jesus (*Yeshua bar Yosef*, to give him his Aramaic name), in his many words about a coming event of suffering and destruction. So here, at the Arch of Titus, I feel myself to be at a junction point of two faiths, the Jewish and the Christian Christ (*Christos*—being the Greek word for the Jewish Messiah). I have at home a cross and a *menorah*, reminders of the rich Jewish heritage out of which my own faith had its beginnings, and a reminder that Christianity had its genesis in a remarkable Jew.

The reliefs include a triumphal procession in which are more Jewish temple artefacts, including golden trumpets and the Showbread Table.

Yes, when I stand by the Arch of Titus I feel myself drawn into those momentous events and times of the destruction of Jerusalem and its temple, the triumph of Titus and the despair of the Jewish nation, a despair which still lives and is perhaps best noted in the Wailing Wall (the remaining wall of the temple) in the modern city. I see the slaves and their masters building this great edifice and I get some feel for the ancient city of Rome and its pride in military and civic achievement.

The arch carries a Latin inscription which can be understood in English to be, 'Roman Senate and People to Divine Titus Vespasianus Augustus Son of Divine Vespasian'.

The north panel shows Titus Triumphant.

The monument is 50 feet in height, 44 feet in width and 15 feet 6 inches in depth (15.4 x 13.5 x 4.75 metres). Its size is the more impressive because its location leaves space around it.

I take you now to the other end of the forum. You will find the Rostra there.

Rostra? As the Arch of Titus is part of my forum, so is the area of the Rostra, perhaps because I have spent so much of my adult life speaking on one public platform or another. The Rostra was the public speaking, public presentation, platform of Rome. This sounds a little strange given that *rostra* is the plural of *rostrum*, but there it is. The Rostra was the platform for addressing the assembled audience.

The *rostrum* was the ram of a ship of battle. The platform gained its name from six rostra captured during the course of the Battle of Actium in 338 BC, and mounted on the platform which took their name.

The modern use of the term *rostrum*, to depict the platform upon which a speaker stands to address his or her audience is derived from the Rostra of Rome. There is of course a public-speaking organisation which takes the name.

The Rostra, then, was the place where orators, especially those of note, called for attention and delivered their orations, or judgements, or whatever else of note they needed to announce publicly.

Here at the Rostra I hear another voice. Marc Antony speaks at Caesar's funeral. Here at this place on the raised platform he gave his heartbroken oration for his friend. I do not have the words he spoke, of course, but I do have Shakespeare's version of them, and I hear so easily the voice which addresses the audience:

Friends, Roman, countrymen, lend me your ears
And especially, I hear the last three lines:
And men have lost their reason. Bear with me; my heart is in the coffin there with Caesar.
And I must pause till it come back to me.

Have nobler lines ever been put to iambic pentameter?

Yes, I hear a noble voice when I stand at the Rostra.

Standing close by the forum is the monument just about every tourist wants to see, the Colosseum, Latin *Amphitheatrum Flavium*, built after the reign of Nero by Flavian emperors from the beginning of construction sometime between AD 70 and 72 and completed in the year 80. It was a massive undertaking, its funding being the reason it is part of my Rome. It was chiefly financed by the wealth taken from the Jewish temple after the Jewish revolt of AD 70 had been put down decisively and ruthlessly.

An inscription on the site, partially reconstructed, tells that the emperor Vespasian ordered the temple to be built from those funds. The labour force was hardly a major budget item, most of the work being done by slaves. Not only were the spoils from the temple used for the Colosseum's construction, but many of the estimated 100,000 Jews brought as prisoners to Rome made their contribution to it. There is, then, an important military link between the Arch of Titus and the Colosseum. It is this link that fascinates me most about the huge amphitheatre. As always, it is a monument's story that makes it compelling. This is a story of Jewish tragedy writ large.

The largest amphitheatre ever constructed, it is estimated that its capacity was 50,000 to 80,000 spectators who were able to see varied spectacles there, including mock sea battles, gladiatorial contests, animal hunts and executions.

Following the great fire in Rome in AD 64, Nero seized a good deal of land between the Caelian, Esquiline and Palatine hills, three of the city's seven. He built his grand house on the site and had erected a huge, bronze colossus of himself, located where part of the Colosseum now stands; hence, the name of the amphitheatre which is itself colossal and which is partly built on the site of the Colossus of Nero. It was built in what was then the heart of Rome, and is now close to the Forum.

Commenced during the reign of Vespasian, it was completed in the emperorship of Titus.

One of my favourite depictions of the Colosseum is a 1747 work by Giovanni Paolo Panini who shows it as a pair with the Arch of Titus. This is not geographically correct, but it is, for me, symbolically perfect.

The Vatican is an enigma. It is legally not part of Italy, yet for many practical purposes, *de facto* it is. It requires the logistical services of Italy, and everything that goes into the Vatican and out of the Vatican has to travel through Italy.

There are many magnificent architectural and painted works to be admired in the Vatican city, yet while I am there, a certain thought is never far below the surface. It is that I am in the headquarters of the force which held up the complete unification of Italy for nine years, and in doing so, postponed the day when Rome could become the capital of the new nation.

The Catholic Church was a major territory holder in pre-unification Italy and was possessor of a military force which became a thorn in the side of the fighters of the *Risorgimento*, the movement for a united country under one administration. The Church refused to give up its lands so that in 1861 unification took place without Rome. That anomaly was corrected in 1870 with the defeat of the papal army at the battle of Milvan Bridge. The Italy with borders approximately those we know today with Rome as its capital came into being.

It was a dark hour for the Church with Pope Pius IX virtually captive in Rome. The unification of Italy had only been possible in the event that the Pope renounced all temporal power in his territories. This he refused to do. Military defeat ended the papal occupations of large parts of Italy. Defeat meant captivity. What the man who taught 'Blessed are the peacemakers' would have made of a Church army I cannot imagine. This state of captivity continued during the papacies of Leo XIII, Pius X and Benedict XV.

The Lateran treaties of 1929 granted the papacy under Leo XI territorial independence, and the Pope became once more the temporal as well as spiritual head of Church territory, now radically reduced to a tiny enclave in the city of Rome. For some, the knowledge that successive Popes were captives in Rome for almost sixty years will be hard to comprehend. However, Pope Pius IX was the last temporal head refusing to give up temporal sovereignty in the face of the popular movement for unification of the Italian peninsula. In the circumstance where ceding of territory was ruled out, the army of Garibaldi was always going to be the solution chosen by the men and women of the *Risorgimento*.

St Peter's Basilica is certainly a building that is both massive and architecturally commanding, though it might not be to everyone's taste. I do not advocate the dull, miserly church buildings found in some denominations (many of which are found in my own), and I believe there is a place for grand architecture and art to the glory of God. But I'm not sure that I am keen on the other extreme either, where servants of Christ are the stewards of great wealth. But I accept that I can easily be wrong in my thinking and mistaken in my assumptions.

217

What, then, matters to me most about St Peter's? My St Peter's is centred upon the necropolis below the basilica. This, for me, is where the history of Rome and of the Roman church are most focused.

It was my privilege to explore the necropolis with a Vatican guide some years ago. It was a thrilling experience, one that my mind revisits often.

It is deep. The depth is not even and varies from five to twelve metres, sufficient for a sense of being very subterranean indeed. I certainly had that sense of the floor of the basilica being far above me as I walked through this extraordinary 'city' (*polis*) of the dead.

There are two levels of appreciation of the necropolis. One is its exposition of ancient burial practices in Rome; the other is the traditional association with the apostle Peter, claimed by the Catholic Church as its first Pope. Were he in fact the first Pope or not, the tradition of his burial in the necropolis is important enough.

The major excavations took place from 1940 to 1949, with further work done in 2003, resulting in my privilege of being able to visit and study the necropolis.

Its location is due to the rule in imperial Rome that no burials were allowed within the city. Burial sites were therefore outside the city walls. The necropolis beneath St Peter's was originally a cemetery close to the Circus of the eccentric Emperor Caligula. The construction of the basilica over the traditional site of Peter's burial means that the visit is now an underground one. The tradition is that he was martyred by 'upside down' crucifixion in the Circus Nero, and buried in what is now the subterranean necropolis.

It should be noted that during the excavation of the grave thought to be Peter's, no human remains were found. However, some bones were found in a recess in what is known as the Graffiti Wall, next to the grave. The archaeologist Margherita Guarducci made the interesting, speculative suggestion, that they might have been removed from the grave during construction of the Constantinian basilica (the basilica built during Constantine's Emperorship), begun sometime between AD 319 and 333, and placed in the recess.

Why? Was it intended that they should be replaced in the grave and somehow it was overlooked? Guarducci pointed out that close to the remains an inscription includes the letters, PETR...EN I, and it could indicate that the bones were those of the apostle. Be that as it may, the conundrum is a fascinating one, and the necropolis should be visited.

As I gazed at the place that might well be the apostle's grave, I wondered if it were my imagination that I sensed the presence of antipathy between the spirits of St Peter and Emperor Caligula.

Tours of about 90 minutes are arranged via the Ufficio Scavi office.

I have one more corner of Rome to take you to. The reader might wonder why I am not I including Trajan's Forum, the Spanish steps, the Trevi fountain and so many more of Rome's great monuments. My response once more is that I am writing about *my* Rome, the Rome which excites me. Much as I have enjoyed the major tourist elements of Rome, they are not the places which stir my blood.

So to another of my favourite places. It is called the Pincio.

It is not one of the better-known parts of the city but is nevertheless a fine place to relax at any time, though especially in the evening. The walk through the Villa Borghese Gardens to get to the Pincio is itself a pleasant experience. The parklands are extensive and a welcome respite from Rome's bustle and noise, especially on a hot day.

When you arrive at the Pincio, an area of the parkland overlooking Piazza del Popolo, you are looking down on one of the city's great evening meeting places, especially of young people. Go to the Pincio on a Saturday evening and you'll be looking down on Rome's favourite young people's *passagiatta.* One of my memorable visits to the Pincio was on a Saturday evening when a great screen had been set up in the Piazza. I had the pleasure of watching *The Hunt For Red October* in Italian from my dress circle vantage point.

One final point. The Pincio is a fine place to spend time in any evening with someone you love. It is one of Rome's settings that invites romance.

Rome is a city as no other is; its history overwhelmingly exciting, its ruins a study for a lifetime, its ecclesiastical importance beyond question, its relaxing places inviting. It is not a place for tourist peering; it's a place for learning about life. For me, it is as compelling, for that matter, as Italy itself.

Epilogue

I set out to write a book about *my* Italy. The emphasis is on the possessive adjective. Italy intrigues me, as a great railway terminus draws the trainspotter. I understand to some degree both, because I am a lover of Italy and a lover of railways and everything to do with them. The man in love with trains knows that in any great railway terminus, anywhere, he does not know quite what he'll find because so many classes of locomotive appear at any given time, and as passengers pour from the carriages, he has a wonderful study of people as well as breathing in the atmosphere of the railway.

My Italy is like that. You never know what to expect when you walk its streets, travel its trains, inspect its archaeological ruins, stand in a queue at Giolliti's. There is no point in my writing about an Italy I do not know and do not love. The Italy in this book excites me. Each time I leave, I am planning for my return. There is so much to learn, so much to enjoy, such depth to nourish in relationships with Italians.

Early last century, E. M. Forster wrote, 'The traveller who has gone to Italy to study the tactile values of Giotto, or the corruption of the Papacy, may return remembering nothing but the blue sky and the men and women under it (*Room with a View*).'

As I think of Italy now, sitting at my computer in South Australia, I see the blue sky over Anacapri, but I think especially of the men and women of Italy who have made my moments in their country special. Mostly, of course, I think of the people I have met, talked with, drunk with, laughed with, some I have even cried with, and one or two I have shared hopes with. But even some who passed into another world many years ago have challenged me and nourished me in the stories of their lives. I fancy that when they passed into their other world, they took their Italian minds with them and stored memories of Italy in their spiritual backpacks.

I could ask for no better for myself, though not an Italian, but a lover of that land and its peoples.

In the meantime, I hear Italy calling.